THE SLEEPING GIANT AWAKENS

Genocide, Indian Residenti~~al Schools, and the~~ Challenge of Conciliation

Confronting the truths of Canad~~a's Indian residential school~~ system has been likened to waking a sleeping giant. In *The Sleeping Giant Awakens*, David B. MacDonald uses genocide as an analytical tool to better understand Canada's past and present relationships between settlers and Indigenous peoples. Starting with a discussion of how genocide is defined in domestic and international law, the book applies the concept to the forced transfer of Indigenous children to residential schools and the "Sixties Scoop," in which Indigenous children were taken from their communities and placed in foster homes or adopted.

Based on archival research, extensive interviews with residential school Survivors, and officials at the Truth and Reconciliation Commission of Canada, among others, *The Sleeping Giant Awakens* offers a unique and timely perspective on the prospects for conciliation after genocide, exploring the difficulties in moving forward in a context where many settlers know little of the residential schools and ongoing legacies of colonization and need to have a better conception of Indigenous rights. It provides a detailed analysis of how the TRC approached genocide in its deliberations and in its Final Report.

Crucially, MacDonald engages critics who argue that the term genocide impedes understanding of the IRS system and imperils prospects for conciliation. By contrast, this book sees genocide recognition as an important basis for meaningful discussions of how to engage Indigenous-settler relations in respectful and proactive ways.

(UTP Insights)

DAVID B. MacDONALD is a professor in the Department of Political Science at the University of Guelph and Research Leadership Chair for the College of Social and Applied Human Sciences.

UTP Insights

UTP Insights is an innovative collection of brief books offering accessible introductions to the ideas that shape our world. Each volume in the series focuses on a contemporary issue, offering a fresh perspective anchored in scholarship. Spanning a broad range of disciplines in the social sciences and humanities, the books in the UTP Insights series contribute to public discourse and debate and provide a valuable resource for instructors and students.

Books in the Series

THE SLEEPING GIANT AWAKENS

Genocide, Indian Residential Schools, and the Challenge of Conciliation

David B. MacDonald

UNIVERSITY OF TORONTO PRESS
Toronto Buffalo London

ISBN 978-1-4875-0349-9 (cloth)
ISBN 978-1-4875-2269-8 (paper)

♾ Printed on acid-free, 100% post-consumer recycled paper
with vegetable-based inks.

Library and Archives Canada Cataloguing in Publication

Title: The sleeping giant awakens : genocide, Indian residential schools,
and the challenge of conciliation / David B. MacDonald.
Names: MacDonald, David Bruce, author.
Series: UTP insights.
Description: Series statement: UTP insights | Includes bibliographical
references and index.
Identifiers: Canadiana 20190087064 | ISBN 9781487522698 (softcover) |
ISBN 9781487503499 (hardcover)
Subjects: LCSH: Genocide – Sociological aspects. | LCSH: Truth and
Reconciliation Commission of Canada. | LCSH: Truth commissions –
Canada. | LCSH: Canada – Ethnic relations – History. |
LCSH: Canada – Race relations – History. | CSH: Native peoples –
Violence against – Canada. | Native peoples – Crimes against –
Canada. | Native peoples – Canada – Residential schools. | Native
peoples – Canada – Social conditions.
Classification: LCC E92 .M33 2019 | DDC 305.897/071—dc23

University of Toronto Press acknowledges the financial assistance to its
publishing program of the Canada Council for the Arts and the Ontario
Arts Council, an agency of the Government of Ontario.

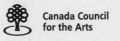

Funded by the   Financé par le
Government   gouvernement
of Canada   du Canada

Canadä

A long time ago, before the residential schools issue came up, an Elder told me to go back to my community because there is a sleeping giant and I had to go and wake it up, gently. I thought he meant the Elders, but when the residential schools issue came up, I knew what he was talking about. He said that when the truth came out, it would reverberate throughout the world.

– Speaker at an Aboriginal Healing Foundation gathering,
Moncton, New Brunswick[1]

Contents

Acknowledgments

I have been working on this book for a decade and a half, and so there are a lot of people to thank. I am grateful that on this researching and writing journey I have made many friends.

I have greatly benefited from the insights, discussions, and/ or conversations with Michael Cachagee, Claudette Chevrier-Cachagee, Liv Pemmican, Marie Wilson, Murray Sinclair, Paulette Regan, Harvey Trudeau, Joe Clark, Paul Martin, James Anaya, Mick Dodson, Kim Murray, Robert Joseph, Wilton Littlechild, Heidi Stark, Robert Innes, Aimee Craft, Audra Simpson, Tasha Hubbard, Tricia Logan, Rupert Ross, Ry Moran, John Milloy, Jim Miller, Mike DeGagné, Jonathan Dewar, Pauline Wakeham, Priscilla Settee, Jennifer Preston, Joyce Green, Valerie Galley, Perry Bellegarde, Shelagh Rogers, Hedy Baum, Scott Serson, Bill Glied, Lori Ransom, Roger Epp, Linc Kesler, Alex Maass, Bill Asikinack, Wes Heber, Payam Akhavan, Alex Hinton, Louise Wise, Makere Stewart Harawira, Jeremy Maron, Karine Duhamel, Malinda Smith, Rosemary Nagy, Matt James, Jenny Kay Dupuis, Pat Case, Tony Barta, Frank Chalk, Bernie Farber, Michael Dan, Brad and Deirdre Morse, Trina Bolam, Ian Mosby, Greg Younging, Madeleine Dion Stout, Kiera Ladner, Myra Tait, Bronwyn Leebaw, Hayden King, Len Rudner, Robert Joseph, Claire Charters, Adam Muller, Frank Iacobucci, Steve Smith, Erica Lehrer, Marika Giles Samson, Greg Sarkissian, Maeengan Linklater, Ted Fontaine, Ajay Parasram, Doug Ervin-Erikson, Steve Heinrichs, Vanessa Watt-Powless, Cara Wehkamp, Rick Hill, Emily Grafton, Rachel Janze, and Tom MacIntosh.

I would also like to thank my current and former students for their hard work and insights: Chelsea Gabel, Graham Hudson, Christopher Ryan, Matthew Chaghano, Malissa Bryan, Curtis Nash, Amber Keegan, Rachel Calleja, Maya Fernandez, Lisa Phillips, David Said, Brian Budd, Jackie Gillis, Joanne Moores, and Sidey Deska-Gauthier.

I would like to thank the good people at the National Residential School Survivors Society who arranged for me to interview many Survivors, and I would also like to thank Ontario Indian Residential School Support Services; the Truth and Reconciliation Commission of Canada; the National Centre for Truth and Reconciliation; Six Nations Polytechnic; the Woodland Cultural Centre, Brantford; the Aboriginal Healing Foundation; the Aboriginal Resource Centre at the University of Guelph; the Zoryan Institute; McGill law school; Saskatchewan Provincial Archives; Library and Archives Canada; Canadian Museum for Human Rights; Te Piringa Faculty of Law at University of Waikato; Ngā Pae o te Māramatanga and the law school and Department of Politics and International Relations, University of Auckland; Political Science and International Relations, Victoria University of Wellington; the First Nations University of Canada; the Political Science Department and Aboriginal Student Centre, University of Regina; the Political Science and History Departments, University of Saskatchewan; the Saskatchewan Indigenous Cultural Centre. Jane Hubbard at Legacy of Hope worked with me so that I could publish excerpts from some Survivor interviews.

Thank you to my parents, Olive and Bruce, and sister, Rachel, who hosted me many times as I visited First Nations University and met with many people in Regina and Saskatoon. My mom took a keen interest in this work from the beginning and collected newspaper and other articles and information for me. As well, I remember fondly conversations with my late Uncle Ivan Amichand on the legacies of residential schools in Regina.

Daniel Quinlan is a fantastic acquisitions editor: extremely helpful, resourceful, and insightful. This book would have been twice as long and half as good without his expert advice and guidance. My thanks to Doug Smith for reading over the historical sections and providing detailed and timely feedback as well as some very useful documents. Andrew Woolford kindly read over my material on genocide, as did Paulette Regan on my conciliation and TRC-related chapters. Sheryl Lightfoot also provided valuable comments and advice. A special thank you to Kent Monkman for his very kind permission to reproduce *The Scream* (2017) on the cover of my book free of charge.

My thanks to the Social Sciences and Humanities Research Council of Canada for four successive grants that have made this work possible: one Standard Grant, two Insight Grants, and a Partnership Development Grant. My thanks to the University of Guelph – in particular, the College of Social and Applied Human Sciences – which selected me as their Research Leadership Chair as I was writing this book.

My thanks to the publishers acknowledged below for permission to cite portions of my work:

- "Canada's History Wars: Indigenous Genocide and Public Memory in the United States, Australia, and Canada," *Journal of Genocide Research* 17, no. 4 (2015): 411–31.
- "Reforming Multiculturalism in a Bi-national Society: Aboriginal Peoples and the Search for Truth and Reconciliation in Canada," *Canadian Journal of Sociology* 39, no. 1 (2014): 65–86.
- "The Genocide Question and Indian Residential Schools in Canada," with Graham Hudson, *Canadian Journal of Political Science* 45, no. 2 (June 2012): 427–49.
- "Genocide in the Indian Residential Schools: Canadian History through the Lens of the UN Genocide Convention," in *Colonial Genocide in Indigenous North America*, ed. Andrew Woolford, Jeff Benvenuto, and Alexander Laban Hinton (Durham, NC: Duke University Press, 2014), 465–93.
- "Indigenous Genocide and Perceptions of the Holocaust in Canada," in *The Wiley-Blackwell Companion to the Holocaust*, ed. Hilary Earl and Simone Gigliotti (Oxford: Wiley-Blackwell, 2019).

My wife, Dana, and son, Gulliver, have always shown kindness, support, and patience with my many book projects and my travelling around. Thanks family!

This book is dedicated to the Survivors, for whom I have the profoundest respect and admiration.

All errors of fact and interpretation in this book are solely my own responsibility.

David B. MacDonald

THE SLEEPING GIANT AWAKENS

Genocide, Indian Residential Schools, and the
Challenge of Conciliation

Introduction: The Sleeping Giant Awakens

Adam Lett worried that he could lose several valuable employees if he could not provide a good education for their children. Lett was principal of the St. George's Indian Residential School near Lytton, British Columbia. In a cordial exchange of letters with Deputy Superintendent General of Indian Affairs Duncan Campbell Scott in late 1926, he suggested that since the "white school" was too far away, he could create a separate classroom in his office. "Like myself," he argued of his employees, "they do not feel that they should expose their children, any more than is necessary, to the low standard of morals, desease [sic] and act inherent in the Indian child." H. Graham, the local Indian agent, concurred: "They do not like the idea of putting a row of desks in the Indian children's classroom, owing to the great amount of tuberculosis which is cropping up amongst the Indians all the time." In February 1927, Scott approved the request, and he advised Lett to place an order for five "silent sanitary adjustable" desks and a style "D" reversible blackboard with Clarke and Stuart of Vancouver.[1]

Inferred in this correspondence was an unspoken context: St. George's was under quarantine for a virulent flu epidemic that had caused the deaths of thirteen Indigenous children, while they confronted a continuing risk of tuberculosis.[2] This short exchange of letters is but one example of countless double standards – what settlers found acceptable for Indigenous children was unacceptable for their own. Then as now, the Canadian government has maintained fundamentally different approaches to Indigenous and settler peoples, not only in terms of health standards but also in its assumptions about morality, mortality, capacity, and rights. Since the 1970s, knowledge of Indian residential schools has been slowly growing, resulting in the Final Report of the Truth and Reconciliation Commission of Canada (TRC) in late 2015. What was once a sleeping giant – public discussion of and engagement with the crimes of colonization and the Indian residential schools (IRS) system – is now awake. Canada faces a conciliation challenge – how to spread knowledge of the IRS system and reverse the destructive impact of the state's crimes against Indigenous peoples and their accompanying legal and political orders.

This year, we commemorate the sixtieth anniversary of the death of Raphael Lemkin, creator of the 1948 United Nations Convention on the Prevention and Punishment of the Crime of Genocide (Genocide Convention, or UNGC), and mark Canada's 152nd birthday. The last 151 years have been destructive for the Indigenous civilizations that flourished on Turtle Island before European exploration, colonization, and settlement. As part of a resurgence of Indigenous peoples, a growing and diverse (re)conciliation movement, discussions of nation-to-nation relationships, conversations about genocide in the Indian residential schools are increasing in frequency. Genocide as an analytical lens is also being used to understand the starvation policies of our first government under John A. Macdonald, and in coming to terms with the Sixties Scoop – the forced removal of Indigenous children from their families and communities.

[To make sense of what genocide is and whether it applies to Canada, I deploy both the UNGC and a larger body of legal and academic work on genocide that predates and follows it. I call these two lenses *legalist* and *pluralist* conceptions of genocide, and both are necessary to my analysis of the Indian residential schools and the Sixties Scoop. Why two versions of genocide and not one?]

The legalist conception is important, first, because its application recognizes decades of claims by Indigenous academics, leaders, activists, and Survivors, who have consistently articulated that the Genocide Convention applies to the IRS system. Such claims continue. In April 2018, former TRC commissioner Wilton Littlechild, at the United Nations Permanent Forum on Indigenous Issues, requested that the UN Special Adviser on Genocide investigate whether the IRS system had violated the UNGC. He requested this in light of Pope Francis's refusal to offer an apology for the Catholic Church's role in the residential schools. Littlechild asked the special adviser to examine the question, "Was this policy indeed, because it happened in Canada, the United States, and elsewhere, was it genocide?"[3]

Second, in the wake of the TRC's work and considerable work by others, there is a growing body of evidence that genocide was committed in the IRS system and during the Sixties Scoop through forcible transfer. Article 2(e) of the convention prohibits "Forcibly transferring children of the group to another group." Third, a legalist analysis recognizes that, in a pragmatic sense, UN-defined genocide is privileged in this country, in that it is recognized, commemorated, and included in educational curricula. The Canadian government has officially recognized seven genocides, and as taxpayers, we fund museums and memorials to the victims of genocide and pledge "Never again," seeking cautionary lessons for the future from the excesses of the past. If the UNGC was violated (as I suggest it was), the IRS system deserves to stand alongside these other, recognized cases of genocide in world history. Otherwise, we do a disservice to Indigenous peoples and to historical truth.

The pluralist conception of genocide is equally necessary because of the narrow framing of the UNGC. First, only two of its elements are found in our Criminal Code ("killing" and "causing serious bodily or mental harm"), meaning that forcible transfer is not seen as genocide in domestic law. Second, pluralism foregrounds the machinations of the Canadian government, along with other settler states, which actively removed elements of the definition of genocide to reduce the potential for Indigenous peoples under settler colonization to articulate a legal case under international law. While the case can be made for violations of the UNGC as currently defined, the definition of genocide should also be expanded if we want to better understand the *fuller magnitude* of what has been done to Indigenous peoples during the creation of the Canadian state.

Third, the Genocide Convention is not retroactive, which means that genocidal crimes before 1948 cannot be punished as genocide under international law. This does not mean that Canadian legislatures or Parliament cannot recognize the IRS system as genocide, since three of our recognized genocides predate the convention. In the concluding chapter, I recommend that the full definition of *genocide* and *cultural genocide* be incorporated into the Criminal Code, and I also recommend that our elected governments officially recognize the IRS system as genocide.

[Despite the political upheavals at the time of writing, we are potentially at a unique moment, a time when the federal government appears interested in questions of genocide and cultural genocide. In their country report to the International Holocaust Remembrance Alliance, published in 2018, the Department of Canadian Heritage identified key questions to be addressed about the nature of the IRS system: "in what ways do the goals of the residential school system fit, or not fit, the idea of genocide; what value is there in conjoining the 'cultural' qualifier to the concept of genocide; and how can we work with cultural genocide in comparison to other forms of genocide particularly the Holocaust."[4] This book sets out to address some of these questions in ways that may have practical import for legislation and policymaking.]

[Beyond a discussion of what genocide means, and how we might apply it to understanding the IRS system and the Sixties Scoop, this book also engages with the formation, goals, and operations of the TRC and how it dealt with the genocide question. This study is based on a decade and a half of archival research, interviews, and conversations with Indigenous leaders, academics, activists, Survivors, settler political leaders, civil servants, and many others. Also important was my participation in the work of the TRC, and in numerous events, gatherings, Survivor reunions, and conferences. I also draw from interviews I conducted with Survivors at the National Residential School Survivors Society in August 2011 through the generosity of Michael Cachagee and his colleagues.]

A caveat is in order: I consider only a segment of Canadian settler history and politics. It is emphatically not my contention that,
in assessing genocide, we should stop at the schools. Others have
already discussed the deliberate starvation of Indigenous peoples
on the Plains as genocide; likewise, the Sixties Scoop fits within
the ambit of the convention, as I discuss in chapter 4. My hope
is that this work can help all of us to more realistically assess the
stakes in *conciliation after genocide* – a very different concept than
reconciliation lite, which focuses on closing gaps while still trying
to assimilate Indigenous peoples within a settler society. I share
Nêhiyaw political scientist Kiera Ladner's conclusion: "Reconciliation is not a great big hug." Instead, it "requires settler society to
acknowledge and accept some really uncomfortable truths about
how they acquired their privileges. It requires settler society to
cede the privilege it has denied Indigenous peoples."[5] This has to
include the return of stolen land, and there is a lot of it to return.

It is fair to say that some readers will feel uncomfortable by what
they read here. In part, this is because the IRS system was not just a
"dark chapter" in Canadian history – it *is* the story of Canada – and
the system was integral to our country's foundation. We walk with
the schools every day and will continue to do so into the future
because many of the institutions, patterns, and processes put in
motion during that time continue. As Cindy Blackstock (Gitksan
First Nation) has observed repeatedly, there are more Indigenous
children in "care" now than during the height of the IRS era, and
the percentage of Indigenous peoples in our prison system is stag-
gering, suggesting to many that these are the "new residential
schools."[6]

I also use the word *conciliation* throughout, because *reconciliation*
implies the need to revisit some point in time when relationships
between Indigenous peoples and settlers were productive, respectful, and healthy. Where the term *reconciliation* works better may be
among Indigenous peoples, where various aspects of colonialism
severely weakened some families and communities, introducing
forms of lateral violence and inter-generational trauma, while also
disrupting several millennia of interdependent relations with animals, plants, waters, and lands.

Indigenous theorist Mary Jane McCallum suggests that the time is ripe for settlers to engage more deeply with the government's Indigenous policies and practices, but she nevertheless notes "a tendency to remain reluctant to acknowledge genocide."[7] This is certainly true for many outside the university setting, although, with time, a growing number of settler and Indigenous historians, sociologists, political scientists, legal theorists, and others have embraced genocide as a focus of analysis. Anishinaabe Elder Fred Kelly has proposed the term *aangone'itewin*, a composite of *aangone* ("extinction") plus the suffix *itewin*, which "refers to the act of exterminating, obliterating, or annihilating living beings; causing extinction of beings."[8] As time progresses, we may see more Indigenous understandings of what genocide signifies, refracted through First Nations languages and conceptual world views. These names will complement the names of genocides provided by other groups: Shoah, Holodomor, Porrajmos, Gorta Mór, and others.

Situating My Analysis

No one should write a book of this kind without first clearly situating themselves. My interest in this topic and my approach to it has something to do with my background as a mixed-race political scientist from Treaty 4 territory – that is, Regina, Saskatchewan (Kisiskâciwan). My mother's family comes from the rural south of Trinidad, and they grew up by the Bronte Estate sugar cane fields, their yard sometimes filled with cane ash during the burning season. My ancestors were brought over from India as indentured labourers in the nineteenth century. British rule in the subcontinent involved power politics and the use of famine as a tool of colonial policy. My mother attended a mission school originally run by the Presbyterian Church of Canada. My father's family is from Jersey and Scotland and goes back to the 1760s in Nova Scotia. They came as farmers after the Highland Clearances, after the Acadians had been forcibly removed from the region, and during the long-term destruction of the Indigenous peoples in that area.

In Regina, I spent my formative years in a stucco bungalow in the south end, enrolled in a French immersion program, and raised within a small Caribbean community, with a multitude of uncles, aunties, and cousins. I delivered the *Leader Post*, a newspaper founded by one of the architects of the IRS system – Nicholas Flood Davin. It was virtually impossible to live in Regina and not be unsettled by the stark segregation of the city between the affluent, largely white suburbs and the poor east-downtown core and North Central, home to a large proportion of the city's Indigenous peoples.

As someone who looks visibly different, I was often unsettled by the racial and social dynamics in my community and was sometimes a target of these dynamics. Bullying and physical abuse were common at my school, and they gave me a low opinion of human nature and authority figures as I was growing up. My Indigenous friends were (inexplicably to me then) raised in white adoptive homes. When discussion of the residential schools surfaced during my high school years, I had little problem believing that something was very wrong with our prairie society. In an overview of Saskatchewan in 2016, *Maclean's* reported that of the 265 most powerful positions in the province, 4.5 per cent were filled by Indigenous peoples. Only 2 of 101 judges are Indigenous, in a province where 81 per cent of inmates in provincial jails are Indigenous. Saskatchewan was also the home of the last federally funded Indian residential school (Gordon's). One of its Survivors, Darren Maxie, recalls an important lesson he learned about the nature of power in the province: "It is their system, not ours," he observes. "Every institution belongs to them. We are not allowed in."[9]

Indigenous Peoples as Self-Determining Nations

Definitions of Indigenous peoples are contested, not least because of the power dynamics involved in those definitions. Canada's 1982 Constitution recognizes three classifications of "Aboriginal" peoples: First Nations, Inuit, and Métis. Within these categories, the state has divided Indigenous peoples into those with "status" and those without. The 2016 census indicates that there are 1,673,785 Indigenous peoples, comprising 4.9 per cent of the population. Of these, 744,855 are recognized as First Nations with Indian status, with 44.2 per cent living on reserves. The number of First Nations with status has risen by 12.8 per cent since 2006, while the number of Métis has doubled since that time.[10] Having status means, in most cases, being subject to the 1876 Indian Act, a political instrument that has reduced the political power and numbers of Indigenous peoples by dividing them into "bands" and imposing on them a settler colonial administrative and political structure. *Indigenous, Aboriginal, Native,* and *Indian* are settler colonial terms that gloss over the national and political attributes of individual First Nations. In its 1996 report, the Royal Commission on Aboriginal Peoples (RCAP) identified between sixty and eighty Indigenous nations that might viably exercise political rights to self-determination.[11]

This book also foregrounds the specific targeting of Indigenous women by the settler state, which has sought to dismantle matrilineal forms of governance in many Indigenous nations. In a powerful intervention, Kanien'kehá:ka anthropologist Audra Simpson documents how Haudenosaunee women played a central role in all aspects of political life, representing "an alternative political order" to Western settler governance. They had the power to appoint and also dismiss chiefs, control property, and transmit their clan identity to future generations, thereby safeguarding the survival of the nation.[12]

Indigenous women are often forced to make some of the most difficult choices. One Survivor who shared her experiences with me disclosed how she "married a non-Native so my children would never go to the schools."[13] There are many layers to a statement like this. That the Indian Act was overtly sexist is one layer; that women would willingly end their existence as status Indigenous peoples and choose to pass on that non-status to their children to spare them from pain is another. The Indian Act and other legislation has facilitated the abuse of Indigenous women for well over a century, and much of the lateral violence within Indigenous communities traces its origins to the violence of colonialism. Recent statistics provided by the National Inquiry into Missing and Murdered Indigenous Women and Girls (NIMMIWG) indicate that, in 2015, 24 per cent of homicide victims were Indigenous women, making them twelve times more at risk of going missing or being killed than other women in Canada.[14] In this era of #MeToo campaigns, and the NIMMIWG, we must actively counter the disproportionately negative effects of settler society on Indigenous women.

That Indigenous nations were self-determining political actors was affirmed through the 1764 Treaty of Niagara. Some 2,000 Indigenous representatives from twenty-four nations met with William Johnson (speaking for the Crown) and established a system of relationships for selectively sharing lands with the Crown. The treaty recognized Indigenous ownership of the land and premised European settlement on Indigenous consent. The treaty established clear lines of authority, and it gave the Crown responsibility for keeping local colonial administrations in line so they would not bother Indigenous peoples in the practice of their governments and in their use of their resources and lands. At Niagara, Two Row Wampum belts were exchanged, conveying for Indigenous peoples an "understanding of a mutual relationship of peace and non-interference in each other's way of life," as John Borrows carefully describes it. The treaty's oral implications recognized Indigenous self-government and "an alliance between sovereign nations."[15] The Covenant Chain belt, also part of the treaty process, depicted two individuals holding hands, representing distinct peoples who were also interdependent.

The early period of treaty-making coincided with the relative strength of Indigenous peoples. Early agreements dealt with peace, friendship, and trade, and they were often conducted on terms of equality, carefully observing Indigenous diplomatic protocols, such as smoking a calumet, exchanging gifts, intermarrying to promote kinship relations, and other means. Later periods of treaty-making from the late eighteenth century were marked by a decline in Indigenous power and a commensurate increase in the relative power and size of European populations. While decolonization proceeded in much of the world after 1945, Indigenous peoples in settler states were hampered by the UN's "salt water"

thesis from 1960, which asserted that colonies seeking indepen-
dence as sovereign states had to be geographically separated from
the colonizing power by a body of water.

Because I am focusing on the Indian Act as the primary legislative vehicle for forcible transfer, my emphasis is on First Nations
with status, and this emphasis may be less applicable to the situations of Métis and Inuit peoples. Métis comprised about 9 per cent
of the children who attended residential schools, but they were not
a continual target of forcible transfer by the *federal* government,
as they were deemed to fall within the purview of the provinces.
Métis were certainly targets for religious conversion alongside
other Indigenous children, and they were an integral part of the Sixties Scoop. The TRC's Final Report notes that Métis were at every
school and "would have undergone the same experiences – the
high death rates, limited diets, crowded and unsanitary housing,
harsh discipline, heavy workloads, neglect, and abuse."[16] In late
2017, I asked Senator Sinclair for his opinion as to whether Métis
were also victims of UN-defined genocide, to which he replied, "I
think the intention with the Métis in residential schools was also to
remove them from their culture and their language and to assimilate them into mainstream Canada. And that implicates the forcible
removal with the purpose of doing away with the culture, with the
cultural group."[17]

Equally, this study does not offer a detailed focus on Inuit peoples, as they were not brought under the colonial umbrella of the
Indian Act until 1939, following a Supreme Court decision. The
federal government had little interest in the North initially, and it
was only during the 1950s that the situation changed. Before 1940,
residential schools were run by the churches, and few children
attended them. This increased, beginning in the 1950s, to such an
extent that at the height of the IRS system, a higher proportion
of children attended residential schools in the North than in the
South. Many schools comprised a hostel and integrated school for
Indigenous and non-Indigenous children. There were important
differences but also similarities – in the disruption of values and
skills, levels of abuse, loss of language and culture, and estrange-
ment from families when children returned to their communities.[18]

Settlers

While a mental image of Euro-Canadians may leap to mind, there is sometimes a question mark about racialized peoples since we function within a system that marks out European identities as normal and unproblematic, while representing others as "ethnic" or "multicultural." Thus, we have divisions between those who are "tolerated" and those who do (or do not do) the "tolerating." It is true that people like my mother's side of the family were not envisaged in the British North America Act (BNA Act), were purposefully barred from entry into the Dominion, and were denied a legal relationship with Indigenous peoples by exclusion from treaties. However, given that many racialized peoples see their primary identity as "Canadian," a self-identity as a settler may be valid. One might define *settlers* in its broadest sense as everyone who is not Indigenous, while also making distinctions, where appropriate, between European settlers and racialized settlers, and those whose ancestors were brought to this continent against their will, such as the descendants of enslaved Africans.

I share Métis writer and lawyer Chelsea Vowel's suggestion to understand *settler* as a "relational term," signifying someone who engages in the "deliberate physical occupation of land as a method of asserting ownership over land and resources."[19] Settlers, as Stó:lō scholar Dylan Robinson observes, can also be defined as those who bear "intergenerational responsibility" for "intergenerational perpetration."[20] This definition is useful in helping us understand that whether we are newly arrived in Canada and are non-white (like my mom's family) or mixed, or are white settlers (like my dad's) who trace our families back generations, our choices right now determine whether we are contributing to ongoing problems of colonization, or working to help roll back and alleviate those problems.

At the same time, Anishinaabe legal theorist Aaron Mills reminds us that settlers and Indigenous peoples are not simply one thing or another. Many people have both Indigenous and settler ancestry and identify with one or both groups. The key issue for Mills is not so much a label as, rather, what view of reality we adopt, whether it be a settler view of the earth as property and commodity or an "earth-centred Anishinaabe view of treaty constitutionalism," which can frame our role as settlers within Indigenous legal traditions, instead of those principally derived from Europe.[21]

Survivors

Throughout this book I use the term *Survivor*, which the TRC defined as "a person who persevered against and overcame adversity … someone who emerged victorious, though not unscathed … someone who had taken all that could be thrown at them and remained standing at the end."[22] Ted Fontaine, former chief of the Sagkeeng First Nation, in his memoir *Broken Circles*, describes the situation this way: "Most survivors left school in their teens or early 20s, and most didn't live long."[23] Arthur Bear Chief credits his ability to endure to his traditional Blackfoot teachings, observing that those who were able to create good lives for themselves did so because of "our Indian spirit and our determination to overcome obstacles even in the most difficult situations. I praise my ancestors and grandparents for giving me both."[24]

The Schools: An Overview and Context

It is difficult to pinpoint where legacies of the IRS system begin and end because the creators of the system wanted their effects to complement larger, parallel processes of settler colonization. At the beginning, as military allies, and as invaluable partners in the fur trade, many Indigenous peoples had clear economic value to the early explorers and colonizers. The change in economic focus from trade to resource extraction and agriculture eroded and eventually destroyed any semblance of partnership, to be replaced by a sense that Indigenous peoples were an impediment to a larger settler colonial project of taking over the land and substituting Indigenous civilizations with transplanted European forms.

In the first half of the nineteenth century, the settler population of Upper Canada increased from under 100,000 to almost one million, while the Indigenous population dropped to 1 per cent of the total.[25] The Treaty of Niagara, which informed some of the early relations between Indigenous governments and colonial authorities, gave way to a far more coercive relationship through policies of "civilization" and assimilation. By 1860, the Indian Affairs portfolio was transferred to pre-Confederation Canada from the British imperial government. After Confederation, the British Crown devolved many of its responsibilities to the new government, violating Indigenous understandings of the original treaty.

Certainly, John A. Macdonald refused to see Indigenous peoples as treaty partners, cynically describing them as being like children, "incapable of the management of their own affairs," a sentiment that legitimated his paternalistic policies of "guardianship."[26] The 1876 Indian Act consolidated the pre-existing colonial legislation dealing with Indigenous peoples, who became wards of the state, with few political rights within the new country. A male-only electorate was empowered to elect a chief and council, who managed some local affairs, but were largely beholden to Ottawa-appointed Indian agents. In many cases, treaties were requested by Indigenous nations seeking to ward off starvation or to create some framework for the future in a context of European settlement. However, while many Indigenous nations sought treaty under duress, their negotiators were skilled and did not surrender lands in the ways presented in the written treaty texts; their own conceptual world views often did not permit more than sharing responsibility for the land.

The IRS system was created as a partnership between the federal government and the four mainstream Christian churches, building on earlier individual schools established by various Catholic entities and by Protestant missions in Ontario, the Northwest Territories, and British Columbia. The government became very interested in working with the churches to expand the network of residential schools after acquiring, a year after Confederation, Rupert's Land and the lands to the north, both of which contained predominantly Indigenous populations. For the government, the IRS system promised to reduce government expenditure on Indigenous peoples by converting them to Western-style farming

practices and by eliminating Indian status through enfranchisement. The end goal was to do away with Indigenous reserves and
Indian status. The schools were designed to assimilate and to end
the separate existence of Indigenous peoples.

The formal IRS system began in 1883 with the establishment of
three "industrial schools" on the Prairies, built by the government
and run by the Catholic and Anglican Churches. These were larger
than the earlier boarding schools, which had been established by
the churches and funded by government. Boarding schools were
normally located close to reserves, while the industrial schools
were farther away. By 1923, any official distinctions between these
types of school had ended, and both were being funded by government on a per capita basis and run by the churches, an arrangement that continued until 1969.[27] Overall, approximately 150,000
Indigenous children attended a network of 139 Indian residential
schools (as recognized under the Indian Residential Schools Settlement Agreement, or IRSSA). During the IRS era, Indian Affairs
expanded significantly, from a branch of the Interior Ministry to
a department in its own right, slowly building up its power and
influence across the country.

The system was but one aspect of a much larger settler colonial
project, which used coercive instruments, including starvation,
forced removal, and the concentration of peoples onto small and
isolated reserves, often away from fertile lands, which the government then opened up to European settlement. Particularly implicated was Macdonald, whose practice was "to starve uncooperative
Indians onto reserves and into submission." James Daschuk documents how the government targeted food, clothing, shelter, and
tool sources such as the buffalo, and used the denial of rations and
targeted starvation as techniques for herding nations onto small
reservations by the 1880s. Once on these reserves, most people
were largely dependent on and subject to government control.[28]
When I interviewed Senator Murray Sinclair on Daschuk's conclusions in 2017, I asked whether the crimes outlined in his book could
be violations of the UNGC. He replied, "No doubt in my mind …
that if it happened now, it would be an act of genocide because it's
a deliberate infliction of conditions of life upon a group of people

for the purpose of, essentially, either annihilating them or forcing them to give up their identity. And so that amounts to the same thing."[29] Over the twentieth century, a larger climate of cultural, spiritual, and political suppression made it exceedingly difficult to resist the coercive nature of the system, as I discuss in chapter 3.

The End of the IRS System, Public Awareness, and Compensation

Indigenous resistance to settler colonialism goes back to the beginning. By the twentieth century, groups such as the League of Indians of Canada, the Allied Indian Tribes of British Columbia, and the council of the Six Nations near Brantford, Ontario, vocally advocated for the return of stolen lands and many other issues. The denouement of the IRS system began as the Second World War drew to a close. In 1944, some Indian Affairs officials, notably the superintendent of welfare and training, Robert Hoey, articulated the need for a policy shift from the residential system, which, he argued, should "slowly and gradually close." In 1949, the Special Joint Committee of the Senate and House of Commons promoted integrated day schooling over residential schools as a preferred vehicle for assimilation.[30]

As the IRS system very slowly wound down, the provinces began to assert a larger role in the lives of Indigenous children, heralding the era of the Sixties Scoop. The 1951 amendments to the Indian Act, specifically section 88, delegated to the provinces the power to make general laws that Indigenous peoples would be obliged to obey, despite their lack of consent to such changes.[31]

By the mid-1960s, Indigenous organizations were able to better assert their interests. In 1967, Métis leader Howard Adams chaired a national conference at which delegates and speakers publicly outlined problems of the IRS system, opening up a larger debate about colonialism; the conference resulted in speaking-out assemblies, talk-ins, powwows, and increased links with the American Red Power and Black Power movements.[32] In 1969, the funding relationship between the federal government and the churches ended, and by 1970, the process of transferring control of some of the schools to

Indigenous bands began; the first school to be transferred was the Blue Quills School in St. Paul, Alberta. Over the next two decades, approximately a dozen schools were transferred to band operation. By the 1980s, organizations such as the Children of Shingwauk Alumni Association began to help Survivors. Co-founder Michael Cachagee (Chapleau Cree First Nation) and his colleagues were instrumental in promoting awareness of the crimes in the schools and organizing to achieve healing, redress, and compensation.

As Survivors organized, North America was rocked by growing public awareness of the sexual abuse of children in Catholic-run schools, scandals that in Canada culminated in the 1989 outcry over widespread abuse at the Mount Cashel Orphanage in Newfoundland. This period created a window of opportunity to engage with the IRS system. Phil Fontaine (Sagkeeng First Nation), who later became national chief of the Assembly of First Nations (AFN), openly discussed his history of physical and sexual abuse and encouraged others to come forward. Fontaine's revelations took place against the backdrop of the Oka crisis in Quebec, where Kanien'kehá:ka warriors faced the Quebec military and the Canadian Armed Forces to defend their traditional lands (including a burial ground) from being expropriated by the Oka town council for a golf course expansion.

This standoff, together with the public revelations about the IRS system, laid the foundation for the RCAP in 1991. Its 1996 report documented the extent of the physical and sexual abuse in residential schools (as well as their goals of assimilation and cultural destruction). The RCAP advocated that a public inquiry be established to listen to Survivors, collect evidence, and recommend forms of compensation. It was hoped that the government would issue a formal apology and help rebuild damaged lives and communities, while promoting public knowledge of IRS abuses through education.[33]

In response, the federal government released its "Gathering Strength" report in 1998, which led to the formation of the Aboriginal Healing Foundation (AHF) in the same year, and Indian Residential Schools Resolution Canada in 2001.[34] An alternative dispute resolution process to compensate Survivors was established during this time. Compensation varied by province, and it was skewed against Indigenous women and their experiences of abuse. Those who had attended Catholic-run institutions received only government money – no compensation from the Church.[35] Consequently, the next decade saw widespread litigation against the churches and the federal government. By early 2005, some 13,400 individual suits had been filed, with large class-action suits such as *Baxter*, in which 90,000 Survivors sought $12 billion in compensation.[36]

During this time, a number of key legal changes created more permissive conditions for Indigenous peoples to hold the churches and the federal government to account. Provinces changed their Limitation Acts during the 1990s to remove limits on the amount of time within which adults could be charged with the sexual assault of a minor, while provincial legislatures permitted class-action suits to be undertaken.[37] Many forms of abuse, however, were never actionable in Canadian courts, such as "loss of culture and language, alienation of parental love, alienation from community, deprivation of life skills required for living in remote communities."[38] From 1995 to 2005, a range of court decisions also allowed for vicarious liability – holding the institutions that controlled the schools liable for crimes committed by their employees.[39] Less positive were court decisions from 2000 to 2003 that ruled that only living former residential school students could claim compensation. Their heirs could not. This allowed courts to compensate individual living IRS Survivors, but not the estates of those who had died before the class-action suits were concluded.

In 2004, the AFN played an instrumental role in securing a settlement that was to move well beyond seeking money for sexual and physical abuse. While most lawyers aimed primarily to maximize monetary settlements for their clients, the AFN sought a truth and reconciliation commission as well as commemorative, healing, and other activities. The IRSSA was signed by the parties in April 2006, following which courts in all nine jurisdictions that had heard the class-action suits had to approve it. By January 2007, the courts had certified and approved the agreement, which was formally adopted in September of that year.[40]

The agreement set out a variety of compensatory mechanisms, including Common Experience Payments (CEPs), an Independent

Assessment Process (IAP) for more serious abuses, a commemoration fund, funds to promote healing and health support, and the
mandate for the TRC. It also laid the foundation for pressuring the
government to deliver an official apology, something the Conservative government initially refused to do. In 2008, Prime Minister
Harper finally delivered an official apology on the floor of the House
of Commons; he even recognized that "some sought, as it was infa-
mously said, 'to kill the Indian in the child.'"[41] The IRSSA was hardly
perfect, and it covered only certain categories of Survivor and certain
schools. Schools run by provincial governments were excluded, as
were religious schools without government funding and day schools.
Métis students in provincial residential schools were not included,
nor were Indigenous children who had attended church-run residential schools not primarily designed for Indigenous children.[42] According to the TRC's legal counsel, Tom McMahon, over 1,500 residential
institutions for Indigenous children were not included as part of the
IRSSA, as per the federal government's decision.[43]

Both Newfoundland and Labrador also had residential schools,
but as Newfoundland joined Canada only in 1949, its schools were
not part of the agreement. Only recently have these one thousand IRS Survivors obtained a $50 million settlement, followed in
October 2017 by an official apology.[44] Another outstanding issue
concerned Survivors caught in an "administrative split," where,
typically, a student residence was operated by a church and a day
school by the federal government. While the government funded
both, some IAP claimants were denied compensation "on a tech-
nical argument that certain schools were transformed into day
schools during an individual's attendance."[45] At the time of writing, the challenges for Survivors are far from over.

Structure of the Book

In chapters 1 and 2, I critically examine how genocide is defined in
international and Canadian law, and I discuss how we might apply
a commonly accepted legal definition to the Indian residential
schools. The first chapter features analysis of what we might call

the "legalist" tradition, whereby genocide is understood through the Genocide Convention and case law from international and domestic legal settings. In the second chapter, I explore "pluralist" conceptions, where strict legal understandings are critiqued for their (sometimes) Eurocentric presumptions. Here I engage with the work of some Indigenous theorists and their articulations of collective identities, including interdependence with lands, animals, plants, waters, and other aspects of the natural environment, as well as webs of relations between peoples and fluid forms of group membership, including kinship relations.

In chapter 3, I begin with a brief history of the IRS system, present an overview of government legislation, and feature a discussion of church and government intentions in establishing and maintaining the system. I also explore how we can best understand processes of transfer through a detailed engagement with the fate of Indigenous children within the system. Chapter 4 on the Sixties Scoop follows closely from the previous chapter, exploring how policy responsibility for forcible transfer moved from an exclusive reliance on federally funded residential schools as a vehicle of genocide to a more province-based, decentralized system of forcibly removing Indigenous children through child welfare agencies.

The TRC is the focus of chapters 5 and 6, in which I first discuss its mandate and its lack of judicial power under the IRSSA. Second, I provide an overview of the TRC's structure and some of its activities over its six-year timeline. Third, I analyse how the TRC addressed the question of genocide during its mandate and in its voluminous Final Report. Chapter 6 provides a short analysis of how the TRC broached the painful subject of missing children, and whether, through its work, we can understand these deaths as genocide.

My focus in chapter 7 is on academic contestation of genocide claims. Here I critically consider three arguments in the literature on residential schools that refute the application of the UNGC to forcible transfer. In chapter 8, I offer a post-TRC analysis of how genocide has largely failed to be recognized in Canadian settler society. A portion of this chapter will examine how the Canadian Museum for Human Rights has privileged five officially "recognized" genocides, while presenting a more ambiguous account of the IRS system. In the second half of the chapter, I consider what settlers understand about Indigenous peoples by examining three governance models and narratives that are deployed (often simultaneously) to define what Canada is and, by omission, what it is not.

In chapter 9, which concludes this short volume, I focus on the future – what does conciliation look like if we understand the IRS system as genocide? Much of this chapter is about the return of Indigenous land, and it explores other ways that those of us who are settlers can work to roll back the settler state in the lives of Indigenous nations so that the current resurgence has a meaningful chance of leading to practical, purposeful, and successful forms of Indigenous self-determination. I conclude with some observations as to how Canada can achieve forms of (re)conciliation into the future. I stress that the process will be slow and will involve rethinking the nature of Canada as a Westphalian state possessing absolute sovereignty over the territory and peoples it occupies and administers. The federal government's support of Romeo Saganash's Bill C-262, which will incorporate the UN Declaration on the Rights of Indigenous Peoples (UNDRIP) into Canadian law, could be an important step forward. The bill passed its third reading in the House of Commons in early 2018 and was then introduced to the Senate in November of that year.

I am aware that there is opposition to the idea that the IRS system was genocidal, and debate and discussion is really just beginning. In his 2017 book *Residential Schools and Reconciliation*, the eminent historian James R. Miller critiqued my earlier writings on genocide (alongside similar claims by criminologist Andrew Woolford). He cautions that "the use of an explosive term like 'genocide' is socially dangerous: it can be a barrier to progress to reconciliation."[46] I agree with Miller's general proposition that genocide may be explosive if used merely for rhetorical effect, but this is not my goal here. Rather, as will become obvious throughout this book, genocide is neither hyperbole nor an unwarranted accusation. Rather, I use genocide as a carefully considered analytical tool to better make sense of Canada's past and aspects of its ongoing actions into the present. My conclusions echo those of Senator Sinclair, the work of a large number of Indigenous academics and activists, and the AFN's determination of genocide in 2002.

In promoting reconciliation, there is always the temptation, as Tuck and Yang predict, to attempt "moves to innocence," which would "reconcile settler guilt and complicity, and rescue settler futurity."[47] I see this book instead as a *move to responsibility*, in the hope that a clear focus on genocide will disabuse those of us who are settlers of the notion that conciliation will be easy. Genocide recognition may help settlers to realistically appraise the stakes involved. I suspect that these stakes will be readily apparent to many Indigenous readers. I devote much of the final chapter to a discussion of what a move to responsibility might look like. If this book accomplishes its limited goals, it will provide useful insights for further dialogue and discussion about the IRS system and settler colonialism more generally, as we work to build better and fairer societies for us all, societies that embody forms of respectful and complex sovereignties.

chapter one

Understanding Genocide: Raphael Lemkin, the UN Genocide Convention, and International Law

I'm pretty sure that their legal thinkers would have been well aware of the fact that if they simply had adopted the convention into Canadian law that everything they did after the convention would have rendered them culpable to a claim of genocide. Anything they did before the convention, they might have been able to free themselves and argue that they were not subject to the convention because it didn't exist in law before then.

– Senator Murray Sinclair on Canada's restrictive definition of genocide in the Criminal Code (2017)[1]

In June 2012, I drove a Hertz rental car, a white Chevy Malibu, up Broad Street and then along the flat ribbon of Highway 11 from Regina to Saskatoon to attend the TRC's Saskatchewan National Event. It was not my first National Event, but it was the first in my home province, a province that included twenty-two residential schools. Saskatoon was similar to other National Events in its careful planning, crowds of people, including large numbers of Survivors, health support workers, and church officials and volunteers. It was also similar in the frequent invocation of genocide by Survivors. An understandably emotional Ted Quewezance, the former chief of the Keeseekoose First Nation, said it plainly during a Commissioner's Sharing Panel: "This is genocide, Mr. Commissioner. ... We, as little boys and girls, lost our innocence. ... We lost our lives, our identity, our language, our culture and our family."[2]

Most Survivors with whom I have spoken have a clear understanding of what genocide means, and many do not hesitate to apply that understanding to their experiences. In late 2012, I became one of many academic consultants for the TRC; in my case, I had the responsibility to write a draft chapter on genocide for the commissioners to consider for their Final Report. While my work for them was confidential, this book draws in places on that research, while also reflecting the influx of much new information since that time.

Legal theorist William Schabas, who has spent many decades writing on genocide and working on war crimes tribunals, puts the matter starkly: "In any hierarchy, something must sit at the top. The crime of genocide belongs at the apex of the pyramid."[3] This chapter focuses primarily on the UN Genocide Convention of 1948 and how genocide is officially defined in international and domestic law. In the next chapter, I will argue that the convention is a far-from-ideal lens through which to make sense of genocide against Indigenous peoples as part of colonization, given that the legal definition is intimately tied to state power, and that states (some of whom were committing genocide) have exerted control over how genocide is defined, both internationally and domestically.

In this book, I use the terms *legalist* and *pluralist*. The first refers to those who centre their understandings of genocide on the UN convention, while those in the second group may or may not use the convention as a basis of analysis, and critically explore the problems behind its creation and the groups it actively excludes. Legalists tend to focus on state agency and anchor their understanding of genocide within a Holocaust paradigm. Pluralists, by contrast, are far less focused on states and political objectives and are more interested in the genocidal impulses and social forces within a given society. They may also seek to significantly redefine what genocide means and should mean.[4]

This chapter will focus primarily on legalist means of defining genocide, with the next chapter highlighting aspects of the pluralist turn and what it means for understanding colonial genocides. Legalist scholars, who pioneered genocide studies, were influenced primarily by the Jewish Holocaust and the Armenian genocide.

Genocide theorist Alex Hinton has observed that the Holocaust constitutes *the* prototype of what most people think genocide looks like. With it, Rwanda and Armenia figure as the "triad," followed by a series of "core" genocides of the twentieth century, a "second circle," a "periphery," and "forgotten genocides."[5] This triad represents uncontroversial cases for the applicability of the Genocide Convention. These are deliberately planned mass murders on a grand scale, in the context of an international or interstate war, with an obviously racist perpetrator using its full range of bureaucratic and military instruments to affect the annihilation of a relatively defenceless minority population, who have been actively and publicly demonized through propaganda.

Indigenous genocides in settler colonial states do not always fit this standard view of what "real" genocide should look like. Often, there are no international or localized wars taking place. One or more groups are certainly targeted by the state, but settler populations, animated by racist sentiments, may play a larger role in the unfolding violence. Their racism might be overt or even unconscious, merely an assumed understanding of what is desirable and what is not. The targets are often numerous groups who are artificially lumped together because a colonizer, usually European, has assumed control of an expanse of territory that encompasses them all. Genocide can consist of a perpetrator literally creating-by-identifying a group that never existed before, then seeking its destruction at the very same time.

Raphael Lemkin's Neologism

Born in 1900, Polish Jewish legal theorist Raphael Lemkin coined the term *genocide* in 1944 and, through dogged persistence, laid the foundation for the UN Genocide Convention only four years later. There is a certain tragic quality to Lemkin, a pale, balding, bespectacled man, forever, it seems, down on his financial luck, living hand to mouth in the fleabag hotels of New York, yet driven to seek justice for oppressed peoples in the world. He was raised in an atmosphere of racial violence and poverty, where anti-Semitic pogroms were not uncommon. His interest in law was kindled by a sense of needing to right injustices, and he was particularly taken by state crimes against minorities such as Armenians and Jews. Governments, it seemed, had legal impunity to massacre their own populations without any international consequences, while members of minority groups striking back often felt the full brunt of domestic law.

Developing a legal framework for the protection of minority populations was a central preoccupation for Lemkin, and it grew all the more pressing as Nazi Germany prepared to invade Poland in 1939. Lemkin fled to Sweden that year, eventually making his way to the United States, where he later taught at Duke and Yale Universities. Forty-nine members of Lemkin's family stayed in Poland, and they were consequently shipped off to the Treblinka death camp and gassed in 1943. During his time in Sweden, Lemkin penned his magnum opus, *Axis Rule in Occupied Europe*, offering a comprehensive overview of Nazi policies in the lands they conquered. In trying to make sense of the horrific events swirling around him, Lemkin combined the Greek word for "tribe" or "race" (*genos*) and the Latin suffix *cide*, used in words such as *homicide* and *fratricide*.

What stands out prominently is how broadly Lemkin applied his new term to a wide range of crimes. Genocide, he observed, was "a coordinated plan of different actions aiming at the destruction of the essential foundations of the life of national groups, with the aim of annihilating the groups themselves." Yet killing was not crucial, and as such, "The objectives of such a plan would be disintegration of the political and social institutions, of culture, language, national feelings, religion, and the economic existence of national groups, and the destruction of personal security, liberty, health, dignity, and even the lives of the individuals belonging to such groups."[6] Indeed, killing marked only the final stage of genocide, and Lemkin was clear that "the machine gun" was often "a last resort" instead of the primary means of destruction.[7]

The fundamentally tragic element of genocide was that each culture and group had something unique to offer to humanity as a whole. Lemkin observed in 1946:

Our whole heritage is a product of the contributions of all nations. We can best understand this when we realize how impoverished our culture would be if the peoples doomed by Germany, such as the Jews, had not been permitted to create the Bible, or to give birth to an Einstein, a Spinoza; if the Poles had not had the opportunity to give to the world a Copernicus, a Chopin, a Curie; the Czechs, a Huss, a Dvorak; the Greeks, a Plato and a Socrates; the Russians, a Tolstoy and a Shostakovich.[8]

Culture was the bedrock from which these people and ideas flourished. Contributions might be seen in two primary ways. First, the group, by virtue of its existence, provided an intrinsic service to its members, who wished to belong to the group and perpetuate its identity. At a second level, the group contributed certain extrinsic functions, acting as an incubator for talent that enriched not only the group but the wider human population as well.

Eventually basing himself in New York near the fledgling United Nations, Lemkin worked tirelessly to have genocide adopted as a crime in international law. His broad-based World Movement to Outlaw Genocide lobbied UN member states to have a genocide convention drafted into law. Behind the scenes, he was an adviser to the secretary general, and he took to occupying unused offices at the UN as a means of cajoling, badgering, and flattering state delegations, often in equal measure.

In late 1946, the UN General Assembly met for the first time, and Lemkin worked with India, Cuba, and Panama on a genocide resolution, which was passed in December. Lemkin and two other legal theorists then worked with the UN Secretariat to create a draft text, consequently revised by a committee formed by the Economic and Social Council, then followed in 1948 by discussions and further refinement by state delegations at the Sixth Committee of the General Assembly. By late 1948, the final text was submitted to the General Assembly, which unanimously adopted it.

There are differences between the 1947 and 1948 drafts, and they are of crucial importance to understanding how Indigenous genocides are often ignored in international law. In particular, the 1947 draft envisaged genocide in three forms: physical, biological, and cultural. Of these, it saw cultural genocide as an integral component of genocide, as Lemkin outlined in June 1947:

National, racial or religious groups do not exist only physically. Their main characteristics lie within the provinces of spirit and culture. If one destroys these valuable elements of their life, members of such groups are reduced to the stage of robots. Their contribution to world civilization ceases.[9]

For Lemkin, there was something special about groups that inherited cultural, linguistic, religious, and/or other traits from their ancestors and passed them down to succeeding generations. A human group was to him "a living entity with body and soul," whose destruction would leave "a vacuum in human society." He reasoned, "Our whole cultural heritage is the product of the contributions of all peoples, races and creeds."[10] For Lemkin, it was never central to the definition of genocide that members of a group be targeted with death because the key issue was the group's ability to continue its existence into the future.

The original May 1947 draft included cultural genocide as one of its three aspects. While Lemkin saw cultural genocide as another type of genocide alongside the other forms, the process of codification separated out cultural genocide and described five methods of destroying the specific characteristics of a group:

(a) forcible transfer of children to another human group; or
(b) forced and systematic exile of individuals representing the culture of a group; or
(c) prohibition of the use of the national language even in private intercourse; or
(d) systematic destruction of books printed in the national language or of religious works or prohibition of new publications; or
(e) systematic destruction of historical or religious monuments or their diversion to alien uses, destruction or dispersion of documents and objects of historical, artistic, or religious value and of objects used in religious worship.[11]

Of these, only part (a) survived the vote of the Sixth Committee of the General Assembly and eventually made it into the final draft. Lemkin viewed this as a personal failure, lamenting, "It meant the destruction of the cultural pattern of a group, such as the language, the traditions, the monuments, archives, libraries, churches. In brief: the shrines of the soul of a nation. But there was not enough support for this idea in the Committee. ... So with a heavy heart I decided not to press for it."[12] The excision of cultural genocide is significant for those of us trying to interpret Indigenous genocides in settler colonial contexts, given that settler and colonial states were committing many of the above acts, while often at the very same time deliberating how genocide should be interpreted in international law. The final draft of the convention defined genocide as follows:

> Any of the following acts committed with intent to destroy, in whole or in part, a national, ethnical, racial or religious group, as such:
>
> (a) Killing members of the group;
> (b) Causing serious bodily or mental harm to members of the group;
> (c) Deliberately inflicting on the group conditions of life calculated to bring about its physical destruction in whole or in part;
> (d) Imposing measures intended to prevent births within the group;
> (e) Forcibly transferring children of the group to another group.

In the remainder of this chapter, I review several salient aspects of genocide in international law, using the convention and later international case law to help situate my analysis. Legal decisions pertinent to this analysis include definitions and findings from the International Criminal Tribunal for the former Yugoslavia (ICTY), the International Criminal Tribunal for Rwanda (ICTR), and the International Criminal Court (ICC), all of which have helped refine the UN definition.

Who or What Can Be Charged with Genocide?

While Lemkin was clearly interested in the fate of human groups as groups, his focus on collective responsibility did not make it into the convention. While sub-state units such as the National

Socialist German Workers' Party could be disbanded for their role in genocide, the state itself could escape such accusations and would retain its sovereignty, whatever actions were taken in its name or on its behalf. Instead, individuals would be charged with genocide, while states could continue their existence, although potentially with a change of government. This individual focus is obvious throughout the convention. Article 4 states that *"Persons* committing genocide or any of the other acts enumerated in article III shall be punished." Article 5 obliges contracting parties to "provide effective penalties for *persons* guilty of genocide," while Article 6 outlines the procedures for trying *"Persons* charged with genocide or any of the other acts."[13] This raises important issues, such as those the TRC raised in 2015, when it argued that cultural genocide had been committed. Had it made a case for genocide under international law, the state itself would not be liable for a genocide prosecution. Rather, individuals, most of whom were long dead, would have been the targets of any legal action.

International Case Law and Key Elements of the Crime of Genocide

At the top of the definition of genocide is the *chapeau* (French for "hat"), which lays out the ground rules for interpreting crimes. Proving genocide in international law is uniquely difficult because the legal bar is set extremely high, at the level of a specific intent (in Latin, *dolus specialis*) to "destroy, in whole or in part, an identifiable group of persons." Under the UNGC, general intent is insufficient. A group's destruction, in whole or in part, must be clearly and explicitly sought by the perpetrators. The Holocaust set a near-impossible benchmark for the burden of proof, given that we have the minutes of the 1942 Wannsee Conference, which set out plans for the murder of eleven million European Jews in thirty-five regions. To this we can add an enormous number of supporting documents outlining the goals and scope of Nazi plans. This unique situation is not replicated in other cases, and it was largely a fluke of history that the Wannsee minutes, owned by Foreign Ministry official Martin Luther, were discovered at all. Given that a smoking gun or "direct evidence of genocidal intent" is rare, the ICTY Trial Chambers in the 2016 trial of Bosnian Serb President Radovan Karadžić concluded that intent could instead be "inferred from all the facts and circumstances." The judges concluded that one could, therefore, analyse such factors as "the general context, the scale of atrocities, the systematic targeting of victims on account of their membership in a particular group, the repetition of destructive and discriminatory acts, or the existence of a plan or policy." Further, "Display of intent through public speeches or in meetings may also support an inference as to the requisite specific intent."[14]

Additionally, and curiously, genocide does not require a specific motive, meaning that while a perpetrator must intend to destroy the group "as such," genocide need not be the key motivation at all. A 2001 Appeals Chamber decision from the ICTY helps clarify this somewhat counterintuitive reality: "'The personal motive of the perpetrator of the crime of genocide may be, for example, to obtain personal economic benefits, or political advantage or some form of power.'"[15] Genocide scholar Ben Kiernan explains that one may interpret genocide as "a means, rather than an end it itself." He expands on this concept:

> Many perpetrators bent on another purpose – such as forcing the surrender, dispossession, or departure of a victim group – have threatened genocide, committing it only when the threat alone failed to achieve those goals, or desisting once they are fulfilled.[16]

While prosecutors must prove that the perpetrators set out deliberately to commit genocide, it does not really matter *why* they want to commit the crime or even whether this was the first option. It could have been the final option after the perpetrators attempted a range of other horrific policies. Indeed, the perpetrators do not have to have an existential hatred of a group of people to seek their destruction. They could, for example, be after the group's land or other resources – the group might be perceived to be simply "in the way" of their vision of the future.

Negligence and Omission

It is important for us to distinguish between omission and negligence (what we might call "extreme carelessness"). As the ICTR argued in *Akayesu*, a person cannot be charged with genocide in a situation "where he did not act knowingly, and even where he should have had such knowledge."[17] Negligence, however, is distinct from omission, which is covered by the UNGC. Schabas observes in a passage worth citing at length:

> An individual may intentionally omit to perform an act, thereby participating in a result. Where the result is an act of genocide, the individual may participate with the required level of intent. Omission is not an issue of intent so much as one addressing the material element of the crime. Depending on the circumstances, an omission may occur intentionally, although it may also be the result of negligence.[18]

This is particularly relevant when we are discussing Article 2(b). In this case, omission might involve someone "inflict[ing] conditions of life on a group by failing to provide it with essentials for survival." Here, "The crime is committed by omitting to take action, rather than by taking action. Obviously, such an act can be committed with the specific intent to destroy the group."[19] This distinction brings to mind Daschuk's history of the colonization of the Plains, which documents the deliberate use of starvation by the federal government against Indigenous peoples to ensure their compliance. This is also an important distinction when we examine the negligence of the federal government in the IRS system, by allowing disease to spread unchecked, and by laying the basis for the widespread malnourishment of children. According to the UNGC, the defence that no one knew, or did not understand, the longer-term ramifications is insufficient to evade responsibility.

"In Part"

No tribunal has ever provided us with a clear percentage for "in part." Most international case law is deliberately vague so as not to embolden would-be perpetrators to advance to the red line, but not cross it. Noting that the Nazis did not realistically intend to destroy all Jews, but only those in Europe, and that the Hutu extremists in Rwanda sought to kill Tutsis only within Rwanda, the ICTR Appeals Chamber said, "The intent to destroy formed by a perpetrator of genocide will always be limited by the opportunity presented to him. While this factor alone will not indicate whether the targeted group is substantial, it can – in combination with other factors – inform the analysis."[20] The ICTY in the Krstić Appeal (2004) concluded that "in part" must represent "a substantial part of that group"; the proportion targeted "must be significant enough to have an impact on the group as a whole."[21] As I argue in chapter 3, the number of Indigenous children targeted with residential schooling fulfils the in-part criteria and is somewhat larger than the proportion of the group targeted in the genocide of Bosnian Muslims in 1995 and larger than the percentage of Aboriginal children taken in Australia as part of the Stolen Generations.[22]

Elements of Article 2

The most obvious form of genocide for those unfamiliar with the UNGC is "Killing members of the group." As I will discuss in regard to the IRS system, a finding of genocide as Article 2(a) is complicated by the fact that it is not clear how many children died or were murdered and what were the intentions behind the deaths.

"Causing Serious Bodily or Mental Harm to Members of the Group"

This is the second element of Article 2, and international case law has been very useful in defining what these elements mean in practice. In *Gacumbitsi*, the ICTR defined *serious bodily harm* as "any form of physical harm or act that causes serious bodily injury to the victim, such as torture and sexual violence." However, this harm need not be "irremediable," and the Trial Chambers outlined that "serious mental harm can be construed as some type of impairment of mental faculties, or harm that causes serious injury to the mental state of the victim."[23] More recently, the Trial Chambers in *Karadžić* made clear that serious bodily or mental harm must result "in a grave and long-term disadvantage to a person's ability to lead a normal and constructive life." The *Karadžić* decision also provides some examples of what this harm might include – that is, "torture, inhumane or degrading treatment, sexual violence including rape, interrogations combined with beatings, threats of death, and harm that damages health or causes disfigurement or serious injury to the external or internal organs of members of the group."[24]

"Deliberately Inflicting on the Group Conditions of Life ..."

Here, the ICTR's *Akayesu* judgment has become a standard for interpreting how these conditions should be understood. The Trial Chambers clarified that Article 2(c) "should be construed as the methods of destruction by which the perpetrator does not immediately kill the members of the group, but which, ultimately, seek their physical destruction." A perpetrator's actions can include "subjecting a group of people to a subsistence diet, systematic expulsion from homes and the reduction of essential medical services below minimum requirement."[25] Similarly, the Trial Chambers in *Karadžić* was clear that Article 2(c) could be understood as "the methods of destruction by which the perpetrator does not immediately kill the members of the group, but which, ultimately, seek their physical destruction."[26]

"Forcibly Transferring Children of the Group to Another Group"

Without doubt, this is the most contentious element of the UNGC and also the most relevant for Canada. Schabas is a notable critic of treating forcible transfer as genocide, and he observes that Article

2(e) was included "almost as an afterthought, with little substantive debate or consideration."[27] In other words, while it does technically count as genocide, it really should not. In later chapters, I will discuss how Schabas's misgivings reflect "common sense" views about what genocide should mean in mainstream settler society. While politicking removed cultural genocide from the convention, forcible transfer was returned by the Greek delegation and was the only part of the cultural genocide section to be included.

In parting company with Schabas in my support of 2(e), I am on solid ground, given that Lemkin always saw cultural genocide as being a form of biological genocide. This he articulated in 1951, when he posited that "genocide can be committed either by destroying the group now or by preventing it from bearing children or keeping its offspring."[28] He further responded to the question, "Can genocide be committed by kidnapping children?" by stating emphatically, "The answer is yes!" He went on to provide the examples of Genghis Khan abducting European children in a policy of "tartarization," the Ottoman Empire's abduction of Greek children, and the abduction of Greek children in 1948 by communist guerrillas. Kidnapping, he argued, was certainly a form of biological genocide in that, "From the point of view of genocide or the destruction of a human group, there is little difference between direct killings and such techniques which, like a time-bomb, destroy by delayed action."[29]

An analysis of Lemkin's voluminous correspondence confirms that he consistently upheld forcible transfer as real genocide. For example, in a draft "Memorandum on Action against Genocide" from late 1949, Lemkin wrote that genocide could be accomplished by "stealing children so that the continuity of the group as such is disrupted."[30] In a letter on how women's organizations could promote ratification, Lemkin offered, "Breaking up of families is a technic of genocide," and "Stealing of children is a technic of genocide."[31]

The ICTY in *Blagojević & Jokić* reflected Lemkin in concluding that forcible transfer can lead to the physical destruction of a group, reasoning that "the physical or biological destruction of the group is the likely outcome of a forcible transfer of the population when this transfer is conducted in such a way that the group can no longer reconstitute itself." It concluded that "the forcible transfer of individuals could lead to the material destruction of the group, since the group ceases to exist as a group, or at least as the group it was."[32] In defining what *force* means, the Rome Statute of the ICC concluded that this "may include threat of force or coercion, such as that caused by fear of violence, duress, detention, psychological oppression or abuse of power, against such person or persons or another person, or by taking advantage of a coercive environment."[33] All this is relevant to the IRS system, where we can observe both overt force deployed by the state and its agents as well as parents and guardians feeling under threat to surrender their children.

Canada's Excessively Narrow Definition of Genocide

Canada's role in the UNGC process was not benign, and our contribution, as outlined in the *Travaux Préparatoires* (the lengthy, two-volume discussion of the minutiae of the UNGC's passage), was to actively exclude cultural genocide, while at the same time stressing the English and French heritage of the country. For example, the minutes described how one of the Canadian delegates, Hugues Lapointe, rejected cultural genocide, but it then paraphrased him: "The people of his country were deeply attached to their cultural heritage, which was made up mainly of a combination of Anglo-Saxon and French elements, and they would strongly oppose any attempt to undermine the influence of those two cultures in Canada, as they would oppose any similar attempts in any other part of the world."[34] Lapointe's narrow conception of Canada as the arena for English-French political negotiations signally ignored Indigenous peoples and demonstrated a disturbing irony.

Stephens, another Canadian delegate (unfortunately, his first name is unrecorded), saw no reason for Canada to go beyond including physical and biological genocide given that his was "a country with two main and abiding cultural traditions, and with a great variety of minority groups." Painting a narrow picture, the *Travaux* minutes recall, "He [Stevens] knew of no country where the government, and the people generally, were more concerned to ensure the preservation of the culture, language or religion of minority groups."[35] Canada's federal government was certainly on the same page regarding cultural genocide, and in July 1948, Louis St. Laurent, prime minister and secretary of state for external affairs, sent a telegram to his delegation with clear instructions: "You should support or initiate any move for the deletion of Article three on 'Cultural' Genocide. If this move [is] not successful, you should vote against Article three and if necessary, against the Convention."[36]

Lester Pearson, who was secretary of state for external affairs from 1948 to 1957, before becoming prime minister in 1963, also took an active role in reducing the ambit of the UNGC to just the first two elements of Article 2. At first, he had no interest in having the convention incorporated into Canadian law, arguing, "I do not think any legislation is 'necessary' inasmuch as I cannot conceive of any act of commission or omission occurring in Canada as falling within the definition of the crime of genocide contained in article II of the convention, that would not be covered by the relevant section of the criminal code."[37]

In early 1964, a private member's bill was introduced in Parliament, which did not succeed beyond second reading, but nevertheless led to a parliamentary committee to examine whether the full UNGC should be incorporated into Canadian law. In 1966, the committee advised the government that only Articles 2(a) and (b) should count as genocide. In particular, forcible transfer was seen as a measure "intended to cover certain historical incidents in Europe that have little essential relevance to Canada where mass transfers of children to another group are unknown."[38] When questioned why some aspects of the UNGC were to be excluded, Maxwell Cohen, chair of the committee, replied, "We thought they were not relevant to Canadian life and factual needs."[39] Much of this book refutes that contention.

This narrow version of the convention was incorporated into domestic law in 1970, with the result that our Criminal Code, in section 318, lists only Articles 2(a) and (b) as genocide. This definition has remained more or less unchanged since that time, with the notable exception of updates on the nature of the "identifiable group." An amendment in June 2016 added "mental or physical disability" to the list of groups, previously defined as "any section of the public distinguished by colour, race, religion, ethnic origin or sexual orientation."[40] These changes demonstrate a selective largesse on the part of the federal government to create a more "inclusive" definition of who can suffer from genocide – ironically, in the general context of excluding two-thirds of the actual crimes from being recognized or liable for prosecution. In other words, more groups are protected, but from fewer crimes.

There is, however, some ambiguity about whether Canadian law recognizes the full convention in other government legislation. For example, in 2000, Parliament passed the Crimes Against Humanity and War Crimes Act (CAHWCA), implementing the 1998 Rome Statute of the International Criminal Court. Of interest here is the fact that the CAHWCA gives the attorney general the authority to criminally prosecute citizens and non-citizens in domestic courts for committing genocide, either in Canada or abroad. Genocide is defined in this confusing, clause-laden passage as

> an act or omission committed with intent to destroy, in whole or in part, an identifiable group of persons, as such, that at the time and in the place of its commission, constitutes genocide according to customary international law or conventional international law or by virtue of its being criminal according to the general principles of law recognized by the community of nations, whether or not it constitutes a contravention of the law in force at the time and in the place of its commission.[41]

In practice, Canadian courts have not recognized the retroactivity or the full definition of genocide, which has meant that Indigenous peoples have not found the settler legal system particularly useful. Senator Sinclair outlines this particular problem in the interview quotation that opens this chapter. In 2005, in *Malboeuf v. Saskatchewan*, Indigenous plaintiffs filed civil action over abuses at residential schools, alleging that the Canadian government had contravened Article 2(e) when it forced "the Plaintiff and other children of First Nations heritage ... to be systemically assimilated into white society and in pursuance of that plan, they were forced to attend school and contact with their families was restricted. Their culture and language were taken from them with sadistic punishment and practices." Lawyers for the government of Saskatchewan countered: "As the events giving rise to the claim predate the adoption of the Convention, the Government submits that it is irrelevant to the claim and the entire paragraph should be struck."[42] The court agreed with the government, striking out any references to the UNGC.

In a second case, *Re Residential Schools*, a Saskatchewan court struck down claims of genocide, focusing on the narrow definition in the Criminal Code. In this case, the plaintiffs were not after financial compensation, but wanted a declaration from the court that the IRS system had contravened the UNGC. The government, as defendant, countered by arguing that since the only legislation in Canada prohibiting genocide was in the Criminal Code, which "refers only to the physical destruction of peoples and not 'cultural genocide,'" the plaintiffs had no case.[43] The court sided with the government, and ruled that it lacked "the jurisdiction to award a declaratory order on the basis of a non-legal or political code of conduct."[44]

Is the act of narrowing the definition of genocide itself a breach of international law? Nêhiyaw legal theorist Tamara Starblanket has argued that Canada violated Article 18 of the 1969 Vienna Convention on the Law of Treaties when it failed to incorporate the full UNGC into the Criminal Code. The government did not have the right to pick and choose sections of the UNGC to include or exclude in domestic law. She puts it this way:

> The significance of Article 18 to the legal question is that states should not be engaging in possible acts of genocide prior to entering into a treaty on genocide and then continue with genocidal conduct after the treaty is acceded to by the state. ... It is well established that genocide is a norm of customary international law and most recently a principle of jus cogens. A state cannot pardon itself of criminal conduct by creating loopholes internationally and domestically.[45]

Starblanket's objective, as I understand it, is to see whether Canada can be held legally liable for purposefully narrowing its understanding of genocide domestically at a time when it was committing genocide. Should Canada be found to be in violation of the Vienna Convention, and given the state-centric nature of the international legal system, it is not clear what would happen next. The more cynical students of politics and law will not be surprised if little happens. The international legal system is composed of sovereign states, and while the case can be made that Canada *should* have incorporated the full definition, no other state has chosen to call Canada to account on this matter. Indeed, Canada is one of those rare Western settler states that ratified the UNGC early on and then incorporated it (albeit incompletely) into its domestic criminal legislation. The United States did nothing until the 1980s, Australia only in 2004.

Cultural Genocide

As mentioned previously, international law does not recognize cultural genocide, which is precisely why the TRC, with its restrictive post-judicial mandate, could claim that Canada had committed something that was not considered a crime in domestic law. Indeed, Canada played a key role in eliminating this aspect of the Genocide Convention, and the *Travaux Préparatoires* provides several examples of European and settler colonial delegations volubly backing off from endorsing cultural genocide. The French delegation advanced a now familiar objection – that "some of the acts which it has proposed to include in the concept of cultural genocide might have a lawful basis" and that, therefore, the proposed convention could "incriminate States exercising their powers in a normal way."[46]

Similarly, the US delegation averred that genocide "should be limited to barbarous acts committed against individual[s]," while cultural genocide, it argued, should be "dealt with in connection with the question of the protection of minorities."[47] The Americans also raised objections to the words "in part," arguing instead that, to trigger the convention, genocide must be focused on the entire group. This objection seems to have arisen out of fears in the US Senate that the frequent lynching by white racists of African Americans could qualify as genocide. US delegates worried that "sporadic outbreaks against the Negro population" might be seen as genocide.[48] The British delegation reported to the Foreign Office that the Americans were "afraid of accusations which may be made against them as a government in respect to the negro and Red Indian populations of the United States."[49]

Had decolonization been more advanced in the late 1940s, cultural genocide might have been retained as part of the UNGC, although it is also possible that the major economic and political players might never have agreed to support it. The Canadian, French, and US delegations who spearheaded opposition to cultural genocide were, as Elisa Novic recently noted, "involved in widespread campaigns of colonization to conquer territories already inhabited by other peoples."[50] Beyond this hypothetical proposition, it is certainly true that developing countries and Indigenous peoples were largely ignored. Delegates from newly independent countries and the developing world – including Egypt, China, and Pakistan – were more inclined to support the inclusion of cultural genocide. This was not coincidental as cultural genocide was often a vehicle of colonialism and settler colonialism.

Indeed, when Indigenous peoples had the chance to return cultural genocide to international law, they tried to do so. In the 1993 draft of the UNDRIP, Article 7 introduced "ethnocide" and "cultural genocide," which were defined as

(a) Any action which has the aim or effect of depriving [Indigenous peoples] of their integrity as distinct peoples, or of their cultural values or ethnic identities; (b) Any action which has the aim or effect of dispossessing them of their lands, territories or resources; (c) Any form of population transfer which has the aim or effect of violating or undermining any of their rights; (d) Any form of assimilation or integration by other cultures or ways of life imposed on them by legislative, administrative or other measures; (e) Any form of propaganda directed against them.[51]

These comprehensive definitions were removed when the declaration was put to a vote at the General Assembly in 2007, largely because states worried about their potential outcomes. Currently, genocide receives only a brief mention in Article 7(2): "Indigenous peoples have the collective right to live in freedom, peace and security as distinct peoples and shall not be subjected to any act of genocide or any other act of violence, including forcibly removing children of the group to another group."[52] Note that forcible transfer figures prominently in this definition.

Conclusions

I have designed this chapter to highlight those elements of the UNGC that are relevant to a discussion of genocide in the IRS system and in the Sixties Scoop. Raphael Lemkin's original conception of genocide was fairly broad and could indeed cover crimes in colonial and settler colonial contexts. However, as genocide moved from an academic term to being legally codified, the definition narrowed as the self-interest of the drafting states became paramount. On the other hand, as I will discuss in the next chapter, Lemkin's understanding of genocide was undeniably Eurocentric, focusing on European conceptions of how a group was constituted, how it expressed and practised its identity, and how it might be dissolved. Further, Lemkin needed to negotiate with some of the very states engaged in genocide during the drafting of the convention, including Canada and the United States, to turn his idea into law.

chapter two

Pluralists, Indigenous Peoples, and Colonial Genocide

Let us understand that what happened at the residential schools was the use of education for cultural genocide, and that the fact of the matter is – yes, it was. Call a spade a spade.

– Former prime minister Paul Martin,
Quebec National Event (2013)

On a cold April day in Montreal, Paul Martin announced to rousing applause that it was time to recognize the IRS system as cultural genocide. It was a landmark occasion, that day in 2013, but I was curious. Had Mr. Martin gone as far as he was willing to go with this conclusion? At a dinner in Toronto some time later, I saw Mr. Martin and plucked up the courage to chat with him. He is a thoughtful man, so I pushed him a little and asked whether he would go so far as to say that UN-defined genocide had been committed in Canada, and I inserted the issue of forcible transfer into the discussion. This for him appeared to be a stretch, and he intimated an understanding of genocide as primarily about mass killing, a legalist view that predominates in this country.

At another conference the year before, I met in Winnipeg with a number of Indigenous and non-Indigenous theorists to discuss genocide in settler colonial contexts and how we could best interpret these experiences. While most participants argued that forcible transfer and cultural genocide should be seen as genocide, there was a notable detractor. Clinical psychologist Joseph Gone, of the Gros Ventre tribal nation of Montana, volubly advanced a legalist position, stressing that genocide should be reserved only for cases in which a group had suffered mass murder. While Gone readily acknowledged genocidal episodes during the colonization of the Americas, he took exception to activists, historians, and others seeking to cast the entire history of colonization as a larger genocidal project.[1]

Gone later wrote that since genocide's appeal "is based on the fact that it occupies the extreme end of a continuum of moral evaluation relative to group-based violence," we needed to safeguard our use of it since it risked being "undermined by expanding its descriptive function to instances beyond mass murder proper."[2] This is a view long promoted by legalists, and indeed, distilling genocide to mass killing has been an academic preoccupation since at least 1959, when Dutch theorist Pieter Drost explicitly argued for a narrow understanding of it as "group murder."[3]

This chapter picks up from the previous one, critically examining problems with the "common sense" understanding of genocide as mass killing, with forcible transfer as a loophole or technicality in the Genocide Convention. And if there is debate about applying the black-letter legal elements of the convention, it becomes even more problematic for some to interpret the decimation of the buffalo, the theft of Indigenous lands, and the Sixties Scoop as genocide. Many highly destructive aspects of colonization fall outside the convention, or at least outside how Western courts and legal theorists have chosen to interpret them.

In this book, I articulate the case that the IRS system and the Sixties Scoop violated the UNGC, but I also make the additional claim that the convention is itself too narrow, and that to better understand Indigenous experiences of colonization, we need to broaden the academic understanding of genocide. How might we do this?

In this chapter, I lay out four possible ways to better understand Indigenous experiences of colonialism, building on the work of many thoughtful people, with the important caveat that the list is hardly exhaustive. The first way is to *critically* situate Lemkin, to employ his work to cast theoretical light on colonialization and Indigenous experiences, while also carefully positioning him as a product of his time. We must understand that there were two distinct Lemkins: Lemkin the thinker/idealist and Lemkin the pragmatist/lobbyist. A second avenue for better reflecting Indigenous experiences is to problematize *specific intent* as embodying only one type of genocidal motivation, and to turn our focus to relations of destruction. We might see genocide as a broad-based phenomenon that extends beyond governments, ruling ideologies, bureaucracies, and/or the military. Genocidal intent can be rooted in the evolving norms, patterns of thought, and behaviours in a settler society as much as they are found among policy planners and political and military leadership.

Third, we can move beyond Eurocentric understandings of what constitutes group identity. European forms of identity, promoted by Lemkin's work and underwritten by the UNGC's ratifying states, exclude many aspects of Indigenous identities. Finally, we can increase the importance of cultural genocide to better understand Indigenous genocides. Given the many and sometimes incommensurable differences between Indigenous and European ways of governance, spirituality, and holistic relationality, a focus on the differences might alert us to ways in which those of us who are settlers have destroyed Indigenous groups without having the legal or conceptual lenses to fully comprehend what we have done.

Raphael Lemkin's Mixed Messages

Embedded within the UNGC from the beginning were double standards, which seemed to privilege settler states. This situation arose not just from the self-interest of the countries involved but also from Lemkin's own work. On the positive side, Lemkin the thinker/idealist was attuned to colonial genocides, and his analysis of Nazi occupation was refracted, in part, through the lens of his studies of European colonialism in Africa, Australasia, and the Americas. His unfinished book on genocide included a number of chapters on Indigenous and colonial cases. They were to include Germany's actions in its African colonies, including massacres of the Herero; genocide by the Belgians in the Congo; and genocides against Indigenous peoples in Australia (with a separate chapter on Tasmania), Latin America (including chapters on the Aztecs, the Yucatan, and the Incas), New Zealand, and the United States. However, his final draft excised most of these case studies, and the manuscript was never published, leaving us with a mishmash of typed and handwritten notes on letter paper and index cards.[4]

On the negative side, Lemkin poorly served the study of Indigenous genocide by his overt gratitude to Western settler states. Indebted to several countries for saving his life, and cognizant of the fact that champions were needed to prevent future genocides, he failed to dig too deeply into the politics of European colonial and Western settler states. For Lemkin, the United States represented a haven for European Jews and a guarantor of a better international order. He begins *Axis Rule* by extending a not-so-subtle olive branch to the Western allies, laying out the violence of the Nazi crimes for his "Anglo-Saxon reader," who, "with his innate respect for human rights and human personality, may be inclined to believe that the Axis regime could not possibly be as cruel and ruthless as it has been hitherto described."[5]

This gratitude resulted in myopia – an inability to see the United States through the eyes of its poorest and most marginalized peoples, and Lemkin remained deeply uncritical of his adoptive country. Of that country he was clear: "Genocide does not happen here and is not likely to happen. But this country has always been and still is on the receiving line at this evil because it has to provide leadership and means for rehabilitation of millions of victims of genocide abroad."[6] In search of champions, Lemkin also befriended members of the Canadian delegation to the Genocide Convention, whom he viewed as straight shooters who were honest and reliable. In 1949, Lemkin met with and was favourably impressed by then foreign minister Pearson and observed, "One could also recognize what is so appealing about all Canadians: they basically reject the theory that international feeling must necessarily be devious. 'Let us first try it straight,' they seem to imply by all their behavior, and they remain at that point."[7]

Lemkin's gratitude resulted in a singular inability to denounce racism in the United States, especially with regard to African

Americans. In 1951, prominent African American activists, including the singer Paul Robeson, advanced a petition denouncing their treatment as genocide "as the result of consistent, conscious, unified policies of every branch of government."[8] Lemkin condemned the petition in the *New York Times* as "un-American," claiming that African Americans, while victims of discrimination, had certainly escaped "destruction, death, annihilation."[9] In a general sense, Lemkin helped legitimate the racial inequality and white supremacism of much of the United States, and was retrograde in his perceptions of the civil rights movement.[10]

Second World War–era enemies were also quickly rehabilitated in the service of the convention. Lemkin courted Japan by highlighting the abuse of its prisoners of war in China and the Soviet Union, and he sought West German support, alleging that Germans expelled from Eastern and Central Europe might also be victims of genocide.[11] When persuading Italy to sign on to the convention, Lemkin lobbied the Order Sons of Italy in America, a fraternal organization, raising the spectre of genocide against Italians in Italy's former colonies. He stoked fears among Italian Americans that their 200,000 compatriots left in Eritrea after the departure of the British would be in danger, and thus "the necessity of international law protecting the Italian minorities from the natives will become very urgent."[12]

Weiss-Wendt observes that, in the end, Lemkin was pushed into a vicious circle by the political realities of the Cold War: "He had a noble idea, which he wanted to see implemented. But he had to fight for his idea. As the fight dragged on, more and more compromises had to be made."[13] Irvin-Erickson has similarly documented the frustration among Lemkin's supporters, "believing he was too willing to allow the United States, UK, USSR, and France to dictate the contents of the law." There was good reason for this frustration since these states were consequently "able to write their own genocides out of the law, narrowly defining the acts that constitute genocide."[14]

Given that Lemkin has been dead for six decades, there is an obvious "So what?" question that arises here. My reply is that Lemkin's studied aversion to probing into the practices of Western settler states gave countries like the United States, Australia, and Canada a free pass and allowed them to continue their ongoing forms of genocide and other crimes against humanity. Rather than take a principled stand in favour of all victims of genocide, Lemkin picked his battles, and he sided with the victors of the Second World War. These countries, in his view, would constitute the international champions of the convention in preventing genocide abroad, but not at home.

This myopic view of history created several problems. First, in helping to draft the convention, Western settler states actively excluded elements that could be compromising in their own domestic contexts. Second, in supporting the convention during its evolution, they gained rhetorical assurances from Lemkin that their adversaries were genocidal while they were not. Third, in promoting a high level of respect for the sovereignty of states, states could effectively shield themselves domestically by choosing how they would incorporate or not incorporate the convention into their own legislation.

Moving beyond *Specific Intent*

A central focus of legalist analysis is *specific intent*; this is often lacking in cases of Indigenous genocide, sometimes because the evidence has been destroyed, in other cases because the general climate of the time made genocide against Indigenous peoples a widespread and normal expectation. Those whom I call pluralists have moved beyond the UN definition, recognizing the politics behind the convention, how some groups were excluded, and other issues. They have moved beyond the seminal role of settlers in colonial genocides, to explore how settler societies and settler norms can, in fact, be genocidal in and of themselves. In this view of genocide, no state ideology targeting Indigenous peoples and calling for their destruction is necessary.

One of the trailblazers of this type of analysis was historian Tony Barta, who famously developed the term "relations of destruction" when describing the genocide of Aboriginal and Torres Strait

Islander peoples over two centuries of Australian history. In 1987, he argued persuasively that many genocides, especially those in colonial contexts, had relied on unintended consequences rather than specific intent.[15]

While white settler Australians often claimed that they had no directly genocidal relationship with Aboriginal peoples, Barta countered that such a relationship existed through settler exploitation, land appropriation, and other means, even if settlers had never actually met an Indigenous person. Indeed, unequal, exploitative, and ultimately genocidal relations were "fundamental to the history of the society in which they live; and that implicitly rather than explicitly, in ways which were inevitable rather than intentional, it is a relationship of genocide." Moving beyond state responsibility for genocide, Barta explored Australia as a "genocidal society," marked by the "remorseless pressures of destruction inherent in the very nature of the society."[16]

Through a logic of competition, Indigenous peoples were presented as being in the way of lands and other resources needed for settlement. A settler logic that saw the "vanishing," or "melting away," of Indigenous peoples as inevitable excused their widespread "disappearance" in the face of Western colonization. In the Canadian case, Daniel Francis has traced an unquestioned belief among many settlers that Indigenous peoples were fated to physically disappear. This was simply expected, and little effort was expended to actually reverse the process other than trying to assimilate them into settler society. There were, he argued, "no plans presented for halting their seemingly inexorable plunge toward extinction. In part, this was because such plans were unthinkable."[17]

Why unthinkable? Because, as Francis argues, Indigenous peoples were wrongly seen as being inferior to white Europeans, and so when these groups confronted one another, their decline was conceived as inevitable. In such a scenario, their disappearance need not be overtly stated as a policy goal. Rather, it might occur by the omission of any policies to save Indigenous ways of living, or Indigenous lives, or by not stopping the spread of European diseases that decimated the Plains peoples during the eighteenth and nineteenth centuries, causing the elimination of many nations. The idea that Indigenous peoples were genetically susceptible to dying from European diseases led to a high degree of settler apathy when trying to stop the causes of disease and save lives. Take, for example, an official response to the spread of tuberculosis and other diseases by Frank Oliver, deputy superintendent general of Indian affairs. He put it this way: "The excessive mortality occurs mainly among Indians in process of transition from the aboriginal to the civilized environment." While he predicted that the situation would improve as Indigenous peoples became more "civilized," his report suggested an inevitably high number of deaths before this would occur.[18]

Myths of the inevitability of Indigenous disappearance, Sherene Razack argues, have allowed successive Canadian governments to evade responsibility for the negative impacts of colonization, since they are only there to promote Western civilization and law, while Indigenous peoples are "dying due to an inherent incapacity to survive modern life."[19] Similarly, Andrew Woolford's sociological understanding of genocide moves beyond the need for specific intent and looks instead to the ways in which intent is "negotiated under structural and discursive conditions." A settler colonial society may establish the basis for the destruction of Indigenous peoples through a range of settler institutions and actions. Absent any sort of military chain of command, as in a wartime situation, those carrying out genocidal destruction may do so in different and potentially contradictory ways. Looking for the Wannsee minutes or a smoking gun may be unrealistic in a scenario where group destruction is enabled through societal pressure and narratives that inferiorize Indigenous peoples, together with situational factors such as biased institutions, ingrained settler racism and fear, and hunger for Indigenous lands and resources.[20]

This type of theorizing provides tremendous range for pluralistic thinking about genocide that can largely be distinguished from specific intent, speed, or war. It helps develop the case for revisions to the definition of genocide under international law, which would seek to move beyond the emphasis on *dolus specialis*. We might explore genocide as a series of processes that seek group attrition over a long period of time, which, following Sheri Rosenberg, can include "forced displacement, the denial of health and health care, the denial of food, and sexual violence."[21] Robert Nixon's concept of "slow death" details how people die in ways that fail to appear on the radar of public consciousness. The public, he argues, is conditioned to respond to certain types of events, which are usually short in duration, highly visible, and explosive in content. Slow violence, however, is not terribly newsworthy because it happens over time, as a result of processes that are neither exciting nor quick, "a violence of delayed destruction that is dispersed across time and space, an attritional violence that is typically not viewed as violence at all."[22]

Paradoxically, some can take for granted the slow death of a group, even while seeking the health of individual members. In his 1936 essay on the dangers of tuberculosis in Indigenous communities, David Stewart (medical superintendent of the Sanatorium Board of Manitoba) made the case that since Indigenous peoples would inevitably be merged into the settler population, as individuals they should be cured as soon as possible. The general logic of colonization and biological absorption held that the "mixture of blood, which has gone on for nearly two hundred years ... will no doubt continue until the red race is absorbed into the general population." Stewart reasoned, "This forecast surely gives a special motive for doing the best we can for the Indians." In other words, since the Indians as a separate racial category would either die off or become assimilated, it made good sense to combat tuberculosis right away, largely as protection for settlers.[23]

Countering a legalist focus on war, specific intent, and mass murder, many pluralist arguments suggest that lack of speed and deliberation do not necessarily mitigate the long-term genocidal impact on the affected groups. In a settler colonial situation, the government already exercises considerable control, so the strategy is more about management, about conducting policy in a manner that will ensure consistency over a long time. Several authors writing on Indigenous genocide in Canada have articulated this slow but steady approach. In an early work published in 1973, Davis and Zannis called for a wider definition of genocide, one that included not just "mass homicide" but also cultural destruction through the forcible transfer of people in the North.[24] Later works like Menno Boldt's *Surviving as Indians* described the reserve system as a form of "Indian genocide," in which the concentration and isolation of Indigenous peoples led to heightened levels of alcoholism and drug abuse, alongside violence and suicide.[25]

Chrisjohn and Young's well-known book *The Circle Game* similarly likens Indigenous genocide to a "slow, lingering death" over a long time period, genocide with no end point, with little fear of domestic resistance or international accountability.[26] In her work, Andrea Bear Nicholas also outlines the case for the convention's applicability, given Indigenous experiences with "extreme social, cultural, physical, and spiritual dislocations, which lead, in turn, to dramatically increased rates of death as a consequence."[27] To this we can add Neu and Therrien's *Accounting for Genocide*, which analyses parallels between Indigenous and Jewish genocides. A marked difference in Canada, they argue, was that the genocide was slower and more subtle, using "assimilation and absorption, compulsory enfranchisement."[28] The slow and steady process of demonizing Indigenous peoples, stripping them of their lands, and outlawing their spiritual traditions and languages brought about genocide without international warfare or industrial-scale mass murder.[29]

The lack of war, and indeed the lack of necessity for war, potentially marks out Indigenous genocides as distinctive. European Jews, Rwandan Tutsi, Armenians in the Ottoman Empire, Bosnian Muslims – these were all self-sufficient and demographically thriving communities. They were not suffering from dramatic reductions in mortality resulting from foreign diseases and rapid environmental changes. In a sense, European and African perpetrators *needed* to use war as a means to destroy target groups. However, Indigenous genocide in the context of the Indian residential schools took place when Indigenous peoples in Canada were already experiencing demographic decline; this situation marks a very different confluence of events.

Indigenous Genocide: Beyond Human Groups

The non-human world – that is to say, the actual world – does not form a part of Lemkin's cosmology or the Genocide Convention, which is focused on protecting human national, racial, religious, and ethnic groups. We should consider how colonial genocides of Indigenous peoples present particular circumstances that necessitate us seeing genocide differently. Without being essentialist, we might observe that many Indigenous perspectives privilege an interrelated, holistic approach to humans and their environment, an environment that is very much alive, moving, expanding, and changing. For Leroy Little Bear (Blackfoot), many Indigenous paradigms stress "ideas of constant flux, all existence consisting of energy waves/spirit, all things being animate, all existence being interrelated, creation/existence having to be renewed, space/place as an important referent, and language, songs, stories, and ceremonies as repositories for the knowledge that arise[s] out of these paradigms."[30]

Similarly, in her overview of Indigenous-settler history, Indigenous scholar Lisa Monchalin has focused on the sacred links between human beings and everything around them, including plants, rocks, and the land, which are "equal, interconnected, mutually dependent, and embracing a sacred relationship with this world."[31] Similarly, Nêhiyaw legal theorist and novelist Tracey Lindberg elaborates on the concept that "the earth is our mother" by describing an expanded understanding of Indigenous group identity, distinct from European conceptions: "Included within that familial relationship is the understanding that we have a relationship with the land that is reciprocal. It has cared for us. We must care for it."[32]

Western views are often seen as being fundamentally different, even incommensurable with Indigenous realities. Nêhiyaw-Saulteaux Knowledge Keeper Blair Stonechild has observed that, for many Indigenous peoples, "*all entities* – whether animal, plant, reptile, insect, and even what others consider to be inanimate objects – have life, energy, and supernal significance. In other words, *all* entities in this world – animate and inanimate – are purposeful *beings* in their own right."[33] Without a sense of how a group understands its identity in relation to its own group members and to those not of the group, it becomes impossible to engage with whether the group was actually targeted for destruction. Land and the environment, for example, are often seen as not just supporting group life but also being "key components of group life."[34]

Anishinaabe Elder Fred Kelly outlines the scope of the violence committed by the state in stealing Indigenous lands: "To take the territorial lands away from a people whose very spirit is so intrinsically connected to Mother Earth was to actually dispossess them of their very soul and being; it was to destroy whole Indigenous nations."[35] Land, in addition to its spiritual significance, may also play a central role in cultural memory and cultural reproduction. Lynne Kelly's study of oral memory highlights some of the many mnemonic strategies of Australian Aboriginal peoples – in particular, their use of songlines. Here, the "method of loci" ties a complex memory of events in the life of the group with specific locations, which as ceremonial locations are also spaces of memory.[36]

Indigenous conceptions of group identity may also include close familial interrelationships with non-human animals, like the buffalo in Nêhiyaw filmmaker Tasha Hubbard's seminal studies of buffalo communities and buffalo genocide, which include both academic writing and films (such the 2013 animated work, *Buffalo Calling*). Hubbard sees aspects of genocide in the near-extinction of the buffalo, which deprived Plains people of their traditional food, clothing, and shelter, and hastened their deaths. However, Hubbard goes further and, in applying an epistemological framework appropriate to her people, believes that animals who share their lives with humans can be members of the group, even though they are of a different species. Hubbard reflects on her teachings that "the buffalo people take care of us and teach us how to live, much like a benevolent grandparent."[37] Further, "Indigenous peoples saw the buffalo as their protector, who took a position on the front line in the genocidal war against Indigenous peoples."[38] Hubbard's contribution offers tremendous scope for reflection on how a group can include non-humans and how genocide can involve the targeting of relationships between humans and non-humans. Her work also suggests that genocide can involve targeting the relations among different groups and that these relationships may also perform a central role in group identity.

From some Indigenous perspectives, relations of destruction can be the result of omissions, inaction, silences, and the squandering and exploitation of the non-human world. Sylvia Saysewahum McAdam (one of the founders of Idle No More and a Nêhiyaw legal scholar) outlines several concepts worth considering. Particularly important for an understanding of groupness is *ohcinêwin*, "the breaking of a law(s) against anything other than a human being." Here humans are understood to have obligations to maintain respectful and harmonious relations with everything around them. Cruelty to animals and the environment and not respecting traditional hunting laws and relationships between humans and animals – these are considered to be part of *ohcinêwin*, "to suffer in retribution for an action against creation." McAdam puts it clearly: "Animals are regarded as persons in their own right; the relationship between the Nêhiyaw and animal-persons is governed by the same legal considerations that govern human relationships."[39]

If we understand groups as being inseparable from animals, plants, water, and air, group identity can never be reducible to a small number of European-defined characteristics like languages, famous heroes and battles, novels, and religious practices. Given the multidimensional nature of some Indigenous identities, methods of committing genocide may also be more complex, concentrating their attention on areas that are not traditional targets of genocide in Western literature. Thus, Nêhiyaw scholar Matt Wildcat articulates a view of genocide focused on the destruction of the "webs of relationships and kinship" among groups of Indigenous peoples.[40] The destruction of these "inter-Indigenous bonds" was a strategy of the settler state to weaken Indigenous identities and resistance to colonial expansion, yet does not form part of the UNGC.

There have been recent efforts to consider the many forms of Indigenous collective identities. Robert Innes's work on kinship, which is based on research with his own Cowessess First Nation, stresses pluralism in group membership and a lack of rigid boundaries demarcating inside and outside. In his Cowessess nation, membership was largely based on kinship practices. People could marry into the group, and membership was largely understood by who was related to whom, in a "fluid, flexible, and inclusive" arrangement. "Band membership, then, served to strengthen social, economic, and military alliances with other bands of similar cultural origins." As such, by the 1870s, Innes's nation was, in fact, "multicultural" in the sense of being based on kinship relations and including members of five Indigenous groups.[41]

Innes problematizes the idea that there were clear and distinct tribal boundaries, and he notes that many bands did not aim to create a single culture based on hybridity, but practised multiple cultures in the same group.[42] In many cases, he notes the mixed lineage of many influential leaders (Chiefs Pîhtokahanapiwiyin, Mistahimaskwa, and Payipwât, for example) and the fact that Métis were integral members of bands, despite how they were later seen as distinct, and administered by the provinces and not the federal government.[43] A key point here is that settler colonial explorers, traders, and officials have tended to stress the differences between Indigenous peoples, while downplaying the commonalities, connections, and intermarriage between families and groups as well as the fluidity and interchanges of group identities.

From a settler historian's perspective, James Daschuk explores the phenomenon of "ethnogenesis" in his work – the joining together of groups that were once distinct in the aftermath of high rates of mortality during the eighteenth century. He focuses in his work on the Western Ojibwa (Saulteaux), the Plains Cree, and the Plains Métis. While at one time, the Indigenous peoples of the Plains were some of the tallest and healthiest in the world, they became one of the sickest due to high rates of tuberculosis, smallpox, and other diseases.[44]

The sometime fluidity and multiculturalism of group membership does not mean that these were somehow not "real" groups for the purposes of the UNGC. Jews were, after all, defined by Nazi Germany based on complex racial laws passed in 1935, not on religion, language, geographic region, or other criteria, while Tutsis in Rwanda were targeted based on characteristics defined from 1926 by Belgian colonial officials. Nevertheless, this argument serves to alert us to the Eurocentrism of the Genocide Convention and its focus on certain types of assumed group boundaries, which generate insides and outsides that may not correspond to some Indigenous traditions.

The Return of Cultural Genocide

Cultural genocide has a distinguished legal pedigree, and while it has no legal standing now, it certainly had *potential* legal standing when the residential schools were in operation. Indeed, but for the actions of Canada and other settler colonial and colonizing states, cultural genocide might have been accepted as authentic, UN-defined genocide. Lemkin clearly saw cultural genocide as an inseparable part of genocide, and he realized that the primary reason that cultural genocide was hived off and voted out from the Genocide Convention was that colonial and settler colonial states did not want to enact laws that would clearly bind their hands in dealing with Indigenous peoples. We also need to better understand that when there is a wide divergence between the cultures of perpetrator and target groups, especially in how groupness and group membership is determined, cultural genocide can be disastrous for the reproduction of group life. Those studying genocide have generally failed to adequately examine the key differences between oral and written cultures and how knowledge is transmitted from one generation to the next. Does cultural genocide make a bigger impact when the targeted group and the perpetrator are starkly different?

We see a clear example of how the IRS system impacted Indigenous identities by understanding oral history and culture. A Survivor of three residential schools, Michael Cachagee (Chapleau Cree First Nation), served as the executive director of the National Residential School Survivors Society. He offered an example to me, in an interview, of how the residential schools had broken his continuity with the past and impeded the transmission of his culture. When he was three, in the spring of 1943, he was taken to residential school and lost the ability to communicate with his family, including his grandmother:

> I didn't see my Granny when she died, she died in 1955, my Granny was 103 years old ... being 103 she could probably go back to 1860 and have vivid memories of 1860 and in that, from 1860 she would have had the opportunity to talk to people directly that could remember back two centuries. ... I'm cut off from that resource as a person of oral history ... what's the difference of burning a history book or destroying people whose history is based upon oral translation?[45]

Mr. Cachagee has consistently argued in favour of applying the convention to his experiences, and he articulates a strong case for understanding the intergenerational breaks among parents, grand-parents, and children as a form of cultural genocide.

To this, Woolford suggests that, in oral societies, where language and culture are transmitted through children, child removal will mean far more than simply "an interruption of reproductive and socialization patterns."[46] If a society depends on its language and its children to continue its culture and maintain the identity of the group, cultural genocide may be a clearer road to group extinction among Indigenous peoples than Europeans. If relationships with animals, plants, and waters are central to identity, destroying these living beings and networks may have far more significant ontolog-ical consequences for Indigenous peoples than simply removing water and food "supplies" might for European peoples.

Western settlers like me may find it difficult to understand how different our imposed systems may be, and how destructive, but we are starting to learn. Patrick Wolfe's observation that "settler colonialism destroys to replace"[47] expresses the processes I exam-ine later in this book: the means by which our government and church representatives sought to destroy Indigenous societies and replace them with something altogether different. The greater the differences, the more traumatic that replacement could be. In com-ing to terms with Indigenous genocide, genocide theorists will need to prioritize and privilege Indigenous peoples and their own understandings of group composition, identity, and destruction.

Conclusions

From pluralist perspectives, the IRS system is but one manifes-tation of much larger processes of colonial genocide at work, at varying degrees of intensity and in different regions. Expanding our understanding of genocide to better capture Indigenous expe-riences may lead those of us who are settler academics to question the human-centred nature of groupness and to problematize how group identity is presented as being a relatively impermeable shell dividing insiders from outsiders. Expanding our understanding also involves better engaging with group identities in relation to land and waters, and the spiritual practices derived therefrom.

These views of genocide take the term well outside its legalist confines and may lead to a range of new understandings that better reflect historic and ongoing Indigenous experiences of colonization. However, to reach out to a larger settler public, many of the Indigenous writers discussed in this book make ample use of the Genocide Convention. This may be because it is the most expedient path *right now* to create a "ground floor" for understanding genocide in the IRS system. Further, the convention is the standard by which Canada's provincial and federal elected bodies have chosen to officially recognize seven genocides (about which more in chapter 7). This indicates that there is a commonly accepted standard of what genocide is, and public institutions like the Canadian Museum for Human Rights are using this standard to teach about genocide and genocide prevention. In this context, however, we also need to work for a more just convention, one that reflects the types of crimes to which Indigenous peoples were and are still subject.

chapter three

Forcible Transfer as Genocide in the Indian Residential Schools

I remember screaming. I remember my mom doing the same thing. But the police officer held onto her. When Mr. Findlay threw me in the car, I went out the other door and I ran. But he ran after me and caught me. I like to think of the word *abducted*. After he caught me he threw me into the back seat again and they tied me with my hands like this (indicating). And we drove away.[1]

At the age of five, Arthur Fourstar was forcibly taken from his mother and transferred to an Indian residential school. An RCMP officer and another white man burst into his home and physically restrained his mother, while he was grabbed and thrown into a waiting car. Mr. Fourstar's recollections are one of many hundreds compiled by the former AHF, to which we can add seven thousand Survivor reflections gathered by the TRC, and tens of thousands more compiled by the federal government, as part of the compensation process for the IRS Settlement Agreement.

In this chapter, I apply legalist and pluralist conceptions of genocide to the IRS system. In line with my own reading of IRS history, I prioritize Article 2(e), "Forcibly transferring children of the group to another group," and carefully consider how we might understand *forcible* and *transfer* in this case. Most of this chapter will discuss the types of force used and the methods of transfer; it will also establish the intent to commit genocide against Indigenous peoples using the IRS system as a vehicle. While I base my discussion on the framework of the UNGC and the international case law that has developed from it, I also argue that these sources are insufficiently narrow. The bigger picture concerns the settler colonial context of the Canadian state as well as the colonial and settler colonial context of the development of the UN and the UNGC itself, which was, in part at least, a product of state interests.

This chapter covers a range of issues, beginning with an examination of group size, then moving on to a detailed discussion of what both *forcible* and *transfer* mean in this context. This chapter also engages with key questions about how the IRS system developed. What did government and church officials intend when they established it? How did federal laws facilitate forced removal, while making Indigenous resistance to colonialism extremely difficult? This chapter lays the foundation for further exploration of forcible transfer as the IRS system wound down, through the Sixties Scoop and the devolution of some Crown powers to the provinces.

Group Size and Significance

What proportion of a group must be targeted to invoke the UNGC? James R. Miller notes that, in 1910, the number of First Nations children in government-run schools of any kind was 6,784 students in 241 day schools, 2,229 in boarding schools, and 1,612 in industrial institutions out of a total population of 19,528 Indigenous children with status aged between seven and fifteen. This translates to 54.4 per cent attendance by status Indigenous children in any form of federal government–run school, and 19.7 per cent in residential schools. By 1927, the number of school attendees had increased to approximately 20,400 Indigenous children aged between six and fifteen, about 6,600 in residential schools, and 8,000 in day schools. This proportion remained consistent for some time, until, at its high point, the system consisted of about eighty schools, and they would not have been able to house more than about one-third of Inuit and status Indigenous children.[2] In reviewing one of my publications, Miller asks, "If one-fifth or fewer 'Aboriginal' children attended residential school, can the experience be judged as genocide?"[3]

This is an important question, and both case law and the literature on genocide suggest that one-fifth does indeed represent a significant proportion of a group. This is especially so when we understand that residential schooling was but *one* aspect of government policy towards Indigenous peoples that aimed at their disappearance as groups. In other cases, one-fifth is sufficient to apply the UNGC. First, we can examine the massacre of Bosnian Muslim men and boys in 1995 by Bosnian Serb forces in the city of Srebrenica. There, 7,500 people were massacred out of a total community population of 40,000, a number that represented only a fraction of the total Bosnian Muslim population of Bosnia Herzegovina itself.[4] Should the percentage of targeted people be higher if the focus is on forcible transfer and not mass murder? This question is not articulated in the UNGC and is not answered by international case law.

Second, one-fifth aligns with the case of Australia, where thousands of Aboriginal and Torres Strait Islander children were forcibly removed from their home communities in the early twentieth century. In that case, between 10 and 30 per cent of Indigenous children were subject to forcible transfer. In 1995, the Australian federal government tasked the Australian Human Rights Commission with investigating the full extent of the country's child removal policies, in order to recommend what legal and others changes should be made in Australian law to remedy past and current abuses. After a detailed study and many hearings, the commission produced the *Bringing Them Home* report in 1997, which classified this period of forcible transfer as genocide, despite the fact that the crimes had largely predated the UNGC and that the UNGC had not been incorporated into Australian law until 2004.[5]

One-fifth is also sufficient when we understand that opportunity is a key part of any finding of genocide; thus, the fact that a proportion of Indigenous children were beyond the reach of the state does not mean that the IRS system was not genocidal. The system can be understood as one part of a coordinated strategy of different actions, which included starvation and disease. To this we can add that the federal government viewed Indigenous "groups" differently than Indigenous peoples themselves viewed group identity. The government made divisions according to the Indian Act and also, to some extent, by treaty or the lack thereof. Indigenous peoples, by contrast, often identified themselves by their connections to land, plants, waters, animals, and the world around them; and by their own communities, kinship, and treaty relationships. Given the wide range of Indigenous peoples – languages, cultures, and ways of living and knowing the world – it would be grossly inaccurate to see Indigenous peoples as a coherent group that can easily be segmented into fractions for the purpose of denying the applicability of the UNGC.

We also need to consider the overall depletion and sometimes amalgamation, fracturing, and change in group identity and composition over the course of Canadian colonial history, which we already saw in relation to Innes's and Daschuk's work in the previous chapter. As Mi'kmaq historian Daniel Paul carefully documents, the physical genocide of the Beothuk and Mi'kmaq occurred primarily during the eighteenth century, and it involved starvation, the forced spread of disease, and bounties placed by colonial leaders on Indigenous scalps.[6] The fact that there was (only) one residential school in the Maritimes, at Shubenacadie, does not mean that Indigenous peoples there were less affected by colonial genocide, only that genocide had occurred earlier and through other means.

The decimation of Indigenous peoples and nations as a result of disease, massacres, destruction of food supplies, and other purposeful and/or inadvertent methods during the processes of colonization is well documented. These disasters, both natural and colonizer-derived, changed the nature of group identity by physically and culturally weakening many nations, while also creating new nations through processes of ethnogenesis. Thus, in some cases, there was no long-term and historically continuous, demographically stable "base" populations and "base" identities from which to work when assessing the impact of residential schools on groupness. This lack of a stable base population distinguishes the IRS system from other genocides, where there were relatively settled populations of German, Polish, or Czech Jews in Europe, for example, or Tutsis in Rwanda. In Canada, the size of the base was steadily diminishing as its food supplies were deliberately destroyed and its land holdings eroded by government trickery.

At another level, while Indian Affairs divided Indigenous peoples into three "legal" categories for its own purposes of classification, it also classified them by language, tribal affiliation, and other criteria, and some tribal groups were targeted more than others. The Plains was the region in which the most aggressive assimilation occurred, and Duncan Campbell Scott argued that the Plains Indians, "whose hatred of work [is] proverbial," were most in need of residential schooling.[7] This was also the region that government policy planners were most anxious to populate with European settlers.

Forcible Transfer

I will focus in this section on the concept of *forcible*. I do this by describing four aspects; the first two are settler-state-inspired *push factors*, and the other two are settler-state- and church-inspired *pull factors*.

The first push factor is the intent by policy planners to do away with the separate existence of Indigenous peoples, resulting in specific legislation that created a climate in which children were pushed to go to schools lest their guardians be imprisoned or otherwise punished. The second push factor was the general climate of suppression of Indigenous governance traditions, lands, peoples, and spiritual practices, which weakened Indigenous legal and political institutions. It is worth reiterating that *force* under the UNGC can include the threat of force or, as the ICTR put it in its *Akayesu* judgment, "threats or trauma which would lead to the forcible transfer of children from one group to another."[8] These push factors became more pronounced after 1920.

Of the pull factors, the first is the fact that children were removed from their homes and/or communities – in some cases, actually kidnapped without their guardian's knowledge. The second relates to the often violent, transformative force used in the schools themselves.

Transfer, as I define it here, occurs when children are in the control of another group and are being actively assimilated into that group, while key aspects of their identity from the group of origin are suppressed. They do not necessarily have to be fully integrated into the perpetrator group, just taken from their group, with various impediments placed on them to prevent their return. As a secondary factor, parents and other members of the group targeted with genocide are discouraged – through legislation, through force or threat of force, or through other means – from either preventing the transfer from taking place or rescuing the children during and after they have been taken.

James R. Miller has critiqued the claims of genocide advanced by Andrew Woolford and me, asserting that "it is demonstrable that many who went to residential school maintained their Aboriginal identity, albeit with difficulty."[9] However, genocidal policies do not have to entirely destroy group identity and cohesion to be considered genocidal. Ultimately, transfer never meant full transfer in the sense of Indigenous children somehow "becoming" white. Due to the racism of the time, the IRS system could never have created an egalitarian society, nor a truly level playing field. This marks an important distinction from other efforts at forced removal such as the *Lebensborn* program, which I discuss in chapter 7. The system was designed to ensure that Indigenous peoples would be subservient and no longer, as Scott once put it, "an undesirable and often dangerous element in society."[10] Indigenous people were to enter mainstream society primarily as workers and servants, at the lowest rungs of the economic ladder. My argument is consistent with that of other genocide scholars, such as Eliza Novic, who stress that transfer was not focused on assimilation and the merging of Indigenous peoples into a homogeneous group, but was intended to bring them in to serve the "already-established dominant group."[11]

We might say that *transfer from* was always far more important than *transfer to*. The RCAP's 1996 report understood the chief goal of the schools as "a concerted attack on the ontology, on the basic cultural patterning of the children and on their world view." The success of the IRS system, it concluded, would be determined by the extent to which Survivors understood "the world as a European place within which only European values and beliefs had meaning," while similarly seeing that "the wisdom of their cultures ... [was] to them only savage superstition."[12] Agnes Grant notes that the success of the schools depended on their ability to "alienate children from their parents and their tribal customs."[13] As the system evolved, the planners seemed to envisage a new group, one comprised of Survivors caught in a sort of limbo between Indigenous and settler societies – one in which people would be racially Indigenous (insofar as this was possible) and culturally working-class, semi-skilled, and European.

A History of the Schools and the Intentions of Their Creators

Certainly, Canada has a long history of residential schooling, going back to the seventeenth century. While the federal government initiative created a network of schools, there were already residential schools in existence, such as the Mohawk Institute, Shingwauk, Wikwemikong, and Mount Elgin in Ontario.

My focus here is on the mid- to late nineteenth century, the period in which the federal government and the four mainstream churches entered a partnership to establish a network of schools as a complement to the expansion and deeper colonization of the country. In my introductory chapter, I briefly outlined some of the larger context for the creation of the IRS system: the pre-Confederation history of the school system and several key discriminatory policies arising from the BNA Act, the Indian Act, and other such documents. The 1842 Bagot Commission recommended the establishment of boarding schools, focused on agriculture, to which educator Egerton Ryerson in 1847 added recommendations for a small network of religious schools funded by government. By that time, a series of legal changes had signalled a shift of political power from the British imperial government to the fledgling Province of Canada, which assumed control of the Indian Affairs portfolio in 1860. A series of important pieces of legislation – the BNA Act (1867), the Gradual Civilization Act (1869), and the Indian Act (1876) – underwrote the conditions for the active colonization of Indigenous peoples and their incorporation into an expanding settler colonial state.

Journalist Nicholas Flood Davin, together with a number of influential political leaders later in the century, was interested in using schools as a vehicle for the destruction of Indigenous identities. Davin was commissioned by the federal government to write a report on residential schooling, which he submitted in 1879, making thirteen concrete suggestions. He viewed adult Indigenous peoples as both irredeemable and also cognizant that their days were numbered: "He is crafty, but conscious how weak his craft is when opposed to the superior cunning of the white man."[14] Children, however, were seen as more malleable and could potentially be transformed into productive members of settler society. While such schools would be expensive to establish, Davin envisaged, as did later planners, that they could be self-supporting, and they were preferable to day schools on reserve since "the influence of the wigwam was stronger than the influence of the school."[15] He was cautious, however, about ceding the churches too much control over education and also argued in favour of high salaries for teachers to attract the best people. These recommendations were not followed up as the churches would run the schools, with teachers and other staff often paid well below the equivalent rate outside the system.

Davin's report found support in Ottawa. Public Works Minister Hector Langevin made it clear to Parliament in 1883 that day schools would be insufficient in assimilating Indigenous children: "The fact is that if you wish to educate the children you must separate them from their parents during the time they are being taught. If you leave them in the family they may know how to read and write, but they will remain savages, whereas by separating them in the way proposed, they acquire the habits and tastes ... of civilized people."[16] The government subsequently provided $44,000 to fund the creation of three residential schools in Battleford and Qu'Appelle, Saskatchewan, and High River, Alberta.

The intention of ending the separate existence of Indigenous peoples as such was expressed in 1887 by John A. Macdonald, when he argued, "The great aim of our legislation has been to do away with the tribal system and assimilate the Indian people in all respects with the inhabitants of the Dominion, as speedily as they are fit for the change."[17] Certainly, Macdonald saw Indigenous education as being distinct, arising from his perception of different needs. If he conceded that "secular education is a good thing among white men," he thought that "among Indians the first object is to make them better men, and, if possible, good Christian men by applying proper moral restraints."[18]

In its annual report of 1889, the Department of Indian Affairs provided further rationale for the system: "The boarding school disassociates the Indian child from the deleterious home influences to which he would otherwise be subjected. It reclaims him from the uncivilized state in which he has been brought up."[19] Superintendent General of Indian Affairs Edgar Dewdney promoted similar views at around the same time: "It would be highly desirable ... to obtain entire possession of all Indian children after they attain the age of seven or eight years, and keep them at schools of the industrial type."[20] Similarly, the archbishop of St. Boniface, Manitoba, advocated that children be "caught young to be saved from what is on the whole the degenerating influence of their home environment."[21]

To this, Deputy Superintendent General of Indian Affairs Hayter Reed expressed his department's perspective in the 1890s, that the IRS system should make "every effort ... against anything calculated to keep fresh in the memories of the children habits and associations which it is one of the main objects of industrial education to obliterate."[22] On another occasion, Reed observed that for the IRS system to operate effectively, children had to be physically isolated: "The more remote from the Institution and distant from each other are the points from which the students are collected, the better for their success."[23] In 1894, Reed reasoned that day schools were a futile exercise in the wholesale transformation of Indigenous peoples. Transferring children "for a long period," and under "constant care and attention," could remove the taint of their traditional ways and therefore offer "the solution of the Indian problem."[24] Later officials such as Frank Pedley, who also served as deputy superintendent general of Indian Affairs, articulated the

IRS system's role in 1904 as being "to bring the Indians as near the status of the white man as can be and make them a moral, industrious and self supporting class."[25]

Duncan Campbell Scott, deputy superintendent general of Indian Affairs from 1913 to 1932, expressed similar sentiments about ending the separate existence of Indigenous peoples. Scott had an interest in removing Indigenous identity from the country, and in his early writings, he referred to Indigenous peoples as "a real menace to the colonization of Canada." As to the future, Scott predicted that traditional practices such as trapping, fishing, and hunting would have to give way to farming or some other form of Western settled existence, which might invariably involve working within the "industrial or mercantile community." The schools would then form an essential part of the transformation of the Indigenous person, embodied by "the substitution of Christian ideals of conduct and morals for aboriginal concepts of both."[26]

However, as Brian Titley explains in his seminal biography of Scott, schools would never be sufficient, given Scott's view that the eradication of "primitive instincts" could take generations. Western industrial and agricultural employment was "foreign to [an Indigenous person's] natural bent," while "altruism is absent from the Indian character." While the schools could help improve the situation, Scott had still grander plans, which involved intermarriage with settler populations. Given his perception that the primitive instincts of Indigenous peoples were genetically encoded and thus transmitted through each successive generation, intermarriage would be the best way of creating a race of people more suited for his concept of civilization. This was the larger context for understanding Scott's well-known conclusions: "The happiest future for the Indian race is absorption into the general population, and this is the object of the policy of our government. The great forces of intermarriage and education will finally overcome the lingering traces of native custom and tradition."[27] We might understand the goals of the policies as being to make Indigenous individuals *palatable* to the settler, but not necessarily *like* the settler.

In 1920, Scott delivered a famous speech justifying many of his new amendments to the Indian Act, in which he said, "I want to get

rid of the Indian problem. ... Our object is to continue until there is
not a single Indian in Canada that has not been absorbed into the
body politic and there is no Indian question, and no Indian Department."[28] This does not encapsulate the entire history of the schools,
but it does provide a useful snapshot of Scott's thinking at the time,
and, when combined with the views of other government officials,
it allows us to make inferences about the nature of the schools and
the intentions behind them.

The Churches

Most residential school overviews of any detail note that the actors
involved had a range of complementary and conflicting motives.
The churches engaged in keen competition to convert Indigenous
peoples to their particular denomination, and they sought to divide
Canada into spheres of influence for proselytization. Negative
perceptions inflamed all sides. Protestants were sometimes seen
as being too close to the British and their imperial system, while
Catholics were seen as supporting a foreign leader, engaging in
the worship of saints and idols, while also flying the French rather
than the Dominion flag above their missions.

The churches and the federal government sometimes maintained diverging views of their priorities in the transfer process.
The churches generally sought to convert Indigenous peoples and
to instil in them scriptural knowledge, religious discipline, and a
particular world view that would make them God-fearing and
law-abiding in a Western context. Governments, by contrast, were
often more interested in creating useful workers, who spoke some
English or French, were adept at some useful trade, were trained to
be subservient, and had culturally turned their back on Indigenous
ways of living, knowing, and relating to the world.[29]

The interests of the churches and government converged in the
sense that both wanted to maximize the number of children attending some form of schooling, and both sought to use the schools as
a vehicle for transforming children. Both groups, in some respects,
lamented the fact that Indigenous peoples were disappearing; yet

both accepted this as an inevitable outcome when a superior civilization confronted an inferior one.

Joseph Hugonnard, the Qu'Appelle school's first principal, was clear that Christianizing and civilizing Indigenous children would be facilitated by "get[ting] them out of that pagan environment and plac[ing] them and teach[ing] them in a school with the goal of making them into good citizens and good Christians." Battleford school principal Edward Matheson promoted the Anglican policy of getting children "away from the reserves, if possible." This, he argued, "is the sure way to solve the long debated 'Indian Problem.'" The general secretary of the Missionary Department of the Methodist Church of Canada is quoted as writing, "The only way in which the Indian of the Country can be permanently elevated and thoroughly civilized is by removing the children from the surroundings of Indian home life, and keeping them separated long enough to form those habits of order, industry, and systematic effort, which they will never learn at home."[30] In a report prepared in 1911 for the Methodist Church's Executive Committee of the General Board of Missions, the authors concluded, "The Indian is a weak child in the family of our nation," and, as such, "we have reached the conclusion that the day-school on the reserve cannot possibly accomplish the end in view."[31]

This is not meant to be an ahistorical treatment of the intentions and actions behind the schools. At different times and locations, and among different actors, there were divergent opinions about the best ways forward. Policy convergence among actors was ephemeral, and there were continual debates regarding day schools versus residential schools; conflicts over costs and the best means of allocating limited funds; and, of course, debates as to why funding was often so low. At various times in the lengthy chronology of the IRS system, government officials sought to reduce the number of residential schools in favour of day schools. Sometimes they promoted integration into settler-dominated schools, only to be thwarted by the churches, particularly by the Catholic Church and its various entities. Chief Inspector Glen Campbell, for example, favoured day schools on reserves, outlining in 1912 several clear arguments for reducing residential schools and creating an educational system more aligned with provincial standards.[32]

Coercive Legislation

The sentiments of individual officials are important, but unless they were implemented into policy, they remain primarily statements of opinion. More important, perhaps, are the legislative outcomes of these opinions. Attendance was poorly regulated in the late nineteenth century, and there were few laws before 1894 covering mandatory attendance at residential or other schools. Regulations from Indian Affairs were largely on a case-by-case basis, devoted to particular schools, with few, if any, national standards or guidelines. This changed in 1895, when an amendment to the Indian Act made attendance at day schools, where available, compulsory, and it allowed the government to commit students to boarding schools if Indian agents thought they were not being properly educated or cared for. This early legislation was not rigorously or universally applied.[33] There was also considerable parental resistance to enrolment during this time. Yet while enrolment was primarily voluntary, parents who enrolled their children found that they could not withdraw them without the permission of Indian Affairs. While one parent fought this policy in court and won, the government continued to enforce it until 1920.

In that year, attendance was made compulsory for all status Indigenous children aged seven to fifteen at a day school, boarding school, or industrial school. Truant officers, RCMP officers, priests, and ministers could lay complaints, which would be heard by Indian agents, who, as justices of the peace, could prescribe fines or imprisonment for those who did not comply. Later, stricter legislation greatly increased the numbers of children attending residential schools.[34] Curiously, the Harper government kept this legislation on the books until 2014 – fully six years after the apology. That year, billed as a "gesture of reconciliation," a private member's bill repealed portions of sections 114 to 122 of the Indian Act, which dealt with schools for Indigenous children.[35] Until 2014, subsection

115(c) had empowered the minister to "enter into agreements with religious organizations for the support and maintenance of children who are being educated in schools operated by those organizations." Subsection 119(6) had permitted a truant officer to "take into custody a child whom he believes on reasonable grounds to be absent from school contrary to this Act and may convey the child to school, using as much force as the circumstances require."[36]

Legislation achieved policy success in the sense of increasing overall enrolment in government-funded schools, while also increasing the proportion of children in the residential stream. Under the tutelage of Duncan Campbell Scott, the IRS system grew considerably. Titley provides some illuminating statistics on enrolment from the beginning to the end of Scott's tenure in office: "From 11,303 in 1912 to 17,163 in 1932 – an increase of 51 per cent. During the same period, the increase for day students was from 7,399 to 8,775 (an 18 per cent increase), and for residential students from 3,904 to 8,213 (a 110 per cent increase)."[37] Summing up the goals of the IRS system and Scott's role in the process, Titley paraphrases his thinking: "Education was to be nothing less than an instrument of cultural annihilation, which would at once transform the Indians into an unskilled or semi-skilled workforce while forcing them into the mold of Anglo-Canadian identity."[38]

If the laws compelling Indigenous children were the same as those for non-Indigenous children, this might raise some interesting philosophical discussions, but this was not the case. Charles and DeGagné make this exceptional situation clear: "Throughout Canadian history it was only Aboriginal children who over an extended period of time were required to live in institutions because of their race."[39] Compulsory schooling was not common for non-Indigenous children, and in Manitoba, for example, such schooling was introduced only in 1916.[40]

For many Indigenous peoples, there was little choice but to comply with the laws. Refuting the idea that the rules were not enforced or the coercion not feared, Constance Dieter has highlighted numerous instances in which children were forcibly returned to schools under police escort, while parents who refused to send their runaway children back were fined, imprisoned, or denied rations. Whether or not the laws were consistently applied, a large proportion of Indigenous parents believed they were enforced.[41] One Survivor at an AHF gathering in Vancouver in 2006 recounted what was a regrettably common story:

> A Priest came into my parents' house to see who I was and asked, "Why isn't she in school?" And my mother said I wasn't very strong. The Priest said I would have to go to school or we would both go to jail. She thought about it for a while, and then she sent me to school. I didn't want my parents to go to jail, so I went to school.[42]

Isaac Daniels recalled how, in 1945, the Indian agent for the James Smith Reserve in Saskatchewan threatened his father with imprisonment if he and his brother did not attend residential school. Daniels chose to go to avoid his father being jailed. Similarly, an Indian agent visited the home of Donna Antoine in British Columbia and made threats, forcing her to go with him lest her parents be imprisoned. Numerous other Survivors recount similar experiences.[43]

In some cases, force was overt, and children were violently rounded up. Arthur Bear Chief relates how he and his brother were taken to the Old Sun residential school in Gleichen, Alberta, when "three white men and an RCMP officer" ran into his house: "They dragged my brother down as he was screaming and kicking. They dragged him out, and my parents could not do anything."[44] Some children were taken without anyone reporting the abduction to their parents. Howard Stacy Jones was forcibly removed from a day school in Port Renfrew, British Columbia, at the age of six. He recalls how two witnesses, including his aunt,

> saw me fighting, trying to get away with, from the two RCMP officers that threw me in the back seat of the car and drove off with me. And my mom didn't know where I was for three days, frantically stressed out and worried about where I was, and she finally found out that I was in Kuper Island residential school.[45]

In his harrowing account of life in the Mohawk Institute Residential School in Brantford, Ontario, Bud Whiteye recalls how, on the way home from their grandmother's house, a large, black car picked up him and his three brothers and sister, luring them with promises of ice cream and jello at a nearby restaurant. Instead of returning home, Bud was taken to Brantford, and it would be a year before his father found out where he had been taken. He endured six years of brutal abuse.[46]

The above cases demonstrate overt coercion and force, including the use of threats to induce people to surrender their children. Additionally, government decisions to stop funding day schools reduced the options for parents considerably. In 1895, for example, Hayter Reed promoted closing day schools and expanding the IRS system because "home influences so readily counteract any good which may be attained through them." While the Blood Reserve had three day schools, Reed introduced a residential school, which had the effect of closing down two of the day schools within a decade.[47]

Food rations were sometimes withheld if parents did not send their children. Grant outlines the role that government-mandated starvation sometimes played in coercing parents to give up their children to a school "where they would at least be warm and fed." Despite the obvious drawbacks of the schools, Grant recalls how "children in the schools during this era were at least guaranteed a regular supply of food, however inadequate, which was not always the case for children who stayed at home."[48] On at least one occasion, Indian Commissioner David Laird advised an Indian agent to reduce rations to induce more children to attend residential school.[49]

While starvation was used to both quell Indigenous political resistance and encourage attendance at residential school, such schools could also mitigate the potential for resistance by keeping children ostensibly as hostages. School inspector Andsell Macrae observed in 1886 that "it is unlikely that any Tribe or Tribes would give trouble of a serious nature to the Government whose members had children completely under Government control."[50]

A larger climate of cultural, spiritual, and political suppression made it difficult for Indigenous parents and communities to resist the coercive nature of the system. Many laws, while sometimes inconsistently applied, were nevertheless used to deny Indigenous peoples their right to continue to exist as groups in the ways they had done traditionally.[51] Notable here is the outlawing of many aspects of the potlatches in 1884, give-away ceremonies among prairie First Nations, the Thirst Dance of the Saulteaux and Nêhiyaw, and the Blackfoot Sun Dance. Reed developed the pass system in 1885 and, in 1886, issued passbooks to many Indian agents, documents designed to severely restrict the movement of Indigenous peoples. While fully aware that "this is hardly supportable by any legal enactment," Reed nevertheless thought that common sense and the public good were on his side. Individuals wishing to leave a reserve required written consent from the Indian agent or employers. Selling cattle, farm produce, or any goods similarly required written permission.[52]

Scott brought in other legislation to reduce the numbers of status Indians. In 1919, he mandated that Indigenous women who married non-Indigenous or non-status Indians would lose their status. This was followed in 1920 by a compulsory enfranchisement bill, defined as "the enfranchisement of an Indian against his will following a report by a person appointed by the Superintendent General on his suitability."[53] Effectively, Indigenous peoples with status could be stripped of that status and made Canadian citizens without their consent. Scott was also instrumental in quashing the ability of Indigenous peoples to address the injustices of the IRS system in Canadian courts, and in 1927, it became illegal for them to seek legal remedies against the government. Until 1960, status Indigenous peoples did not have the right to vote, which meant that they were essentially voiceless in Canadian politics. All these actions, taken together with the extreme and embedded racism of the time, made life exceedingly difficult.

Control as an Element of Transfer

Coercive actors such as Indian agents, police, and others directly initiated aspects of transfer (we might call these push factors), while the impact of general discriminatory government legislation, intergenerational trauma, and poverty indirectly created pull factors, driving children towards the gates of the residential schools. Both the push and the pull factors were discussed in chapter 2.

Parents and guardians were obliged to sign over guardianship of their children to the school principal, with official application forms to that effect created and circulated by Indian Affairs after 1891. The 1892 application form required parents to consent that "the Principal or head teacher of the Institution for the time being shall be the guardian" of the child, wording that was very similar to the later consent form of 1900.[54] The principal then had the power to decide whether children could be released for vacations or outings, and could determine when a child could ultimately be released. Scott made this point clear in 1913: "The principal of a boarding school remains the guardian of a pupil while on vacation, and he may recall a pupil should he deem it necessary for good and sufficient cause."[55] This marked a significant element in the transfer process, although its legality was questionable.

Symbolically important in the process of transfer were what sociologist Eviatar Zerubavel has called "rites of separation," events "specifically designed to dramatize the symbolic transformations of identity involved in establishing new beginnings," even in essence to "socially engineer a new type of person who would embody the dramatic historical break between the old and new 'eras.'" In his work, these are seen as positive, although potentially emotionally challenging, developments.[56] In the IRS case, however, such rites of separation were involuntary.

They were designed to demarcate a line between an often positively remembered time in the child's home community with family (although not always) and a shocking and far more negative experience in the schools. Survivors often describe having their hair cut, losing their personal possessions, being given a uniform, and losing their name. Elder Fred Kelly notes of his experiences: "Braids were immediately shorn. Traditional clothing was confiscated and replaced by standard issue uniforms. Our traditional names were anglicized and often replaced by numbers."[57] The purpose of the initial dislocation seems to have been to create a disjuncture, a temporal break between the past and present, where nothing would ever be the same again. This was marked by processes designed to destabilize, to dislocate, to make the Indigenous child into a darker-skinned settler on settler lands controlled by the growing white population.

A key aspect of this type of education was what Bear Nicholas has called "the hidden curriculum," designed to instil deference to Western forms of authority, a regimented lifestyle, and a belief in hierarchical organization as legitimate. Equally important was "methodological individualism," with a focus on individual hard work in order to climb higher in a hierarchical, meritocratic system. Thus, people deserved what they received, and equality of outcomes was deemed illegitimate. Indigenous values stressing "non-interference, responsibility, community, and respect for all beings" were to be replaced with Western views.[58]

Some institutions were strongly influenced by forms of monastic discipline associated with the Oblate order. For example, the strict and unrelenting Durieu system, created by Oblate father Paul Durieu, had a marked influence on some Indian residential schools. Other models of control were overtly penal, echoing nineteenth-century reformatories in Europe, such as the Cîteaux juvenile institution in France, where boys under sixteen who had been found guilty of criminal offences were subjected to physical abuse and hard labour. The prison-like atmosphere of the residential schools did not escape many children. Nora Bernard, a survivor of Shubenacadie in Nova Scotia, recalled, "Once you entered those big doors in the front and they slammed behind you, it was just like going into a prison." On the other side of the country, the Kuper Island Residential School in British Columbia was known as "Little Alcatraz."[59]

Dennis George Greene, who attended Ermineskin Residential School in Hobbema, Alberta, describes a high-stress atmosphere of violence:

I've never been in jail, but I understand. I had the same experience. Every day was about survival. Only the toughest survive. So at one point I became a protection racket because when I was younger, I used to be under somebody else's protection, so I in turn became one. ... It was about survival, not just from the students, the kids coming in during the day, even the teachers. Some of them used to fight the teachers. It was a world of violence.[60]

Robert Tomah similarly recounted a carceral atmosphere at Lejac Residential School in Fraser Lake, British Columbia, which corrupted a child's sense of right and wrong: "It was easy to lie because the system taught us that if you lied you got away with a lot of things." The upshot of his education was the development of a "criminal mind." This Catch-22 of being forced to break the rules in order to function created a climate of criminality and evasion of responsibility: "In order for me to survive, I had to collaborate to learn and start thinking criminal-wise, learning how to steal, learning to blame other people, learning to let go [of] responsibility."[61]

Forced Conversion

Implicit in the Indian Act was the condoning of religious conversion as a concomitant to the transfer process, and Indigenous spiritual beliefs and practices were especially targeted. Martina Pierre, who attended St. Mary's Mission in Mission, British Columbia, from 1950 to 1964, noted the efforts of the nuns and priests to destroy her spirituality, who instilled the belief that everything she did was a sin and that all her people's practices were "witchcraft."[62] Forcible conversion had very negative impacts on many children. Lucille Mattess describes debilitating fears from her time at Lejac: "I feared God, and I feared going to hell. When that fear is there, it's a block to my growth … it's like you're dammed if you do and you're dammed if you don't, eh, the teaching of heaven and hell and God and the devil. I really suffered a lot of psychological problems."[63]

Name Changing

Name changing occurred in two ways: in a temporary manner, with the assignment of numbers within the confines of the school environment; and in a more permanent way, through new names given through baptism. Since conversion could require adopting a "Christian" name, many children were forced to abandon their traditional Indigenous names. Many Survivors chose to return to their original names, while some had entirely forgotten them. In the first of its two historical volumes, the TRC notes, "At Alert Bay, Tlalis became Charles Nowell. At Qu'Appelle, Ochankugahe became Daniel Kennedy. At the Anglican school on the Blackfoot Reserve, Medicine Pipe Rider (itself a translation of a Siksika word) became Ben Calf Robe." Missionaries would often select French or British names during the baptismal process: "In one case, a child on Herschel Island in the Arctic Ocean was named David Copperfield, and in La Pierre's House in the Yukon, there was a Henry Venn, named for a leading figure in the British Church Missionary Society."[64]

Equally insidious was the numbering of each child. One Survivor recalled, "I was number one hundred and sixteen. I was trying to find myself; I was lost. I felt like I had been placed in a black garbage bag that was sealed. Everything was black, completely black to my eyes and I wondered if I was the only one to feel that way."[65] Numbering children was another way of dehumanizing them and aided in the transfer process. Bev Sellars, in her memoir, *They Called Me Number One*, was indeed called Number 1 by the priest and nuns. Her sister was 28, her mother was Number 71 when she attended, and her grandmother – 27. Lydia Ross, who attended the Cross Lake school in Manitoba, recalls being given the numbers 51, 44, 32, 16, 11, and 1 during her time there.[66] Bernice Jacks, at the Kamloops school in British Columbia, describes the dehumanizing process: "I was called, 'Hey, 39. Where's 39? Yes, 39, come over here. Sit over here, 39.' That was the way it was."[67] Children of the same family of varying ages were often given numbers that were far apart so that they would not be able to walk into meals close together, nor would they be seated in proximity to one other. This was another means of separating families and thus further controlling the lives of Indigenous children.

Linguistic Suppression

Forced linguistic change and suppression is another aspect of transfer, and it was one of the hardest for many Survivors because it not only detached them from their own traditional identities but also deracinated them from their siblings, parents, and other family members when they returned home. The suppression of language and its replacement with the languages of the colonizers was government policy. The Indian Affairs program of studies of 1896 concluded, "Every effort must be made to induce pupils to speak English and to teach them to understand it; unless they do, the whole work of the teacher is likely to be wasted."[68] While some schools were more lenient than others, a central goal of administrators was to deprive children of their ability to communicate in their own language. In many cases, siblings and others who spoke the same language were deliberately separated, a practice that eroded their ability to speak, while also depriving them of emotional and social support.

Brutal penalties were often meted out for infractions. Randy Fred recalls how his father, "who attended Alberni Indian Residential School for four years in the twenties, was physically tortured by his teachers for speaking Tseshaht: they pushed sewing needles through his tongue, a routine punishment for language offenders."[69] Meredith Hourie, who attended St. Mary's Mission from 1950 to 1959, recalls, "If other kids spoke their language they were severely punished. It must have been traumatic for those children who didn't know English at all. They were hit on the back of their hands with a yardstick, or strapped several times, every time they spoke the 'devil's language,' as it was referred to."[70]

Allen Kagak, who spoke Inuktitut when attending the Coppermine tent hostel in the Northwest Territories, was beaten and humiliated because he could not speak English.[71] Other children ate soap if they were found talking their language. At La Tuque Indian Residential School in Quebec, Pierrette Benjamin was forced to chew and swallow a big chunk, the principal rationalizing this by saying, "That's a dirty language, that's the devil that speaks in your mouth, so we had to wash it because it's dirty."[72]

Certainly, language was crucial to the ontology of a child, and destroying it was a key means by which the child's cultural inheritance could be broken. The annual report of Indian Affairs for 1895 made this abundantly clear: "So long as he keeps his native tongue, so long will he remain a community apart."[73] The obverse was also true: changing the language could facilitate the transfer of a child from one group to another. Language provides a link to culture, identity, spirituality, heritage, and ways of knowing and interacting. Destroying their language severed children from their families, cut them off from their storytelling and teaching traditions, and inhibited the transmission of collective memories from one generation to the next. As Grant has observed, since "oral histories are the archives of the tribe," suppressing language knowledge foreclosed the ability of children to effectively communicate with parents and grandparents, and perpetuate the culture and identity of the group.[74]

For some church officials and administrators, language was often less important than religious conversion; indeed, the two forms of transfer may have interfered with one another. Some Oblate and Anglican leaders advocated retaining Indigenous languages in some cases, particularly in Christian worship, because this facilitated conversion. Indeed, Indigenous languages were used in worship during the first half of the nineteenth century; this practice changed only later. One could argue that mandatory English or French was designed to help students speaking different languages to communicate with each other as well as with school staff. As Miller recounts, English was adopted more easily in schools where children came from places with different mother tongues, and it could be both "practical and efficient."[75] However, practicality and efficiency fail to account for the widespread and systematic cultural and linguistic destruction that took place within the IRS system, and, as I discuss below, many teachers and administrators associated Indigenous languages with pagan belief systems and superstition.

Abuse and Transfer

Several decades of Survivor testimony and scholarship attest to the widespread use of corporal punishment as well as ubiquitous problems of verbal, emotional, physical, and sexual abuse. These can be seen as means of facilitating the forced transfer of children and promoting the totalizing influence of the institutions. Early studies of Survivor testimony recount that sexual abuse rates at some schools reached 75 per cent, with physical abuse rates even higher.[76] Very high levels of physical and sexual abuse were rampant throughout the system. In January 2015, the government's Independent Assessment Process compiled claims by (living) IRS Survivors for abuses suffered in the system. The IAP received almost 38,000 claims, specifically for physical and sexual abuse. Almost 31,000 claims were resolved.[77] How serious was the abuse? The TRC reports that 21 per cent of the awards exceeded $150,000, a sum provided only for "the most violent, intrusive, and aggravated acts, and the highest levels of harm." It noted the high prevalence of violent and extremely harmful abuse in schools throughout the country.[78] This constitutes only a small representation of the consequences of the IRS system on Indigenous Survivors, their families, and their communities.

In an interview with me, Karen, who had attended St. Anne's (Fort Albany, Ontario) during the 1960s, recalled, "There was a lot of abuse, yeah. And a lot of things I'm not aware of, there was a lot of sexual abuse, there was a lot of this. And there was an electric chair where I went." The children knew the chair was used every day because they would see the lights flicker. As to the purpose of the chair, Karen described how it was used "randomly, just to punish you. I think to them it was an amusement. You know, they were amused just to see to what extent the pain was going, how far you could take it as an individual person."[79] Others also noted an atmosphere of sadism and abuse. Melvin Jack was sexually abused by a supervisor at the Lower Post Residential School in British Columbia. When he told another student about it, the supervisor started beating him: "He laid me over a desk, and he had a fibreglass fishing rod and started to whip me, to the point where I lost control of my bladder, and I was screaming. Every time I screamed, he told me to shut up. That sealed my lips for it seemed like an eternity."[80]

George Guerin, a former chief and Survivor of the Kuper Island school, had his hand permanently injured from severe and repeated beating by Sister Mary Baptiste because he was speaking his language.[81] Velma Page, a former student of Kuper Island, relates the story of her brother's long-term debilitating injuries: "He had a medical problem that could never be fixed because they kicked him so hard in his rectum that he couldn't sit too long, what little bit he revealed to me when he visited me. And the doctors couldn't fix it."[82]

While I am not focusing on this explicitly, this high level of abuse can, in and of itself, constitute an element of genocide. Articles 2(b) and (c), respectively, of the UNGC prohibit "Causing serious bodily or mental harm to members of the group" and "Deliberately inflicting on the group conditions of life calculated to bring about its physical destruction in whole or in part." It is clear from the TRC's six-volume Final Report that while principals and Indian Affairs officials knew about much of the physical abuse, and at least some of the sexual abuse, they did very little to prevent these abuses from taking place. Abuse in the context of forcible transfer (which is my primary focus) can be understood as a vehicle to ensure that the children were so traumatized that the transfer stuck, that they were unable to psychologically return to their pre-IRS childhoods. The range of transformative and abusive processes at work caused an extremely sharp break with the past.

Preventing "Retrogression"

The fear of returning to the Indigenous group (or *retrogression*) was a pressing one in many cases since the success of transfer depended on assimilation continuing after the children had left the IRS system. For some officials, it was clear that every effort had to be made to remove familial or tribal influences during the process of "reorientation." For this reason, Edgar Dewdney fully supported keeping Indigenous visitors off the grounds of the residential schools, even if it meant using the police. He favoured restricting student vacations, especially if this involved a return to the reserve, and reasoned, "Taking children in for short terms and letting them go again is regarded perhaps as worse than useless."[83] Similarly, Hayter Reed saw the merits of locating industrial schools "at a greater distance from their Reserves, than would be the case were they at the Boarding Schools."[84] A key goal was to make it extremely difficult for parents to visit their children and vice versa. Reed was particularly critical of principals who allowed parents to visit their children, and he actively discouraged any displays of hospitality towards parents. In an 1891 letter, he declared, "Visiting must be at once severely discouraged, with a view to its being eventually and at no distant date entirely discontinued."[85]

When parental visits were permitted, they were often strictly controlled. For example, in 1906, the rules governing visits at the Mount Elgin school in Muncey, Ontario, were similar to penal institutions. Visitors had to be accompanied by an officer and could speak to the children only in English. This stringent rule also applied to parents and guardians in situations where, as the principal explained, they had "reason to believe that influence is being brought to bear upon the pupil to create discontent and unrest leading to truancy or removal."[86] Reed had earlier observed, "I have found the result of giving children a short term and then sending them back to the Reserve, not infrequently to be that they are worse than if they had never been taken away from the Reserve at all."[87]

While students were permitted to write to their parents or guardians twice a year, these letters were read and censored by school staff. Vacations were strictly controlled, and students with a history of trying to escape, students who had not voluntarily returned from their previous holidays, and orphans and children from poor or working families who could not make arrangements for their care could and were denied leave to go home. If homes were located too far from the schools, this could also impede a child's ability to return for the summer. If parents did not have the funds to pay for their child's travel to their home communities and then back to school in the fall, vacations could be and were denied. Principals and Indian agents could also deny vacations based on putatively moral concerns, such as the unmarried status of the parents.[88] In many cases, these can be interpreted as excuses. Giving in to parents or guardians was seen as hampering assimilation efforts and was therefore to be avoided.

Forced Marriage

Officials sometimes sought to control the marriage, and hence the reproduction, of Indigenous children as they approached their later teenage years. The File Hills Colony in Saskatchewan is one example, where Indian agent William Graham set aside a portion of the Peepeekisis Reserve, allocating eighty-acre lots for IRS graduates who agreed to abide by his conditions, including consenting to the marriages he arranged. Others, like Joseph Hugonnard, the principal at Lebret, once married six couples at the same time.[89] In an effort to halt Indigenous language and culture, people of different First Nations, speaking different languages, would be paired together.

In 1890, Reed made it clear that parental concerns were incidental to the arrangement of judicious marriages, writing to Hugonnard, "The contention that the parents have the sole right to decide such matters cannot for one moment be admitted. The parents themselves are to a certain extent wards of the Government who interfere in many directions to prevent actions which the ignorance of these people blinds them to the detrimental consequences of." In 1896, Reed elaborated how marriage could be used as a condition for discharging students, that for older students capable of supporting themselves, "It is considered advisable … to bring about a matrimonial alliance, either at the time of being discharged from the school or as soon after as possible." This practice continued well into the 1930s as principals retained the right to refuse to graduate students at age sixteen if they were perceived to be good candidates for an arranged marriage.[90]

Efforts to forcibly assimilate Indigenous peoples into the settler mainstream generally proved impossible due to the racism of the time, limited employment prospects, and the lack of funding for such policy goals. What developed instead were forms of internal colonization, whereby Indigenous peoples departing the schools came to feel inferior to the dominant white settler society. Instilling a deep-seated sense of shame was a key outcome of the schools. Dian Million argues in her landmark work, *Therapeutic Nations*, that Indigenous peoples were made to feel as though their own cultures were inferior, immoral, and indecent. The schools imparted the view to children that "their Indian bodies are by nature sexually depraved and that their entry into white society depends on their eternal vigilance against their own shamed and savage sexuality."[91] Métis scholar and activist Howard Adams described how "the children internalize inferior images as a part of their true selves, often with strong feelings of shame." This sense of inferiority, he explained, helps us understand why "many native people attempt to hide from their Indianness, while others try to pretend that they are white, French, or Italian."[92]

To a degree, this helps account for the period of latency or silence about the residential schools and the lack of widespread discussion. Internalizing an oppressor's reality allows the perpetrator's system to continue unimpeded. The result was often what W.E.B. Dubois conceptualized as a "double consciousness," a process in which students, as Jobin recalls, "internalized the goals of colonial institutions" and therefore "saw themselves through the eyes of the colonizer, seeking recognition and therefore mimicking non-Indigenous ways of being."[93] The process was designed to alienate children from their language, culture, and traditions to complete the process of colonization.[94]

A number of Survivors have recently recalled their experiences of colonization, of how the schools fundamentally changed their identity – at least for a time. Bear Chief describes how he initially felt like "an 'apple Indian,' red on the outside and white on the inside," after leaving school. This occurred to such an extent that "I went along with the ridiculing of Indians, including my own criticisms of them, and laughing at them. Residential school made me ashamed of being an Indian, and, in my case, Old Sun was very successful in making me deny who I was."[95] David Striped Wolf, who attended St. Mary's Indian Residential School at the Blood Reserve in Alberta, describes how his experiences shaped his identity: "These six years I spent, I felt ashamed to be an Indian. I was always looking up to the Whites."[96] The late Campbell Papequash, who published a Survivor memoir, described his state of mind after years in the IRS system:

> I began to resent, despise, and even hated myself as I disconnected from my heritage. Maybe, these missionaries were right; maybe we were

heathen savage and uncivilized? I began to detest myself for being an impoverished stupid Indian. Why was I born Indian? I even tried to wash off the colour of my skin but it didn't work.[97]

Many Survivors report forms of colourism at work, a topic that has not been explored in any great depth with reference to the IRS system, but is well covered in critical race theory, especially in work on mixed-race people, who regularly confront issues about whether they "pass" as white. According to Howard Adams, his relative success in functioning in settler society was in part due to "my appearance [being] predominantly white. Throughout my school years I was favored, because I closely resembled white students."[98] By contrast, William George Lathlin, who attended the All Saints Indian Residential School in Lac La Ronge, Saskatchewan, describes the negative influence of racial hatred directed towards him: "My skin was kind of brown and I tried to wipe the skin off my left hand. You can see the scar today. It's still there. It was all red."[99]

Lorna Rope, a former student at St. Paul's in Lebret, Saskatchewan, discusses how colonization was internalized and how she was taught to dislike her own identity and to prefer whiteness to Indigeneity. She recalls, "We all wanted to be White ... sometimes we would wash and wash ourselves so we would think we were White. ... At the time, we just thought this was something we did. But now that I'm older, I realize that I was trying to – I was losing my identity."[100] This, of course, raises questions about what forcible transfer means in the context of an overtly colonial society, where the perpetrator and target groups, broadly defined, have different skin tones and make fundamental judgments accordingly.

Conclusions

This chapter has privileged forcible transfer, with the goal of laying a ground floor for the discussion of genocide in Canada. For the children involved, the process of transfer, whether beginning in the home or once inside the schools, presented a traumatic, life-changing event, epitomized through a series of path-dependent processes that were difficult, if not impossible, to reverse. *Total transfer* was not conceived as a viable policy option given that the racialized characteristics of Indigenous peoples versus white settlers were sometimes noticeably different. At times, those who could were encouraged to "pass," while those who could not received extra punishment for their darker pigmentation.

Certainly, the TRC was correct to see all this as cultural genocide, and the 1947 draft Genocide Convention provides five elements of this particular crime, beginning with forcible transfer, followed by the four elements that failed to be approved by 1948:

> forced and systematic exile of individuals representing the culture of a group; or prohibition of the use of the national language even in private intercourse; or systematic destruction of books printed in the national language or of religious works or prohibition of new publications; or systematic destruction of historical or religious monuments or their diversion to alien uses, destruction or dispersion of documents and objects of historical, artistic, or religious value and of objects used in religious worship.[101]

Arguably, these elements of cultural genocide were all performed during the lengthy tenure of the IRS system and constituted aspects of the processes of colonization. As should also be clear, I have attempted to demonstrate that forcible transfer is legally as genocidal as any other crime in the convention.

chapter four

The Sixties and Seventies Scoop and the Genocide Convention

In 2011, I had the privilege of interviewing many IRS Survivors in Sault Ste. Marie, Ontario, through the generosity of the National Residential School Survivors Society and the goodwill of the Survivors. Not only did Survivors agree to share their stories with me, but some also acted as health support for other Survivors. As the TRC held regional and National Events throughout the country, I routinely met those I had previously interviewed. Some were there to share their stories, while others wore coloured health-support vests to assist fellow Survivors in their healing journeys.

For many Survivors, being forcibly transferred to residential schools was not the end of their negative encounters with the settler state. Indeed, the legacies of the system continued well after the children had left the confines of the schools, and the state found still other ways to break up Indigenous families. In her discussion with me, Sandra recalled her instances of abuse in the residential schools and then recounted a second trauma she had experienced, this time in her dealings with the Children's Aid Society (CAS) in Sault Ste. Marie. Sandra gave birth to a healthy girl in the early 1960s, but was almost immediately coerced by the CAS into giving up her baby:

> All of a sudden I got all these people around me, and I couldn't leave my room, I couldn't leave my bed, you know? I could stand up there, but I couldn't go out of that room. And you're so naïve when you go to residential school, you don't know because nobody tells you anything,

you know? So, they got these people and then authoritative people, people in authority you have to listen to, you have to do what they tell you, that's what we learned. So they came in and they had these papers that I had to sign, and I signed them, I don't know what I was signing, but I signed them because that's what they told me I had to do, and I went to see my baby, and they said that wasn't possible, and anyway, they had a guard.[1]

As I understand her experience, Sandra never wanted to leave her baby. She felt forced into doing so and regretted the situation immediately, yet felt powerless to take action. When she called the CAS, she was told that her baby had been adopted by an English family and was in Great Britain. The truth, she found out later, was that her daughter was still in Sault Ste. Marie and that, during some parts of their lives, they had lived within blocks of each other and never knew. When we spoke, she was building a relationship with her daughter, an example perhaps of reconciliation after genocide.[2]

This short chapter covers a period of changing strategy in the Canadian settler state's attempt to control Indigenous peoples. Here we move from a specific to a more general intent to commit genocide as some political powers were devolved to the provinces and territories – what John Borrows identifies[3] as a clear violation of the Crown's responsibility to its Indigenous treaty partners from the Treaty of Niagara onwards. From a strictly legalist perspective, it is difficult to prove a specific, across-the-board intent to commit genocide during the Sixties Scoop. From a pluralist point of view, however, it is clear that a general intent existed to forcibly transfer Indigenous children and destroy their specific group identities. Racism against Indigenous families and communities also played a key role.

This chapter provides an overview of federal and provincial policy shifts and continuities, and I argue that as policies of forcible transfer in residential schools began to wind down, new policies, focused on forcibly removing Indigenous children through child welfare agencies, increased. One of these policies was the Sixties Scoop. The Sixties Scoop also saw the widespread targeting of Métis children alongside First Nations and Inuit children, although only status First Nations claimants have so far been successful in class-action claims against the government. An Ontario-based class action, initiated by Marcia Brown Martel in 2009, asked for $1.3 billion. In February 2017, the Ontario Superior Court found in favour of the claimants. In October 2017, treaty and status Sixties Scoop claimants (including Inuit) received a settlement of up to $750 million, which amounts to about $25,000 to $50,000 per child, depending on the number of claimants. A further $50 million would go to an Indigenous Healing Foundation and another $75 million to pay legal costs. Further settlements may be forthcoming from provinces and territories for sexual, physical, and other forms of abuse as well as loss of language and culture.[4]

In this chapter, I also introduce a comparative discussion by exploring Australia's policies of forcible removal of Aboriginal and Torres Strait Islander peoples and how, in 1997, the Australian Human Rights Commission interpreted the fate of the Stolen Generations as being genocidal. If we keep the Australian precedent and its legal innovations in mind, the Sixties Scoop can also be seen as a violation of the UN Genocide Convention.

Changes in Forcible Transfer Policies

The *Sixties Scoop* is a misleading term in the sense that the forced removals that fell within its scope did not end during the 1960s, but rather continued into the mid-1980s, with serious reverberations still. Others prefer the terms Stolen Generations or Lost Generations, which echo the terminology used in Australia.[5] The major permissive cause of the Sixties Scoop was the 1951 package of amendments to the Indian Act, whereby the federal government adopted an assimilationist agenda. Provincial school boards received additional funding (with strings attached) to facilitate more Indigenous children attending day schools. Section 87 of the amendments laid the basis for devolving federal responsibilities for child welfare services for status Indians to the provinces. Once a funding model had been agreed upon, the provinces gained the jurisdiction to apprehend status First Nations children.[6]

The amendments were the product of a joint Senate and House of Commons committee, which met from 1946 to 1948 and made a number of recommendations that were progressive for the time. These included reinstating the right to vote for First Nations people who had opted to retain their status, the creation of an Indian claims commission, the reduction of ministerial discretionary powers, and an increase in band council control over some aspects of their own affairs. While the federal government did not implement these recommendations, there was a policy turn in the direction of using day schools to integrate Indigenous children.[7]

By 1954, the federal government took over funding for IRS teachers. While the residential schools were being slowly phased out, they nevertheless remained an important part of the overall educational system until the end of the 1960s, especially for people living in areas inaccessible to day schools. During the 1960s, there were still approximately ten thousand Indigenous children in sixty residential schools across the country. However, important changes were being made. In 1970, some residential schools were closed down, while in a small number of cases, control shifted towards First Nations; this was the case with the Blue Quills Residential School in St. Paul, Alberta, after the Saddle Lake Cree Nation staged a sit-in. By 1972, the National Indian Brotherhood sought to end government control of First Nations education, and this brought about further changes.[8]

During the 1950s, Indian agents had used the residential schools, in part as child welfare institutions for children whom they deemed were being neglected by their parents or guardians. As the schools closed, children were transferred from one form of institution to another. This practice had less to do with any impartial assessment of the actual care the children were receiving and more to do with Eurocentric perceptions of who should be a caregiver and what constituted good care. In their seminal study, Fournier and Crey outline a legacy of "culturally inappropriate judgments" taking root in settler-controlled child welfare systems, noting, "Orphaned children were quickly scooped up, but so too were those cared for by an aged grandmother or parents living in the impoverished conditions that were endemic on reserves by the early 1950s."[9]

This shift in power was more pronounced after 1966, when the federal government and the provinces agreed to share social service costs – without inviting any input from Indigenous peoples or their organizations.[10] In a detailed examination of the child welfare system in 1983, Patrick Johnson coined the term *Sixties Scoop* after noting an astounding statistic. While in 1955 less than 1 per cent of the children in British Columbia's child welfare system were Indigenous, this swelled to 34 per cent by 1964. Johnson noted similar trends in the Prairie provinces by the 1970s, and he concluded that, nationally, status Indigenous children were 4.5 times more likely to be removed by child welfare agencies.[11] What was going on?

Federal and provincial governments did not take Indigenous forms of identity, community, or family seriously. Rampant paternalism, suffused with overt racism, informed the attitudes and policies of child welfare services. In her study of the Sixties Scoop, Karen Dubinsky notes how, at one level, the "racialization of poverty," coupled with legacies of colonialism, starvation, and residential schooling, contributed to serious problems. At a higher level, colonialism created grossly unequal relations between Indigenous peoples and most agents of the state, including social workers, police officers, teachers, medical professionals, and many others, thereby undermining the ability of Indigenous families to look after their own children.[12]

Racist norms informed provincial child welfare agencies about what a successful family should look like: white, middle-class parents with at least one stable income.[13] Eurocentric notions of family prevailed among social workers. A lack of a Western-style diet convinced some social workers that children were malnourished, even if there was a plentiful supply of Indigenous traditional foods.[14] Even leaving children in the care of grandparents while parents were working could be grounds for removing a child.[15] There was a blatant disregard for Indigenous, community forms of child-raising. As Bev Sellars explains in the case of her people,

> Children were precious and belonged to everyone. They were *our children*, not *my* children. It was expected that if a child lost his or her parents for whatever reason, the extended family would step in and make sure the child remained a part of the community. It was an obligation on

the part of the nation to care for the children just as it was an obligation to care for the elderly, for example.[16]

American adoption agencies became involved in the process in an aggressive campaign to buy Indigenous children to sell to primarily white, middle-class families. In 1981, while 7 per cent of white children were sent out of Manitoba for adoption, the figure for Indigenous children was 55 per cent. Private adoption agencies often paid between $5,000 and $10,000 per child, with little oversight from provincial authorities. Until 1982, there were no legal barriers to removing children from Manitoba or from Canada.[17] Marlene Orgeron, from Shoal Lake, Manitoba, was taken from her home in the 1970s and adopted by a family in Louisiana, who paid $30,000. Willy Fast was sold to a family in Indiana for $10,000. A family in Holland paid $6,400 for Carla Williams, while Alyson and Debra, twin sisters, were sent to Pennsylvania, where they fetched $10,000.[18] Maggie Blacksmith, an Anishinaabe social worker whose son was taken by Manitoba social workers, recalls what it was like:

> Big, shiny American cars would come onto the reserve, followed by the social worker's car. ... When they left, there'd be a little Indian child sitting in the back of the American car, bawling their eyes out. The social worker always had a piece of paper saying it was legal. If parents tried to keep their kids, the social worker called the Mountie.[19]

In the early 1980s, Manitoba began investigating widespread abuses in the child welfare system. This culminated in a judicial inquiry, led by Justice Edwin Kimelman, who released a report in 1985, in which he concluded, "Cultural genocide has taken place in a systematic, routine manner."[20] Kimelman suggested that, in terms of culture and identity, the Sixties Scoop had a more detrimental effect than the IRS system because, in his view, the children in the schools at least knew their families and had the opportunity to return at various points in the school year. By contrast, children who were removed for fostering or adoption were totally separated from their families, and since they were removed at a younger age, sometimes as babies, they experienced a complete severing of ties with their previous identity. In both cases, the guise of benevolence masked a horrific legacy of destruction.

The Kimelman Review Committee, along with organized Indigenous activism, managed to change some of the more egregious aspects of the child-adoption policies. During the 1980s, provinces and territories changed their focus and began privileging the placement of Indigenous children with extended families or other Indigenous peoples. In 1990, Indian and Northern Affairs Canada further devolved child and family services to local Indigenous bands and away from the provinces and territories.[21] In its 1991 report, the Aboriginal Justice Inquiry of Manitoba laid out the case clearly:

> In most provinces, these child welfare services were never provided in any kind of meaningful or culturally appropriate way. Instead of the counselling of families, or consultation with the community about alternatives to apprehending the child, the apprehension of Aboriginal children became the standard operating procedure with child welfare authorities in most provinces.[22]

How many children were removed? Official estimates of 11,132 status children removed from 1960 to 1990 may be too low because the status of many children was not recorded on foster records; as a result, the number, if one includes Métis and non-status children, draws closer to 20,000 people. The vast majority of these children, some 70 to 90 per cent, went to non-Indigenous guardians. The problems generated by this decades-old pattern did not end in the 1990s. Chelsea Vowel recounts that "by 2002, over 22 500 Indigenous children were in foster care across Canada – more than the total taken during the Sixties Scoop and certainly more than had been taken to residential schools."[23]

According to the 2016 census, the situation is actually getting worse. Indigenous children under four represent only 8 per cent of the total number of children in Canada but, in 2016, represented 51.2 per cent of children in foster care, up from 49.1 per cent in 2011. Census data paints a negative picture of ongoing colonization and child removal: First Nations children comprise 41.4 per cent of those in foster care, and disproportionally high rates for both Métis and Inuit children are recorded as well.[24]

South of the border, Margaret Jacobs has documented US efforts to undertake the same process, and she estimates that somewhere between 25 and 35 per cent of Indigenous children were removed from their families by the end of the 1960s, a result of the Bureau of Indian Affairs' (BIA) Indian Adoption Project of 1958, which ran on parallel lines with termination and relocation policies. Rather than working to keep families together, BIA bureaucrats were convinced that Indigenous parents were "inherently and irreparably unfit," and they acted accordingly. Jacobs's comparative work draws in Canada, the United States, and Australia as part of a global process of taking Indigenous children from their families. She notes, however, that while Australia and Canada have had national conversations about forced removal, Americans have scrupulously avoided them.[25]

Can we argue that the Sixties Scoop violated the UN Genocide Convention? Emily Alston-O'Connor's reading of this period suggests that genocide occurred.[26] Jo-Ann Episkenew also supports a claim of genocide, seeing in government policies "the intent to destroy Indigenous nations." From her analysis, it is naïve to impute benign motives to the actions of the provincial governments in these matters.[27] Liebenberg and Ungar, in their work on Indigenous children in the child welfare system, put it this way: "Although the child welfare system purported to be acting in the best interests of the child, this second mass removal of children from their homes and communities paralleled the residential school experience and perpetuated the genocide of aboriginal people."[28]

During a detailed interview in late 2017, I asked Senator Murray Sinclair how he would legally interpret the significance of the Sixties Scoop through the lens of the Genocide Convention. Sinclair pointed out that applying Article 2(e) to the federal government during the Sixties Scoop is difficult, given the key roles of provincial authorities and the courts in the process.

I tend to view that it's more likely that it was than it wasn't, but I tend to view that it was more deliberately infliction of harm as opposed to a

2e situation or infliction of the conditions of life. The removal, the forcible removal of children from one group to the other for the purpose
of doing away with the race of people, is the hurdle that's difficult to
overcome because arguably, and this will be the argument that Canada
and the provinces would muster, [it] would be it wasn't for the purpose
of eliminating the race, it was for the purpose of protecting the children.
And so, every case had to be justified before a judge on the basis that
it was in the best interest [of] the child for the child to be placed with a
foster family.[29]

While courts played a role in legitimating the process of removals, Sinclair points out that they provided very little oversight over
the process, and children could be removed in stages, making it
difficult to assign specific responsibility to any one institution or
actor. As he explains,

The courts very rarely ever supervised the placement. They simply
authorized the child welfare agency to do whatever it thought was in
the best interest of the child. And so, the agency would come to the
court and say, "We believe the child is in need of protection; do you
agree with us, judge?" The judge would agree, and often because the
situation at home, or the situation the child was in, was pretty dire. But
then the question about what was in the best interest of the child often
only became a question of how long should the agency be allowed to
have the child in its care, either temporarily or permanently. And that's
the only thing that the courts decided, so the courts would decide you
can have the child for six months or you can have the child, to make a
permanent ward.[30]

Sinclair equally noted a lack of judicial oversight as to what happened to the children afterwards:

Very rarely did agencies ever say to the courts, "We're going to place
this child for adoption to the States or to a white family." So courts
would often be the unwitting culprit or the unwitting participant in
an overall policy. And we know that many agencies, in fact, had agreements with American agencies to place children for adoption for a fee,

and those children would go into adoptive placements down there with those agencies and pay the fee. So, you know, on the face of it, I think that there is a pretty clear argument to be made that children were being forcibly removed and being placed with non-Indigenous parents at the hands of agencies as opposed to at the hands of the government. It's the extent to which the government can be accountable for what the agencies did that becomes the issue. And so I think that implicates the provinces more than the federal government.[31]

Senator Sinclair's nuanced legal assessment of the role of the courts and the provincial and federal governments outlines some of the difficulties in singling out one institution or level of government for responsibility in forcible transfer. Indeed, the system seemed designed to diffuse responsibility among a range of actors at multiple levels, with no overt intention expressed to do anything negative to Indigenous groups "as such." Rather, everything was framed as being in the best interests of the children, a claim the courts, social workers, and government officials could make by the time the Sixties Scoop began. The commonality was that all these institutions were established by settlers on Indigenous lands and were administered by settlers to take Indigenous lands, to quell Indigenous resistance to settler colonization, while also seeking to assimilate Indigenous peoples into the settler state–dominated system.

The Australian Stolen Generations

In the 1990s, Australia grappled with legacies similar to those we are dealing with in Canada today, and we can look to the Australian precedent to provide further support for a genocide finding. In Australia, forced removals focused initially on mixed, or "half-caste," children, then in 1940 moved to all Indigenous children. Children were removed either to white families or to boarding schools, processes coordinated through a range of state and federal legislation. Under the guise of child neglect, children would be removed, often without the consent of their parents or through pressured consent involving intimidation and threat.[32] Another aspect of this campaign was the active prevention of marriage between "full-bloods" and "half-castes" in favour of "half-caste"/white marriages as a means of "breeding out the colour."[33]

Between 20,000 and 25,000 children were separated from their parents from 1910 to 1970, adopted out and taken to schools far from their home communities.[34] Few people outside Aboriginal communities used the term genocide until 1997, when the Australian Human Rights Commission's report *Bringing Them Home* argued that Aboriginal child removals violated Article 2(e) in that somewhere between 10 and 30 per cent of Aboriginal children had been forcibly separated from their families.[35] As the report's authors explained, "When a child was forcibly removed that child's entire community lost, often permanently, its chance to perpetuate itself in that child. The Inquiry has concluded that this was a primary objective of forcible removals and is the reason they amount to genocide."[36]

The commission made a case for genocide on the basis that the child removals were designed to effect "absorption or assimilation of the children into the wider, non-Indigenous, community so that their unique cultural values and ethnic identities would disappear, giving way to models of Western culture." Citing Lemkin directly, the report's authors argued, "The objective was 'the disintegration of the political and social institutions of culture, language, national feelings, religion, and the economical existence of' Indigenous peoples. ... Removal of children with this objective in mind is genocidal because it aims to destroy the 'cultural unit' which the Convention is concerned to preserve."[37]

Three useful legal conclusions were developed during this process. The first was that seemingly positive intentions on the part of the colonizers did not mean that forced removals were not genocidal; "animosity or hatred" was not required. While some of the intentions, such as job training and education, might be seen as positive, they did not negate the intention of destroying Indigenous groups and merging them into the dominant settler population.[38] A second legal point concerned how genocide could be inferred through practices rather than stated intentions. The report noted, "The continuation into the 1970s and 1980s of the practice of preferring non-Indigenous foster and adoptive families for Indigenous children was also arguably genocidal. The genocidal impact of these practices was reasonably foreseeable."[39]

The commission's understanding of genocide rested on general rather than specific intent, on "proof of reasonable foreseeability" of the actions of the perpetrators. This, it argued, was "sufficient to establish the Convention's intent element."[40] The commission provided the example of New South Wales, where the state had imposed a "general child welfare law," but treated Indigenous and non-Indigenous children differently, applying the law far more severely to Indigenous children. Terms such as "neglected," "destitute," and "uncontrollable" could theoretically be used to describe any child in need of care, but they were far more likely to be used in courts to refer to Indigenous children, and were used far more systematically.[41]

To make such legal pronouncements was to subtly reinterpret international law on genocide, but a commission of inquiry was free to do this. Genocide at the domestic level can be defined as broadly or as narrowly as the state wishes it to be defined. It is, after all, up to individual state governments to decide how they are going to implement or ignore international law. Canada's Parliament, as we have seen, chose to broaden *and* narrow the definition in the Criminal Code. The commission's report reflected the larger debates about genocide in Australian history, which brought in and domesticated a wider definition of genocide based on Lemkin's work.[42]

While *Bringing Them Home* adopted a legalist interpretation of the UNGC, it similarly advocated for a more expansive interpretation. While the report had some supporters, and a reconciliation movement began, with "sorry books" and eventually a government apology, most of the political establishment and the right-of-centre government rejected the term genocide as merely an exaggeration – the outcome of political correctness and left-wing politics.[43] The Stolen Generations case is nevertheless a useful precedent for understanding how we might assign responsibility for the Sixties Scoop. In both cases, sub-federal units (states and provinces) administered the system, buttressed by the courts. Equally important is that, in both Australia and Canada, the federal Crown assumed ultimate responsibility for what occurred within its domestic jurisdiction. Australian Prime Minister Kevin Rudd issued an apology to the Stolen Generations, while in Canada, the federal government was the focus of the class-action suits initiated by Sixties Scoop survivors.

The argument for forcible transfer rests on the dislocation and theft of Indigenous identities. Children were deliberately placed in non-Indigenous homes, and as Fournier and Crey explained, "Their cultural identity, their legal Indian status, their knowledge of their own First Nation and even their birth names were erased, often forever."[44] Chris Benjamin has more recently described how "white parents often encouraged adoptive Aboriginal children to try to pass as white, in order to avoid racism altogether – a loving and unintended assault on their true culture."[45] The long-term legacies were often profoundly negative. In her seminal analysis, Raven Sinclair concludes that while transracial adoptions were generally positive, those involving Indigenous peoples produced "consistently negative outcomes." This was especially true once puberty began, during which time Sinclair noted a "breakdown rate of 95% by the time the adoptee is in the mid-teens."[46] Some of these legacies are described by O'Connor and O'Neal. In the context of total separation from their communities, cultures, and identity, but in an environment where they were the victims of racism, "by the time they reached their mid-teens, the vast majority were running away repeatedly, abusing drugs and alcohol, or turning to crime as a result of identity crises."[47]

Shandra Spears, who was born in 1968 and sent out for adoption at birth, recalls a childhood without her own Indigenous identity, a childhood "robbed of a political, historical, spiritual, linguistic, and cultural base which could have given me a great sense of self-esteem and strength." She has articulated some of her personal challenges as a result of her experiences:

I didn't even know that I was Native. There was no Native "mirror" that reflected my beauty; only a white mirror that reflected my difference. I compared myself to the girls around me, with their small waists and cute noses. I didn't look like them, but I had no reason to believe I was supposed to look any other way. Therefore, I "knew" that I was a white girl – an ugly white girl.[48]

Many Survivors have movingly described their experiences on the Ontario Sixties Scoop class-action case website, highlighting a loss of cultural identity for either themselves or family members. One commentator wrote, "I was born in 1954 and raised in a WASP home without a hint of Native culture or heritage. I ended up being sent to numerous psychologists and psychiatrists in order to figure out what was 'wrong' with me and why I saw the world around me so differently." Still another described how, as a Crown ward, "I was raised not knowing my culture, family or language. ... I believe I am a survivor of cultural genocide and this has greatly impacted me during my lifetime."[49]

Conclusions

The Sixties Scoop presents a different way of viewing Article 2(e), less directly traceable to any overt government policies or official statements about explicitly ending the separate existence of Indigenous peoples. Rather, we are confronted with general intent, with the collusion of provincial authorities and the courts. Yet this is, in many respects, a more compelling example of forcible transfer: Indigenous children were entirely stripped of their identities because transfer was practically irreversible. Whether some individual children may have benefited from adoption, and whether families voluntarily put their children up for adoption (one 2010 study indicates that a significant proportion of adoptees were given up voluntarily),[50] the larger context is more important. The settler colonial system created the conditions through lack of funding on reserves, discriminatory legislation, residential schooling, structural racism, and other means so that adoption was perceived as a preferred option. Further, the system was designed to destroy the ability of Indigenous peoples to perpetuate their governance traditions and cultures on their own lands. To this, Sellars adds, "It didn't matter if the child was cared for in a safe home with good food and a loving family. The determining factor was that the child was Aboriginal and therefore his or her parents and grandparents were not fit to raise their own children."[51]

This was a more successful form of forcible removal in many cases, especially since the records were sealed on adoptions and fostering for a very long time; the result was that the adoptees, often taken by force, had no legal means of finding out who they were, while their parents also had no access to their records. The Sixties Scoop can also be seen as an aspect of the intergenerational trauma produced by the IRS system. Many of the challenges within Indigenous communities can be traced to the legacies of these forms of forcible transfer. In both cases, I have argued that there is sufficient evidence to make a case for genocide under Article 2(e). This may be a popular claim among many Indigenous peoples, but it has little mainstream, settler appeal. In dealing with generations of Indigenous peoples forcibly stripped of their languages, ties to community, and interdependence with traditional lands, animals, plants, and waters, the Truth and Reconciliation Commission faced an extremely challenging task.

chapter five

The Truth and Reconciliation Commission of Canada and the Question of Genocide

Very, very definitely I as a commissioner presided over hearings where Survivors who came forward to us talked about it and qualified their own experience as genocide. They didn't qualify it as cultural genocide, they used the term genocide, and we heard that. I think we actually heard that referenced in pretty well every region of the country.

– TRC Commissioner Marie Wilson on genocide and the Survivors (2017)[1]

I had written a section for the report in which I very clearly called it genocide, and then I submitted that to the legal team and I said, "Can I say this, or, can we say this?" And the answer came back unanimously, "No, we can't as per our mandate because we can't make a finding of culpability, and that's very clear." So, we did the next best thing.

– TRC Chair, Murray Sinclair, on including genocide in the TRC'S Final Report (2017)[2]

In this chapter, I recount the history and formation of the Truth and Reconciliation Commission of Canada and explore its engagement with legalist and pluralist conceptions of genocide. As I approach the topic of the TRC, a post-judicial and Survivor-funded and -led organization, I am extremely conscious of my own standpoint as a non-Indigenous, settler, Canadian male with privilege, able to attend numerous national and regional events on a research grant. As someone who participated in the activities of the commission

and got to know many of the participants first hand, I was personally moved by what I saw. The two quotations above were taken
from recent interviews I was privileged to conduct as I prepared
this book. My impression was that this was work of the highest
importance, performed by people of goodwill who were working
with and for the Survivors and their families (and were often Survivors themselves). However, I acknowledge those who have critiques of the commission, and I have many friends and colleagues
with less positive perspectives. This is my own account of the commission and how it dealt with the topic of genocide.

I have divided this chapter into several parts. First, I discuss the
TRC's mandate and its lack of judicial power, and I discuss why
this may have been the case. Second, I provide an overview of the
TRC's structure and some of its activities over its six-year mandate, including some of its negative encounters with the federal
government and church representatives. What has become clear in
retrospect is how some of the churches and the federal government
sought to hamper the TRC's ability to accomplish its mandate by
withholding key evidence that it needed to make its deliberations.
Third, I analyse how the TRC dealt with the question of genocide
during its mandate and in its 2015 Final Report, examining how
the TRC's work lays the basis for further study into the genocidal
aspects of Canadian history.

The TRC's Post-judicial Mandate

Investigating genocide was not part of the TRC's purview; in its
conception, the commission was meant to be explicitly *post-judicial* –
that is, arising from the settlement of the largest class-action law-
suit in Canadian history. Contrary to some accounts, the TRC did
not pull back from a conclusion of genocide because there was
insufficient evidence or an unwillingness to advance this argument. Rather, it was restricted from doing so in its mandate, as
both Marie Wilson and Murray Sinclair have made clear.

Schedule N, Article 2(b) of the Indian Residential Schools Settlement Agreement set forth that the commission "shall not hold

formal hearings, nor act as a public inquiry, nor conduct a formal legal process." Article 2(c) stated that the commission "shall not possess subpoena powers, and [does] not have powers to compel attendance or participation in any of its activities or events," while Article 2(h) prevented the commission or Survivors from naming names or otherwise identifying people "without the express consent of that individual, unless that information and/or the identity of the person so identified has already been established through legal proceedings, by admission, or by public disclosure by that individual." Article 4 reiterated that since the commission was "not to act as a public inquiry or to conduct a formal legal process, it will, therefore, not duplicate in whole or in part the function of criminal investigations, the Independent Assessment Process, court actions, or make recommendations on matters already covered in the Agreement."[3]

When we spoke, Senator Sinclair observed, "In our report, we were very careful to keep in mind that our mandate was that we were legally unable to, and not permitted to, make a finding of culpability."[4] The commission's post-judicial mandate imposed limitations on what could be stated in published form. Commissioner Wilson articulated a similar point to me:

> We couldn't draw a legal conclusion. We were post-judicial in our nature, and the thing had already been through the courts. One of the terms of our mandate was that we couldn't comment on the settlement itself. ... I said, "Well, talking about the settlement is one thing, being honest in telling in our report what Survivors had said to us – that surely is part of our duty, and when people have come up again and again and spoken about what they felt was genocide, then we would be remiss if we didn't talk about that, and we would run the risk that people would feel like we didn't listen to them or we didn't hear them."[5]

Had the TRC been an official commission of inquiry, it would have possessed a broad range of judicial powers, but would not have been at arm's length from the government. While the TRC was "of Canada," it was not "Canada's TRC" or the "National TRC." It had no power to compel anyone to give evidence, nor could it make any legal determinations, such as stating officially that the Canadian government had violated the UN Genocide Convention or committed crimes against humanity or other violations of international or domestic law. Why was this the case, especially given that the Settlement Agreement had been written by lawyers and that both the first and second chairs of the TRC were judges?

Anticipated Transaction Costs and the Irish Precedent

Katherine Mahoney, a lawyer and law professor, helped negotiate the Settlement Agreement on behalf of the Assembly of First Nations (AFN). She argues that Survivors did not want a commission with judicial powers because such powers would have been "counter-productive and counter to the wishes of the elders and survivors." Notable for Mahoney was the legacy of Ireland's Commission to Inquire into Child Abuse (also known as the Ryan Commission), where "using subpoena powers so paralysed the process with litigation that the commission was disbanded." Given the reluctance of the Irish Catholic entities to fully participate in the alternative dispute resolution process, the AFN, according to Mahoney, predicted that the Church would put up a similar resistance to the TRC. Since most perpetrators of abuse were dead, and a non-judicial mandate would not prevent living abusers from being tried in court, this type of mandate could "avoid the trap of serial litigation."[6] This puts a positive gloss on the process, but it is by no means clear that a judicial inquiry would have been approved had this been a demand of the Survivors. Was it ever on the table?

The RCAP in 1996 recommended a public inquiry into the IRS system to listen to Survivors, collect evidence, and recommend forms of compensation, but no government followed through, nor was there any noticeable public demand.[7] Indeed, as mentioned previously, the Settlement Agreement as an outcome of a class-action suit was hardly about transitional justice, unlike for example, truth commissions in Argentina, Chile, and Peru, where new governments had sought to expose the crimes of past regimes. In other cases, commissions resulted from peace accords between conflict-ing parties, such as in Guatemala, El Salvador, and Sierra Leone. In Canada, there was to be no decolonization, no overhauling of state institutions. The same political parties, government depart-ments, and religious institutions that had planned and run the IRS system continued to exert their influence. As far as the government was concerned, everything was to continue more or less as before, including the perpetuation of self-serving narratives of the settler state. In 2007, Prime Minister Harper ensured that Canada did not sign the UNDRIP. And in 2009, only a year after the official apology to IRS Survivors, he declared,

> We also have no history of colonialism. So we have all of the things that many people admire about the great powers, but none of the things that threaten or bother them about the great powers. We also are a country, obvi-ously beginning with our two major cultures, but also a country formed by people from all over the world that is able to speak cross-culturally in a way few other countries are able to do at international forums.[8]

Whatever Harper had learned about the IRS system, it was insuf-ficient to sway his preconceptions about Canadian history, and his government continued to present a jaundiced image of a country founded by Europeans and developed through multiculturalism. Harper's Canada had little room for Indigenous peoples, and his policies actively sought to undermine them, a reality that dogged the TRC's work.

A Trauma-Informed Process

It is probable that a non-judicial approach was the Survivors' pre-ferred option given their experiences with the tort-based legal approaches to dispute resolution and compensation. In the ADR process established by the government of Jean Chrétien, those seeking compensation often confronted aggressive lawyers, and Survivors could be turned down for compensation if they could not remember specific details.[9] This system compensated only physical and sexual abuse and unlawful confinement; it failed to deal with collective harms such as the destruction of self-esteem, language, spirituality, culture, and ties to family members, traditional territory, and ceremony.[10] The process itself could be incredibly invasive, traumatic, and humiliating.

The later Independent Assessment Process (IAP) replicated some of the same problems. As Schedule D of the Settlement Agreement set out, "Compensation points" would be "awarded" for provable abuses. At the highest level, such abuses included "Repeated, persistent incidents of anal or vaginal intercourse. Repeated, persistent incidents of anal/vaginal penetration with an object." For these "SL5" abuses, one could be awarded forty-five to sixty compensation points, while at the lower end, seemingly lesser harms (SL1) such as "One or more incidents of fondling or kissing" merited five to ten points. "Consequential Harm Compensation Points" could also be awarded based on a Survivor's assessment of their level of harm, from H1: "Modest Detrimental Impact" to H5: "Continued harm resulting in serious dysfunction." Schedule D described a "uniform inquisitorial process," which was to be used to "assess credibility, to determine which allegations are proven and result in compensation, to set compensation according to the Compensation Rules, and to determine actual income loss claims."[11] The process could be highly disturbing for Survivors, a proportion of whom had never disclosed their histories of abuse to their spouses or children.

Garnet Angeconeb, a Survivor of the Pelican Indian Residential School in Sioux Lookout, Ontario, and a board member of the AHF, recalls Survivor reactions to the IAP:

> Some of them walked out of those hearings more wounded than they went in … it was pretty rough for many survivors going through the validation process, being cross-examined, if you will. And so I've heard from many people that it was just as adversarial as going to the regular court.[12]

Based on IAP experiences, an overtly judicial TRC might have obscured the significance of Survivor recollections, silencing important aspects of what they had endured, making them ostensibly function as witnesses for the prosecution. The long-term legacy of the schools would become far less salient than the specific details of abuses for which a criminal conviction might be obtained. While this process might bring certain truths to the surface, it would marginalize other truths. The TRC thus avoided some of these pitfalls by creating what its mandate described as a "holistic, culturally appropriate and safe setting for former students, their families and communities as they come forward to the Commission," which was "committed to the principle of voluntariness with respect to individuals' participation."[13]

A Focus away from Individual Perpetrators and Sentencing

From the perspective of the victims, efforts to punish individual abusers through criminal justice proceedings were often emotionally costly. Abusers often received light sentences, hardly in proportion to the magnitude of their offences. For example, Anglican priest Leonard Hands, from the Pelican Indian Residential School, received a four-year sentence in 1996 for nineteen counts of sexual assault, a poor reflection on his violent crimes, most of which had never made it to court. Likewise, in 1995, Oblate brother Glenn Doughty received only a year for his long legacy of abuse at St. Joseph's Residential School in Fort William, Ontario (now part of Thunder Bay). Cyril Paul, one of Doughty's victims, reflected on the trial: "My life fell apart after I went to court against Brother Doughty – I just couldn't handle the anger and pain. I started drinking again. It really hurt because my life was so damaged by him and then I saw him walk away with a year in jail, which means only four months in a country club prison."[14] Paul later committed suicide, as did Simon Danes, a victim of Plint's who had earlier testified against him.[15] Dian Millions notes how Survivors recounting their experiences were often re-traumatized, and many took their own lives after testifying.[16] While at some level it may have been worthwhile testifying to put an abuser behind bars, Survivor engagement with an adversarial, settler-biased court system did not necessarily deliver the sort of justice they were seeking.

Restricted Access to Information

The black-letter text of the Settlement Agreement appeared to guarantee a high level of access to information for the TRC. In practice, however, the TRC was hampered by obfuscation from the government and church parties. An official inquiry would have had more teeth to secure information, but such access was *already* supposed to be mandated under the agreement. Problematically, there were no properly impartial enforcement mechanisms to ensure that the government and its agencies, and the church entities, complied. Tom McMahon, the TRC's former executive director and general legal counsel, has been an invaluable source of information and reflection on some of the various ways in which the TRC was stymied in its efforts to ascertain the full truth of what was done in the residential schools and why.

McMahon lays out a strong case for the government's violation of the Settlement Agreement, which is worth exploring in some detail. The mandate laid out that the TRC was to be "accessible," "victim-centered," and "accountable," and was to "do no harm." In section 4, the commission was prohibited from "duplicat[ing] in whole or in part the function of criminal investigations, the Independent Assessment Process, court actions, or mak[ing] recommendations on matters already covered in the Agreement." It was also enjoined to "build upon the work of past and existing processes, archival records, resources and documentation" and was directed to "reasonably coordinate with other initiatives under the Agreement."[17] Schedule D of the agreement, which outlined the IAP mandate, allowed Survivors the choice of sharing their information. The agreement reads, "Claimants will also be given the option of having the transcript deposited in an archive developed for the purpose." However, claimants were never offered such an option, which means that the "IAP has been in continuous violation of the IRSSA's requirements for providing choices to IAP claimants and in developing an archive for the transcripts"[18]

McMahon persuasively argues that these processes on which the TRC was to build were to include the CEP and IAP, which would have furnished the commission with a massive amount of documentation. The TRC was supposed to be working *with* the government and the churches, and since it could neither do harm nor duplicate other redress mechanisms, some classes and types of information were unavailable. He recalls, "Very few of the persons who gave statements to the TRC went into any specific details about the physical and sexual abuse they suffered." He suggests,

> In general, the full stories of abuse are in the IAP records, not the TRC records. It could never have been otherwise. To suggest that the TRC could simply duplicate the IAP's work and seek out the kinds of information obtained in the IAP process would violate the principles of being victim-centred and "do no harm."[19]

The case can be made that the TRC should have been granted access – *subject, of course, to Survivor approval* – to the records of the CEP and IAP processes as well as "the civil litigation records held by Justice Canada, the police investigation files, affidavits and transcripts taken over the years relating to abuses at residential schools."[20] Such information would have been invaluable in helping the TRC create a more complete record of the history of and purposes behind the IRS system and, potentially, in making a claim for genocide. The TRC could have cross-referenced and filled in crucial gaps in its information-gathering as it criss-crossed the country. By January 2017, there were IAP statements and documents related to over 38,000 IRS Survivors and, potentially, some one million documents related to the system. By the end of March 2016, there were 105,530 CEP applications, over 79,000 of which were considered to be eligible under the Settlement Agreement. Having access to the CEP information on a searchable database would have constituted an invaluable resource for the commission, but this information was not forthcoming.[21]

When I interviewed Senator Sinclair, he reflected that access to information would not have been a problem had both the TRC and the IAP been run under one body. This, he concluded,

> would have allowed the TRC to have access to what Survivors were saying in the course of those hearings in front of the adjudicators. And the fact [was] that they were placed into a separate process and a separate entity and a separate group in charge, and let me point out that people

in charge of the IAP were largely the government and the churches. And the people in charge of the TRC were largely the Survivors.[22]

Not only was information not available to the commission, it was also to be destroyed, supposedly in the interests of Survivors. In April 2016, the Ontario Court of Appeal, in *Fontaine v. Canada (Attorney General)*, concluded that IAP documents could be destroyed given that fifteen years had elapsed since they had been collected. In October 2017, the Supreme Court voted unanimously to allow the destruction of CEP and IAP records after a period of fifteen years. The Court does allow living Survivors to consent to have their documents retained and archived, but any Survivors who have died since making their statements to the IAP, and those who cannot be contacted, will have their documents destroyed. This destruction runs counter to the Settlement Agreement. Had a consent process been in effect, Survivors could have agreed to have their records archived, or not, and this could have aided the TRC's work. The TRC, like the National Centre for Truth and Reconciliation (NCTR), was working under the same privacy laws as the Canadian government and the compensation processes.

It is important to state this information up front to identify some of the constraints under which the TRC laboured. We can add to this a general lack of settler interest in and support for the TRC, which was the outcome of a class-action suit, not something mandated by the government in response to public opinion polls or a popular movement for change. The commission's hearings also took place during the tenure of a government that took very little interest in Indigenous rights. In retrospect, it is a testament to the tenacity of the Survivors and the commission employees and volunteers that the TRC enjoyed the success it did.

Structure of the TRC

The first iteration of the TRC failed over the course of 2008, in part due to conflicting interpretations of the role of the commissioners. Harry LaForme, of the Mississaugas of New Credit First Nation, a justice on the Ontario Court of Appeal, was to be the chair, with health expert Claudette Dumont-Smith and lawyer Jane Morley serving as the other two commissioners. Disagreement soon arose over the specific powers of the chair. LaForme resigned, lamenting in his letter of resignation that the other two commissioners would not accept his authority, intimating that they preferred a more consensual approach to decision-making.[23] The other two commissioners resigned in January 2009, putting the process in jeopardy.

The second iteration of the TRC began in June 2009 with the appointment of Murray Sinclair as chair and Marie Wilson and Wilton Littlechild as commissioners. All three had close ties to the IRS system and took a personal as well as a professional interest in their work, which soon became all-consuming. The parents and grandparents of Justice Murray Sinclair, an Anishinaabe judge from Manitoba, had attended residential school. Raised by his grandparents, Sinclair found out in 2012 that his father, Henry Sinclair, had been abused in residential school and suffered a range of challenges as a result.[24] While Sinclair was raised a Catholic, he later embraced his own Anishinaabe beliefs, joining the Three Fires Society as well as becoming a "Third Degree Member of the Midewiwin (Grand Medicine) Society of the Ojibway."[25] Sinclair introduced himself at TRC functions using his Anishinaabe name Mizanay Gheezhik, which translates as "images in the sky," or "the one who speaks of pictures in the sky." Sinclair, as a deeply spiritual person, often centred his teachings and beliefs in how he viewed his role, and he presented the commission as "sacred work."[26]

Chief Wilton Littlechild, a lawyer from the Maskwacis First Nation in Alberta, was an award-winning athlete, a former member of Parliament, and very involved in Indigenous rights within the UN system. It was largely due to his influence that the UNDRIP became a central aspect of the reconciliation process. He was also a Survivor of fourteen years at Ermineskin Indian Residential School in Maskwacis, Alberta. Littlechild was candid about his own history: "Of all the abuses experienced, the sexual abuse and witnessing violence was an experience of severe trauma for me." He further reflected, "All of us have been affected in distinct ways, and we think of these collective impacts as a sacred trust to guide our work. This sacred trust ensures that we will use each of our special contributions to ensure that we do not fail in meeting our critical mandate."[27]

Marie Wilson, an acclaimed CBC broadcaster, and the only non-Indigenous commissioner, was married to Stephen Kakfwi, a Dené IRS Survivor who had served as the ninth premier of the North-west Territories. The commissioners became prominent voices for reconciliation and maintained virtually non-stop schedules during the TRC's mandate.

As part of the Settlement Agreement, a ten-member Survivors' Committee worked closely with the commissioners and support staff to help plan National Events and a wide range of outreach activities. Committee members coordinated sharing circles and conducted prayers, the opening and closing of events, and much else. They played a prominent and visible role in the process and represented the country's diverse geography and the multiplicity of Indigenous peoples.

The TRC also had a secretariat, which included an executive director and a research director. John Milloy, the first research director, had occupied a key role in the RCAP, and he had been one of the first to gain access to the enormous Record Group 10 file of Indian Affairs documents at Library and Archives Canada. He later went on to author *A National Crime* (1999), a definitive work on the IRS system. After only a few months in the job he resigned, citing the administrative burden of the task. He had also made negative comments about the Catholic Church, for which he was obliged to apologize. Paulette Regan, author of *Unsettling the Set-tler Within* (2010), served as interim research director after Milloy before moving on to focus on writing the reconciliation volume. A range of academics and others were contracted to write reports and conduct research for the commission on specific themes.

While the commission was independent, structurally it was des-ignated as a department of the federal government, created under the Public Service Employment Act, and the chair was classified as a deputy head for the purposes of regulations and funding. This allowed it to access $8 million "for the additional administrative costs associated with its status as a department."[28] Several employees of Indigenous and Northern Affairs Canada (INAC) also worked for the commission, ranging from a high of forty-seven in 2012 to a low of nine by 2015. These were technically individuals seconded to the commission because, according to Treasury Board figures, no federal employees were directly employed by the TRC at any time during its mandate.[29] In practice, the commissioners stressed that they stood well away from the government and that their $60 million budget came from the Survivors, who had set aside this amount from their $1.9 billion settlement. Their independence became increasingly obvious when they began discussing genocide, critiquing the churches and the federal government, and taking the government to court to release information.

National and Regional Events

As mandated by the IRSSA, seven National Events were held throughout the country. The first was held in Winnipeg in June 2010, following the TRC's move from Ottawa to that city the previous year. Later events were held in Inuvik, Halifax, Saskatoon, Montreal, Vancouver, and Edmonton, with a closing ceremony in Ottawa in June 2015 for the release of the summary of the Final Report. National Events were designed as "a mechanism through which the truth and reconciliation process will engage the Canadian public and provide education about the IRS system, the experience of former students and their families, and the ongoing legacies of the institutions."[30] The TRC also held or participated in regional events, outreach activities, and hearings, visiting over seventy communities. This amounted to over three hundred events, drawing upwards of 150,000 people.[31]

A central focus of the TRC, in line with its guiding principles, was to provide a safe space for Indigenous spirituality, cultures, and languages, the very things attacked by the architects of the IRS system. Indigenous ceremonies, prayers, beliefs, and values played a central role. At the Alberta National Event, for example, simultaneous translation was provided in Cree, Blackfoot,

Stoney-Nakota, Dené, Inuktitut, French, and English. The TRC logo, presenting seven fires arranged in a circle, was based on an Anishinaabe prophecy about the clash and potential reconciliation of Indigenous peoples and white settlers; it also represented the seven sacred teachings of the Anishinaabe: Truth, Humility, Honesty, Wisdom, Respect, Courage, and Love. Each National Event was based on one of the seven teachings, and the banners, posters, coloured vests for health support workers, and educational outlines for visiting school groups were coordinated around them.

Prayers and smudging, water and fire ceremonies, and a focus on traditional spirituality were all key aspects of the commission's operation. Tears were considered sacred, and tissues were collected in small, brown paper bags marked with a blue cross, to be burned in the sacred fire, tended by Firekeepers throughout the National Events. The ashes were ritually collected and stored in a basket, and, at the conclusion of each event, were handed over from one organizing committee to the next. Coupled with traditional ceremonies and practices were new artefacts created for the commission to signal its importance. One of the most iconic was the hand-steamed Coast Salish bentwood box, fashioned from a single piece of cedar in 2009 by Luke Marston. The box became a repository of memories and promises of reconciliation by Survivors, government and church officials, and members of various communities.

National Events came to follow a pattern. The sacred fire would be lit in the early morning by the Firekeepers, followed by prayers and a Survivors' walk, led by Survivors holding honour staffs and flags. Commissioners and TRC staff were followed by Survivors, officials, families, and the general public. In a large, central hall, a procession, often accompanied by traditional drums or other instruments, made its way from the back of the auditorium, while the spectators and participants rose to their feet. Everyone was welcomed to the territory by Elders and TRC officials, who then took part in songs and prayers. The heads of provincial or national Indigenous organizations, and local settler dignitaries such as mayors or a provincial premier, would be involved. These openings were not without controversy. At the Vancouver National Event, then provincial premier Christie Clark faced a stand-off with some activists, who held signs reading, "We are walking money" to protest her support of oil pipelines being run through Indigenous territories.

National Events featured a range of activities. The commissioners held sharing panels during the day, and participants registered on a first-come, first-served basis. Normally, one commissioner would attend each panel, while another attended a concurrent sharing circle. Private statement-gathering took place in another part of the venue from 9:00 a.m. to 6:00 p.m. Other events included academic panels, such as the one on reconciliation that I organized and chaired at the Alberta event. Movies were screened; at the British Columbia event, the films included *A Sorry State*, *We Were Children*, and *Hidden Legacies*, while the Atlantic event's line-up featured *A Windigo Tale*, *My Own Private Lower Post*, *Remembering Inninimowin*, and *The Experimental Eskimos*. The churches maintained a Churches Listening to Survivors Area, where Survivors and others could talk with officials and various volunteers. Exhibits featuring photos of the schools and spiral-bound books of names, documents, and pictures were displayed on each table. There was a separate area where Survivors could go to receive a personal apology. These gatherings played a seminal role in educating the public about the IRS system and its legacies. Each National Event included an education day, which brought hundreds of children to learn about the system. For example, at the 2014 Edmonton National Event, some two thousand school-aged children attended.

The afternoons ended with a Call to Gather at around 4:00 p.m., when the hall would be packed, spotlights brightly illuminating the stage, while music played in the background, like Redbone's 1973 classic, "Come and Get Your Love." The events were often MC'ed by the dapper Stan Wesley from Moose Factory, Ontario. Various dignitaries who had attended sessions throughout the day, the commissioners' sharing panels, or the listening and talking circles, would provide reflections. Many, like National Hockey League star Joe Juneau, shed tears as they described what they had learned. "Gestures of reconciliation" by individuals and community groups would also take place. Video clips of the day's activities and interviews were shown to the audience. One or more commissioners would speak. Following this was a birthday party for all the Survivors, with cupcakes baked by church volunteers. Children who were approximately the age of IRS children stood centre-stage, holding Bristol board letters in different colours, wishing Survivors a Happy Birthday. Those on stage would lead the audience in song, and "Happy Birthday" would be sung in as many Indigenous languages as could be found in the room. The TRC would then remind everyone that children's birthdays were not celebrated in the IRS system.

Concerts were offered at night, and one night was devoted to talent shows, in which Survivors and others were encouraged to perform. These events were often lively and emotional. The talent night at the Vancouver National Event, for example, featured several Elvis impersonators, while at the Montreal National Event, a Mi'kmaq Survivor composed a poem about genocide in the Shubenacadie Residential School. Buffy Sainte-Marie performed three concerts – in Winnipeg, Saskatoon, and Ottawa. She performed "Sing Our Own Song" several times, encouraging a resurgence of Indigenous pride and action and encouraging the audience to be "Idle no more."

Sainte-Marie was one of many "honorary witnesses" inducted by the commission. The first was Governor General Michaëlle Jean, in October 2009. Leaders with public stature in their communities, these men and women were inducted at the beginning of each National Event, after which they attended public testimonies and, at the end of each day, during the Call to Gather, delivered their impressions of what they had seen and heard. Honorary witnesses, according to the TRC, were chosen based on being "accomplished and influential leaders from all walks of life." Knowledge of the IRS system was not a criterion; indeed, the point was to educate the witnesses, most of whom "frankly admitted to their own prior gaps in knowledge and understanding of the residential school system and its continuing legacy." The goal was to send these people out into mainstream society as ambassadors, to "encourage the broader Canadian public to ... learn and to be transformed in understanding and in commitment to societal change."[32] Among the honorary witnesses were two former governors general, two former prime ministers, an auditor general, two genocide Survivors, and a range of other people from Indigenous and racialized communities.

Statements and Documents

Statement-gathering, whether public or private, was a key aspect of the commission's work. It collected some seven thousand statements, mostly from Survivors, but also from former teachers and administrative staff. It also collected approximately five million records, all of which were eventually housed at the NCTR at the University of Manitoba in Winnipeg. As McMahon has discussed, from the outset, the commission encountered serious problems acquiring the documents it needed about the operations of the schools. It also had difficulty accessing information from government departments. The auditor general reminded the federal government in her 2013 report that it had "an obligation to provide all relevant documents to and for the use of the Commission."[33]

In addition to withholding ADR, CEP, and IAP documents, the federal government put up barriers to aiding the TRC in collecting documents. There were constant battles over the interpretation of "relevant" documents. Library and Archives Canada claimed in 2011 that it had created some thirty "roadmaps" outlining where, in thirty government departments, information about the IRS system could be found. It estimated at that time that the number of relevant documents would represent twenty kilometres, or roughly 69,000 file boxes, and would take ten years and $40 million to properly digitize. Eventually, the government came up with $20 million for document collection, to be added to the commission's initial $6 million budget.[34] NCTR director Ry Moran recalls, "While some entities complied willingly, document production would prove to be one of the most challenging elements of the commission's mandate, seeing the TRC in court on five separate occasions for a variety of document collection issues."[35]

Genocide

Thanks in part to the books *The Circle Game* (1997) and *Accounting for Genocide* (2003), both discussed in chapter 2, genocide had been discussed for almost two decades before the TRC released its Final Report. Equally, in *Shingwauk's Vision* (1996), Miller used "attempted cultural genocide" to describe a system that "gradually became the vehicle of the newcomers' attempts to refashion and culturally eliminate the first inhabitants' way of life and identity."[36] In the same year, Agnes Grant published a detailed comparative study of the residential schools and the Holocaust, stressing some commonalities, while also advocating for increased public knowledge of the IRS system.[37]

In 1999, noted Nêhiyaw historian Harold Cardinal similarly called the residential schools "programs of cultural genocide aimed at Indian First Nations," constituting "an integral component of a systematic, intergenerational, state-planned program of brainwashing aimed at removing 'the Indian' from the minds and souls of Indian children."[38] The AFN made a determination in 2002 that the UNGC applied, specifically citing "the forcible transfer of children from one racial group to another with the intent to destroy the group" as being central to the operation of the IRS system.[39] In *Magic Weapons*, Sam McKegney called the system "explicitly genocidal in its intention to obliterate Native societies by rendering their children 'non-Native.'"[40]

Genocide was not widely discussed early in the commission's mandate, although some TRC staff had previously mentioned the issue. Gregory Younging, assistant research director, argued in an AHF publication, "There is ample evidence that the residential school system clearly committed all acts of genocide listed above between 1831 and 1998, and more evidence is sure to emerge during the term of the Truth and Reconciliation Commission."[41] Paulette Regan noted in her book that the genocide issue was important, since some critics "viewed the TRC as a whitewash designed by the government and churches to cover up genocide."[42] As Marie Wilson recounted to me in August 2017, the commissioners, in travelling to regional and National Events, repeatedly heard Survivors describe their experiences as genocide; this prompted internal discussions about how the truth of what Survivors were sharing could be reflected within the TRC's strict post-judicial mandate.

In early 2011, the TRC organized a forum at a downtown Vancouver hotel to canvass a range of international opinions about how best to commemorate the IRS system and preserve future records. Representatives from Holocaust and genocide museums, memorials, and education centres, the founding director of the National Museum of the American Indian, and many others spoke of the importance of memory, representation, commemoration, and preservation. Commissioner Littlechild and invited speakers like Stephen Smith, director of the Shoah Foundation, argued that genocide merited close attention as a descriptor for what had happened in the IRS system.

Senator Sinclair has been consistent in his views about the applicability of the term *genocide* to the IRS system for over a decade, well before the advent of the TRC. His first recollection of using the term publicly was during a 2007 presentation at the University of Manitoba law school. As he told me in his appraisal of the UNGC's applicability,

At that time, without having researched it to any degree at all, I expressed the view that it was an act of genocide. And I still held the view that it certainly fell within [Article] 2[e]. There were also various moments in history when there were other elements of government policy and conduct that brought them into some of the other categories as well. Forced birth control, starvation techniques, conditions of life. So those conditions ... would have also brought government into the convention, if they had occurred after the convention occurred. Now that was the problem ... the convention wasn't in place until 1949, and most of Canada's misdeeds occurred ... before the convention was in place, and the question of retroactivity then became the hurdle.[43]

In 2012, Sinclair made a public conclusion that the system was genocidal, arguing on the CBC documentary series *8th Fire* that genocide had been committed. Such personal opinions and the growing interest in genocide appear to have stemmed from Survivors' comments and widespread interest in investigating this topic. However, apparent dissonance soon appeared between Sinclair's personal comments and official TRC publications. For example, the TRC's Interim Report in 2012 highlighted a four-pronged attack on Indigenous children, families, culture, and nations.[44] It stressed how the IRS system had been "established with the specific intent of preventing parents from exercising influence over the educational, spiritual, and cultural development of their children," but it did not mention genocide.[45]

In his recent book, Miller argues that the TRC's finding of cultural genocide suggests "that the commission had retreated from Chief Commissioner Sinclair's earlier use of the term 'genocide' to describe the schools." He states later, "Although the chief commissioner sometimes flirted with calling the schools an instance of genocide, in the end the commission settled for referring to them as an example of cultural genocide."[46] Miller does not account for why this decision was made, implying that the commissioners may have decided there was not enough evidence for genocide, or perhaps they thought the term was too controversial.

In October 2017, I asked Senator Sinclair about Miller's claim about the TRC's supposed retreat from genocide. I also asked about Miller's statement, "Speaking at the University of Manitoba in February 2012, Sinclair had acknowledged that the schools did not appear to satisfy the United Nations criteria for genocide." My sense was that Miller was in error, both about the reasons why the commission did not directly say that the IRS system was genocide and in his interpretation of Sinclair's words in 2012. When we discussed this point specifically, Sinclair was clear that he had used the term genocide repeatedly since 2007 and that the TRC had concluded cultural genocide because its mandate precluded it from going further: "In our report, we were very careful to keep in mind that our mandate was that we were legally unable to, and not permitted to, make a finding of culpability."[47]

As quoted at the beginning of this chapter, Sinclair stated that he had wanted to include a section in the Final Report describing IRS crimes as genocide, only to be told by his legal team that this was not possible. Commissioner Wilson also recalled internal discussions about genocide and the restrictions of the mandate:

> Yes, we absolutely did ... to figure out how we could talk about it [geno-cide] without, number one, breaking the rules of our own mandate and, on the other hand, not breaking the trust that was put in us with the Survivors, who spoke to us using the language that they used. So that's how we came to that, and that's why the introduction around the issue of genocide is framed and explained in the way it is.[48]

Ultimately, then, the TRC had to navigate the issue without breaking its mandate, but also while honouring the Survivors.

Beyond the personal opinions of the commissioners, the TRC functioned as a platform for the articulation of genocide claims, and it created space for prominent leaders to discuss the issue. Several honorary witnesses invoked genocide. As discussed in chapter 3, former prime minister Paul Martin argued that cultural genocide had been committed. Phil Fontaine went further, charging the Canadian government with genocide, specifically Article 2(e). In 2013, he and former chief executive officer of the Canadian Jewish Congress Bernie Farber penned an article in the *Globe and Mail*, charging Canada with violations of the UNGC. They argued that healing from the effects of a century of genocide would never be addressed until a "national conversation" about this issue had taken place.[49] They then followed up their article with a letter to James Anaya, then UN special rapporteur on the rights of Indigenous peoples, as he was preparing a report on the status of Indigenous peoples in Canada. The letter identified three specific violations of the UNGC: John A. Macdonald's starvation policies on the Prairies, the IRS system, and the Sixties Scoop.

The TRC also inducted two genocide Survivors as honorary witnesses: Éloge Butera, who had survived the Rwandan genocide, and Robbie Waisman, a Buchenwald Survivor. Both gave numerous talks at TRC events and other community gatherings. Waisman never used the term genocide to describe the IRS system in any public address, choosing instead to promote a focus on individual humanity and a message of hope. He argued, "We cannot, and we should not, compare sufferings. Each suffering is unique. ... I don't compare my sufferings or the Holocaust to what happened in residential schools."[50]

In mid-2014, in an interview on the podcast *Red Man Laughing* with Anishinaabe comedian and broadcaster Ryan McMahon, Sinclair laid out the delicate balancing act that the commission had been tasked with performing, arguing that the removal of children "certainly speaks to the fact that this fell within the definition of genocide in the UN Convention." However, the larger question concerned how this conclusion should be operationalized in the work of the commission (or "What do we do with that knowledge; where does it lead us? What do we do about that history – how do we get past it, and how do we come to terms with it?"), which Sinclair dubbed "the reconciliation question." The issue concerned how to not only acknowledge genocide but also create a future-oriented approach to make reconciliation happen.[51]

The Release of the Final Report, 2015

On 31 May 2015, the TRC held its final event, a four-day gathering that brought thousands of people together, beginning with a march for reconciliation, which wound its way from Gatineau, Quebec, past Parliament Hill, and concluded on the lawn of the city hall in Ottawa. A few days before the final event, in a public lecture on 28 May, Supreme Court Chief Justice Beverley McLachlin had called the IRS system "cultural genocide," framing it as part of an "ethos of exclusion and cultural annihilation."[52] At Ottawa city hall, then Ontario premier Kathleen Wynne echoed this conclusion in her opening address. I was interested to know whether there had been some form of coordination among the TRC, Paul Martin, Beverley McLaughlin, and Kathleen Wynne over public discussion of cultural genocide. Commissioner Wilson reflected, "To my knowledge, there was absolutely no coordination, ... and I know that I and others were surprised and thrilled when Justice McLachlin spoke up. That was really, really important. And I didn't know that was coming, and I'm not aware that any of us knew that was coming."[53]

On 2 June, the main floor of the Delta hotel in downtown Ottawa was packed as the commissioners officially unveiled the TRC's summary of the Final Report, entitled *Honouring the Truth; Reconciling for the Future*; a book outlining key principles of truth and reconciliation (*What We Have Learned*); a volume of Survivor testimonies (*The Survivors Speak*); and a twenty-page booklet outlining the TRC's "Calls to Action." They called for the implementation of ninety-four recommendations (not including a number of sub-recommendations) – everything from increased funding for Indigenous programming at the CBC to the adoption into domestic law of the UNDRIP, as well as a national monitoring body to oversee and report back each year on the progress of the implementation of the TRC recommendations.

Sinclair was finally able to reveal the commission's conclusion that cultural genocide had been committed, and he handed out copies of the summary report to the assembled dignitaries, including the leader of the opposition and a disgruntled minister of Aboriginal Affairs. Five hundred paperbacks of the summary were available in the lobby. Those of us who rushed over to collect a copy eagerly opened it to page 1 to read the commission's findings:

> For over a century, the central goals of Canada's Aboriginal policy were to eliminate Aboriginal governments; ignore Aboriginal rights; terminate the Treaties; and, through a process of assimilation, cause Aboriginal peoples to cease to exist as distinct legal, social, cultural, religious, and racial entities in Canada. The establishment and operation of residential schools were a central element of this policy, which can best be described as "cultural genocide."[54]

This excerpt would be quoted extensively in the following weeks. Below this were further conclusions:

> *Physical genocide* is the mass killing of the members of a targeted group, and *biological genocide* is the destruction of the group's reproductive capacity. *Cultural genocide* is the destruction of those structures

and practices that allow the group to continue as a group. States that engage in cultural genocide set out to destroy the political and social institutions of the targeted group. Land is seized, and populations are forcibly transferred and their movement is restricted. Languages are banned. Spiritual leaders are persecuted, spiritual practices are forbidden, and objects of spiritual value are confiscated and destroyed. And, most significantly to the issue at hand, families are disrupted to prevent the transmission of cultural values and identity from one generation to the next. In its dealing with Aboriginal people, Canada did all these things.[55]

Did the TRC conclude that physical and biological genocide had also been committed? The paragraph above was deliberately ambiguous and could be subject to two interpretations, either that Canada had done "these things" too or, alternatively, that Canada had committed cultural genocide and that these other forms of genocide, while not committed by the state, were being discussed by way of contrast. A further oblique reference to the UNGC was embedded deep within the report, where the commissioners concluded,

It is difficult to understand why the forced assimilation of children through removal from their families and communities – to be placed with people of another race for the purpose of destroying the race and culture from which the children come – can be deemed an act of genocide under Article 2(e) of the UN's Convention on Genocide, but is not a civil wrong.[56]

Here there is a suggestion, although again ambiguous, that the removal of children violated the UNGC, but with sufficient wiggle room to suggest that this was not an official conclusion. These ambiguities aside, Sinclair remained consistent in his personal view that the UNGC would apply to the IRS system if it occurred now, making this conclusion to Anna Maria Tremonti on CBC's *The Current* following the release of the summary report. In my informal discussions with TRC staff members at the closing ceremonies at the Delta hotel and Rideau Hall, they suggested that genocide was never going to be officially recognized because the mandate had explicitly prohibited it. However, this legal restriction was not conveyed to the media or the general public. There was no sense that the TRC had deliberately pulled any punches in its analysis of the IRS system or in its evaluation of the malignant intent of successive Canadian governments. Indeed, such a narrative would have reduced the impact of the TRC's findings and their forward-looking approach.

Conclusions

Early in the TRC's mandate, Isabelle Knockwood, a Shubenacadie Survivor, provided testimony at the Atlantic event and noted, presciently, that the TRC had revealed little, if any, information about the perpetrators, the paedophiles, the abusers, the clergy, or the government. "When," she asked, "are they going to tell us how that felt like?"[57] Ultimately, this is not information that the TRC was able to directly provide, given its lack of judicial power to compel anyone to attend and to answer such questions. What we do know of the perpetrators comes from the TRC's collection and analysis of public statements, speeches, private correspondence, reports, and legislation outlining the intent to forcibly remove Indigenous children from their families and communities. The TRC did interview about seventy former school staff, but this was only a small percentage of the overall statements gathered.

In this, the TRC departed from other recent truth commissions that had dealt with abuse. For example, its mandate differed fundamentally from Ireland's Ryan Commission, which focused primarily on the perpetrators, their actions, and their intentions. Its 2009 report was divided into eighty-six chapters, and each Catholic organization had its own detailed section describing its history and the institutions it had operated. In 2009, the Murphy Commission released a report on abuses in Catholic-run institutions in Dublin, featuring a chapter each on the forty-six priests and other church officials whom it had investigated for child abuse. Indeed, most of the report deals with the perpetrators and their crimes.

The difference here, perhaps, was that abuse in Catholic-run institutions was the main story, so individual perpetrators and their manoeuvres to escape justice figured centrally. However, for the Canadian TRC, there were larger contextual issues at stake, about colonization, land theft, broken treaties, the potential renewal of nation-to-nation relationships, and a range of other matters. The Irish cases were straightforward in that both victims and perpetrators were predominantly of the same ethnic group and the same religion, with neither colonizing the other nor implicated in larger crimes that involved the dispossession of peoples from their ancestral lands or the destruction of their forms of government. Indeed, in the Irish case, Catholicism had been present since the fifth century, and would become closely bound up in national identity, which often stood in opposition to Protestantism, seen as an imposition from Britain.[58]

Despite Senator Sinclair's public opinions on genocide, the TRC published little on the topic of genocide, from either a legalist or a pluralist perspective. It did not recommend amendments to the Criminal Code, nor did it recommend that museums (including the Canadian Museum for Human Rights) or any level of government recognize cultural genocide or genocide. In its calls to action regarding education, discussions of cultural genocide or genocide were not included; neither was a discussion of crimes against humanity. In short, there were no recommendations dealing with international legal agreements, conventions, treaties, and so on, except, of course, for the UNDRIP.

Proving genocide was not a key focus for the TRC, and it is fair to say that a focus on genocide may not have reflected the wishes of Survivors. To do so would have reduced the process to an overtly criminal one – charging the state with a specific set of international crimes. In the absence of the sort of documentation that the TRC *should* have received, this would have been difficult to prove, even if its mandate had been different. A genocide frame might also have led to the exclusion of abuses and crimes that did not fit the definition of genocide. That is, it would have had to focus on building a legalist case to the potential exclusion of important pluralist elements that fell outside the ambit of the

UNGC. In pragmatic terms, the TRC's promotion of cultural genocide seems to have been quickly adopted by Survivors, educators,
community leaders, former prime ministers, Supreme Court justices, and many others.

The legacy of the TRC continues with the NCTR, the University of British Columbia's Indian Residential School History and
Dialogue Centre, an interim National Council for Reconciliation
(formed in June 2018 with Grand Chief Littlechild as chair), and a
wide range of activities on the part of governments, universities,
media, and other institutions to engage with the Calls to Action or
to avoid them. It was clear enough, without being explicitly stated,
that the TRC and the commissioners supported a charge of forcible transfer as genocide, and there is sufficient evidence woven
throughout the six volumes of the Final Report to support this conclusion. Where things become more complicated, as I explore in
the next chapter, is in how best to use the UNGC to approach the
issue of the many thousands of deaths in the schools, the deaths
of innocent and vulnerable children who were forcibly abducted
from their families and home communities.

chapter six

The TRC and Indigenous Deaths, inside and outside the Residential Schools

They were places of disease, hunger, overcrowding and despair. Many children died. In 1914 a departmental official said "fifty per cent of the children who passed through these schools did not live to benefit from the education which they had received therein." Yet, nothing was done.

– Gary Merasty, former member of Parliament[1]

During his tenure in Parliament from 2006 to 2007, he rightly became a thorn in the side of Jim Prentice, minister of Indian Affairs and Northern Development, with his frequent questions, asking when the prime minister would apologize for the IRS system and its consequences. Gary Merasty was a member of the Peter Ballantyne Cree Nation and represented the riding of Desnethé–Missinippi–Churchill River. His questions about the fate of the disappeared Indigenous children eventually struck a chord with the minister, precipitating an investigation. Certainly, the search for missing family members and friends, and the lack of knowledge about what had happened to them, was a source of considerable frustration and worry for many Survivors. Rarely were children's small bodies sent to their families for traditional burials, and families were often not informed as to when their children had died or under what circumstances. Most children were buried near the grounds of the residential schools, and costs were kept to a minimum. Indigenous communities sought to find out what happened to their missing community members so that they could identify burial sites, and as Grand Chief Alvin Fiddler of the Nishnawbe Aski Nation argued, for "the remains to be put to rest in an appropriate and respectful manner."[2]

In this chapter, I focus on the thousands of Indigenous children who were killed or died as a result of the IRS system. I review what the TRC was able to accomplish when covering this issue and seek to understand the extent to which we can see the deaths as genocide, based on the evidence compiled by the TRC during its mandate. While the TRC does not make a strong case for violations of Article 2(a), it provides some evidence of violations of Articles 2(b) and (c) – that is, "Causing serious bodily or mental harm to members of the group" and "Deliberately inflicting on the group conditions of life calculated to bring about its physical destruction in whole or in part." This is not, however, the primary focus of my analysis, and my conclusions are speculative because much more research is needed to gauge the full extent of the crimes inflicted by the government and the four mainstream churches on Indigenous peoples.

Accounting for the Missing

The Missing Children and Unmarked Burials Project was an ambitious undertaking, especially given the many challenges it had to overcome, including lack of funding, very limited time, and government and church resistance. Not part of the Settlement Agreement, the mandate arose after Merasty posed his questions in April 2007 and Prentice promised to find out what had happened to the "disappeared children." He was clear: "I have instructed our officials to look into that and to work with oblate records of the churches to get to the bottom of this issue, and this sad chapter in our history."[3]

A Working Group was soon established, comprising Indigenous organizations, Survivors, archivists, and representatives of the federal government. In 2008, it laid out the key questions and goals of what later became the Missing Children research project: ascertaining how many children had died, their names, how they had died, where they were buried, and how many had gone missing. In 2009, a six-member team was formed, led by archaeologist Alex Maass, who had the task of assembling and analysing school, church, and government records – often grainy, handwritten, poorly scanned documents. The team documented who died, and where, and sought also to determine the locations of cemeteries and unmarked burial grounds. Poor access to information before 2011 made the project's work extremely challenging, and even after the number of documents began to increase, the TRC was able to answer only a "small number" of requests by individuals searching for the fate of missing relatives. Overall, Maass recalls problems of incomplete and late production of documents by the churches and the government.[4]

In addition to collecting documents, examining residential school grounds, and other activities, the team sought statements by Survivors, and statement-gatherers were given specific questions that they could ask towards the end of their interviews. Project staff could then review the oral and written testimony. The TRC devoted a portion of its website to seeking information about children who had "never returned home or whose fate is still unknown, or died." The website provided a toll-free number, an email address, and a PDF form entitled "Missing Child or Unmarked Graves Report," although few people printed and submitted the form. Additionally, the team set up a booth in the learning place area at National Events. Maass recalls that, in addition to the large volume of documents the team collected, "the relatives and former students who witnessed deaths and approached us at TRC events were the most useful sources of information. Personal accounts were especially useful when we were able to match and compare these statements against the documentary records – letters etc., from the period."

The initial budget soon ran out, and the government refused to provide additional funding, causing severe financial constraints. As a result, few names were added to the National Residential School Student Death Register when the team wrapped up its work in April 2013, and the project ended in December of that year.[5]

The TRC's summary of the Final Report confirmed 3,201 deaths from 1867 to 2000, divided into two main categories: those who were identified as IRS students and those who were not. Of the students who had died, 32 per cent had not been named, the gender of 23 per cent had not been registered, and the cause of death of 49 per cent had not been recorded.[6] The majority of deaths (2,434) had occurred before 1940, the remainder (691) from 1940 to 2000.[7] According to Ry Moran, who was director of statement gathering for the TRC, the 3,200 figure was very low, and "Justice Sinclair argued that this number is likely higher, perhaps 5 to 10 times as much."[8] Likewise, Commissioner Wilson notes that, of the three thousand named deaths, "at least double that number is suspected, in addition to the many that the records show were sent home, or sent to Indian hospitals in the final stages of illness to die there."[9] In a 2016 publication, Maass put the "documented and recorded" number of deaths at over 4,100, but gave 6,000 as a more realistic figure. The team also created a cemetery database, with over five hundred entries documenting fifty-four burial sites and cemeteries, and the team made twenty site assessments in six regions of the country during the TRC's mandate. While many burial sites have now disappeared, Maass made clear that "IRS burials are not mass graves as they are generally understood, for example, in the context of modern-day genocide."[10]

The death rate for Indigenous children in the IRS system was considerably higher than the rate of child deaths outside the system, and this problem remained significant until the 1950s. The project noted that, even during the early 1940s, "the Named and Unnamed combined death rate for children at residential schools is 4.90 times higher than the general death rate for Canadian schoolchildren."[11] How did the children die? For those who had a reported cause of death, 48.7 per cent died of tuberculosis, which was rampant not only in the schools but also on reserves and in other Indigenous communities. The project's records also indicated a range of other causes of death: fifty-six drownings, six suicides, forty deaths in school fires, twenty deaths by exposure, and thirty-eight deaths due to accidents including falls and car crashes.[12]

The death rate in the schools had been a cause for concern since the nineteenth century, and the issue was brought to public attention in 1907, when Indian Affairs' Chief Medical Officer Peter Bryce submitted a report on the prairie schools, outlining horrific death tolls.[13] Both the *Montreal Star* and *Saturday Night* magazine reported on the high death rates, with *Saturday Night* condemning the casualty rate as "disgraceful to the country," concluding, "Even war seldom shows as large a percentage of fatalities as does the educational system we have imposed upon our Indian wards."[14] The problems Bryce identified were never corrected. Indeed, as the RCAP final report argued, "In those decades, almost nothing was done about tuberculosis in the schools. ... The department did not even launch a full investigation of the system."[15]

Can these deaths be considered genocide? This is not a claim that the TRC advanced in its Final Report. The authors made it clear that information on the number of deaths was incomplete, while concluding that some of the earlier figures provided by Bryce were somewhat misleading, in the sense that he didn't offer an annual death total per school. This would have implied looking at the yearly enrolment of a school and then the percentage of children who had died in that year while attending the school. The authors do their best to take a range of claims, which do not directly correlate to a yearly death rate, to arrive at a yearly total. They conclude that "Bryce's report is evidence of a high death rate, but it is not an annual death rate (or any other sort of death rate). Neither does the report provide sufficient information to determine annual death rates in the schools or to make predictions as to how many of the students then enrolled would die in the coming years."[16] In terms of actual annual death totals, the authors give the example of the Old Sun and Peigan Reserve boarding schools, founded in Alberta in 1890 and 1892, respectively. In the nineteen-year period from the founding of the schools, the authors note an average annual death rate of 4.66 per cent for Old Sun and 4.15 per cent for Peigan. Given that the average annual death rate in Canada in 1901 for children aged five to fourteen years old was 0.43 per cent, the Old Sun death rate is "10.8 times higher than the national death rate for school-aged children."[17]

Overall, while Bryce correctly identified many of the key causes of sickness and death in the schools and on-reserve communities, his quantitative evaluations were far less precise and were prone to a range of errors, many of which have been outlined in other work, such as Michelle Robinson's critical engagement with Bryce's 1907 and 1909 studies. While it is highly likely that far more children died in the schools and soon after than the TRC reported (a point that many TRC staff readily discuss), this does not mean that Bryce's statistics were accurate.[18] This means that any finding of genocide involving mass killing should be based on much more than Bryce's work. Certainly, the TRC authors seemed to be wary of drawing any such conclusions.

In the TRC Final Report's *Missing Children* volume, words such as "deaths" and "missing" are passive, and deliberate killing is rarely discussed. "Abortion," "euthanasia," and "infanticide" are not to be found, while "murder" is used sparingly and never in reference to actions by teachers or administrators against students. The only mention of murder is an incident at the Roman Catholic school in Kenora, Ontario, in 1925, when "a hired man wounded a fellow hired worker, then shot and killed a priest, and finally killed himself."[19] The other mentions concern the horrendous number of missing and murdered Indigenous women and girls, which is discussed in the *Legacy* and *Reconciliation* volumes as well as in the *Honouring the Truth* volume. These references are closely tied with Call to Action 41(1), calling for an "investigation into missing and murdered Aboriginal women and girls." At the same time, the number of the missing and murdered may well be much higher than estimated.

In the *Missing Children* volume, the authors noted that the confirmed death rates might seem low compared to other sources and cited several factors, "the most significant being the overall limitations in the data, which lead to undercounting." They continued hopefully, "As more documents are reviewed, it is likely that the death rates based on the data in the National Residential School Student Death Register will increase."[20] Certainly, information from the IRS system was inconsistent after 1915. Before that time, principals were supposed to provide detailed annual health reports to Indian Affairs, including the number of deaths. However, from 1915 to 1935, their reports of deaths ceased to be published in a consistent way. Overall, the TRC highlighted problems of incomplete reporting and the destruction of documentation (some 200,000 files between 1936 and 1944). Supporting documents were not made available, and the TRC noted "limited and late access to relevant documents from the government and churches, due to problems with document production."[21] In some cases, the commission was flooded with digitized documents, many of which were not organized in such a way as to enable the Missing Children project team to search for death records. A large number of documents were scanned at such low resolution as to be illegible.

It was also clear that the schools had sought to mask the extent of the death rate. There was no guarantee that principals would faithfully report the number of dead children in their schools and no guarantee that, further up the administrative hierarchy, such numbers would be duly recorded. Indeed, principals would more likely be motivated *not* to engage in such reporting. Further, many very sick children were sent home to die so that their deaths would not be recorded on the school register. Death tolls also did not include those who survived the schools only to commit suicide years later, who died from alcohol or substance abuse as a result of their experiences, or who suffered from mental health problems attributable to the system.

Survivor memoirs and recollections detail many accounts of those who survived the schools, but not the aftermath in a settler-controlled society. Basil Ambers (Tunour Island band, British Columbia), who attended St. Michael's Indian Residential School in Alert Bay, recalls, "There's only a little handful of us left. That's all. Dozens committed suicide, drowned, or drank themselves to death. Some went under with drugs."[22] Similarly, Bev Sellars, former chief of the Xat'sull First Nation, adds, "Thousands did self-destruct. If they didn't commit suicide, they became addicted to anything that would numb or distract the pain."[23] The Missing Children project was limited to the records it had. Equally, if children born in the schools were the product of two students, two teachers, or a teacher and a student, the fetus was aborted, the baby was killed, or the infant was sent out somewhere for adoption, these children would likewise not appear in any official death toll. Maass recalls of the team's research,

> Infanticide and abortion were re-occurring themes across the country although I never saw any direct evidence of either; not in the documents nor in my fieldwork. I did have Survivors point to places where "the babies were buried" and discuss the use of school incinerators to dispose of aborted foetuses. This came up in discussions in disparate regions of the country and with unrelated individuals. There were one or two stories of suspected murder, in one case of a "forced" suicide but these were unsubstantiated.[24]

Recollections of forced abortions and infanticide are common. For example, Annis Gregory Aleck discusses the testimony of Paul Johnny, who attended the Kamloops and Williams Lake schools in British Columbia and who told Aleck that sterilization of young girls, as well as abortions, were commonplace, while some girls disappeared, presumably because they did not survive one of these procedures. Two other Survivors with stories about sterilizations died before Aleck could interview them.[25] In one of my interviews, a Survivor named Diane recounted rumours of killings at the Shingwauk school, specifically about a baby thrown into the furnace. She said, "I've heard the bigger girls talking about one person there that, she had a baby and, I don't know, they didn't know what they did with the baby. ... And they said that, that this man had, had this girl. I don't want to say who. ... But it was one of the supervisors." Diane did not disclose much more except that the girl who had the baby disappeared too: "I don't know where they sent her, they must have sent her away or something or kept her someplace in the school. Because it's very easy to keep somebody in that school and not, not find them."[26] Commissioner Wilton Littlechild revealed in a recent interview,

> Then we heard stories about children burying children. A farmer who had a farm by one of the schools said he used to watch the children bring a coffin to the graveyard and bury one of their own classmates.

That impacted me because I still carry those stories, I haven't completely unloaded myself personally.[27]

Overall, the Final Report gives little evidence of violations of
Article 2(a), although it provides evidence of violations of Articles
2(b) and (c). When we discussed this matter, I asked Senator Sinclair about issues of interpretation in 2(b) and (c). He remarked
that, due to the direct involvement of the churches and the indi-
rect involvement of the government, "There's an open question
as to whether Canada as an entity could be said to have deliberately imposed those conditions [or w]hether it was simply by the
creation of the environment in which those conditions could be
imposed by others."[28]

Where we may see evidence of government involvement is in
William Schabas's discussion of genocide by omission, as outlined
in chapter 1: "The crime is committed by omitting to take action,
rather than by taking action. Obviously, such an act can be committed with the specific intent to destroy the group."[29] On harms and
a lack of care, the TRC concluded, "It is clear that the government
and the churches failed to establish the necessary regulations to
ensure ... an acceptable level of care." They outlined failures in
"health, nutrition, building conditions (including sanitation), discipline, truancy, student labour, abuse, and child welfare."[30] With
respect to the conditions of the schools, heating was often inadequate, while overcrowding, poor ventilation, inadequate water
supplies, and poor sanitation resulted in the spread of disease. Little provision was made to halt the spread of influenza, tuberculosis, or other illnesses; sick and healthy children were often housed
together, which encouraged the spread of disease and increased
the death rate.[31]

Despite the demonstrable knowledge that nutrition and health
were closely tied, IRS system planners did little to ensure that
the children were properly fed. Indeed, as the TRC notes, "It was
not until 1958 that residential school funding was increased to
a level thought by the Nutrition Division to allow for the provision of meals that would be 'fully adequate nutritionally.'" Even
in cases where schools maintained farms where they grew their

own produce, much of it was sold to pay the costs of running the schools. During the 1930s and 1940s, Indian Affairs cut funding to the per capita grant at a time when food prices rose considerably.[32]

Mosby and Galloway have traced suggestive links between chronic undernourishment in the residential schools and students' ill health later in life. This ill health includes decreased height, increased chances of obesity, higher insulin sensitivity, and type 2 diabetes. For women, there were serious repercussions for reproductive health: "greater risk of stillbirths, preterm birth and neonatal death; complications with labour, and decreased offspring birth weight." Further, many of the medical effects of chronic undernourishment can be passed on to future generations. The schools themselves were the key cause of these problems, as reported by recent studies, which have demonstrated that "Indigenous children were no more nutritionally stressed than other Canadian children at school entry."[33] These findings build on Mosby's earlier landmark work on various nutritional "experiments" undertaken in the schools without any form of consent.[34] Research such as this supports the contention that as researchers gather more data about the egregious effects of colonization on Indigenous peoples, the UNGC may become an increasingly useful lens through which to examine them.

Outside the school system, as I have outlined elsewhere in this book, the government used starvation to weaken and kill Indigenous peoples, to herd them onto reserves, and to threaten them, in some cases, to relinquish their children to the residential schools. A lack of nutritious food on reserves and in the schools increased risk factors for diseases such as influenza and tuberculosis. As traditional food supplies dwindled, and the lands were taken away by the government, starvation became a serious problem for Indigenous peoples and an opportunity for the government to coerce them into compliance with policies that ran counter to their interests. The government failed to promote economic policies that would allow Indigenous peoples to make a living, particularly in the larger context of the killing of buffalo in the tens of millions.

The spread of tuberculosis also reached severe proportions. One medical study from 1936 put the death rate from TB in the Prairie provinces as "twenty times as great as that among white people," adding that "over 30 per cent of the total deaths from tuberculosis occur among the Indians, who comprise less than three per cent of the total population."[35] Overall, preventable disease greatly reduced Indigenous populations and facilitated the spread of settler colonialism. During the 1930s, the federal government cynically cut funding for Indigenous health, including the care of TB patients and TB prevention. It also cut funding for food. Tuberculosis ceased to be the leading cause of death among Indigenous peoples only in 1960.

When the government did seek to actively address tuberculosis in the early twentieth century, it sometimes had more to do with limiting its spread to white settler areas located near reserves than in stopping the spread among Indigenous peoples. For example, Indian Affairs concluded, in a document from 1908, that because tuberculosis

> is decimating the Indian population of the Dominion and its prevalence amongst the aborigines in thickly settled white districts is a menace to the white population, an evil which becomes apparent in the North West as settlement progresses, it seems necessary to organize a campaign against the disease which will mitigate its results as much as possible.[36]

By 1939, the dangers of Indigenous tuberculosis remained very serious, although, as one co-authored study published in the *Canadian Medical Association Journal* revealed, the problem was not likely to spread to neighbouring white settler populations. In the case of Manitoba, the authors observed that an "average death rate for the reserves is 1,020 per 100,000, while that of the surrounding municipalities is 51 per 100,000, which is definitely lower than the whole death rate of 59 per 100,000 for the province, including Indians. In the case of the Oak River Reserve, where the surrounding population contains few halfbreeds, the rates are respectively 727 per 100,000 and 26 per 100,000."[37]

The TRC's Final Report highlighted Indian Commissioner Edgar Dewdney's use of starvation tactics in the 1880s as "an instrument of government policy" to force Indigenous peoples onto reserves and destroy their governments, and, of the devastating impact of disease and famine, it concluded that "between 1880 and 1885, the First Nations population on the Prairies dropped by more than a third – from 32,000 to 20,000."[38] It emphasized documenting provable harms, including deaths, which suggests the *beginning* of a much larger research agenda, focusing on the Genocide Convention to make sense of the strategies deployed in settler colonialism. The Final Report lays the basis for this important work, but does not specifically set out how it could be done. While the TRC has been criticized for not using stronger language and avoiding any discussion of murder and killing, its report might be better seen as a basis on which academics, journalists, and activists can draw their own conclusions, as I have done here. Certainly, there is ample evidence from which to draw.

Conclusions

Corntassel and Bird have recently critiqued what they see as the TRC's soft language, and they conclude that "Canada is a serial killer," outlining ways in which the expanding settler state "carried out a murderous assault on Indigenous peoples," while over time evolving "more devious and duplicitous" means of doing so. Their work focuses on murder and the various means used by the state to erode the power of Indigenous peoples and their ability to sustain life and their communities.[39] This ties in with Achille Mbembe's writing on "necropolitics," which describes how state governments arrogate power to themselves to determine who may live and who may die. The sovereign state not only becomes the ultimate dealer in life and death, but, moreover, its ability to make these decisions, cloaked in an aura of legitimacy, is what defines that very sovereign power.[40] The TRC never went this far in its analysis. More time, funding, and government goodwill would have allowed it to give a fuller account of how many children died and under what circumstances, and Calls to Action 71 to 76 specifically focus on continuing to find out how many children died in the schools, who they were, and why they died. We need, therefore, to see the TRC's effort as the beginning of ongoing information-gathering processes, which are continuing through the NCTR. It is imperative, if we are to have a fuller picture of the schools, that such work continue; there is still much to be uncovered. In August 2018, for example, a mass grave of over fifty Indigenous children from the Brandon Residential School in Manitoba was found in a campground along the Assiniboine River. Grand Chief of the Assembly of Manitoba Chiefs Arlen Dumas discussed recollections from Survivors "of these things happening, of mass graves existing." Observed Dumas, "Well, here's one example ... there will be more."[41]

When asked in 2016 about the progress of reconciliation, Senator Sinclair put it this way: "I'm feeling that the train is slowly moving. But we still have a ways to go before we can get it up to any kind of speed. And we have a long distance to go once we get to that speed."[42] As I outline in the next chapter, there certainly is a very long way to go. Many settler Canadians do not accept cultural genocide, and certainly not outright genocide. They do not even acknowledge their own identity as settlers or any form of interdependent relationship with Indigenous peoples. While conflict over memory is not as heated as in Australia or the United States, these issues in Canada are far from being resolved, and anti-Indigenous sentiments constitute a major impediment to any agenda focused on conciliation, the return of stolen lands, and Indigenous self-determination.

chapter seven

Genocide and the Politics of Memory: Discussing Some Counterarguments

That Indigenous peoples were subjected to genocidal policies by the state is not a popular conclusion, and several prominent historians, anthropologists, and others have already refuted claims of genocide and cultural genocide. This chapter engages three arguments that seek to counter prospective claims of genocide. The first relates to the legacy of the Holocaust and its influence on how we understand genocide – in this case, forcible transfer through the Nazi *Lebensborn* program. The *Lebensborn* example raises important questions about intent and the permanence of forcible transfer. I then consider two issues that often arise from discussions of the residential schools. The first is the putative goodwill and kindness of some teaching and administrative staff and the positive experiences some students report. To what extent does this mitigate or modify a conclusion of genocide? Can genocide be committed for benevolent reasons by "nice" people? The second issue relates to the wider context of abuse and child removals outside the IRS system – namely, the global nature of abuse in Catholic schools, about which we are learning more on a regular basis. Given that non-Indigenous children in other contexts were also abused, does this mean that genocide directed against Indigenous peoples should primarily be seen as a subset of larger crimes and not distinct in and of itself?

While Canada has never had the overtly buoyant exceptionalism of the Americans, settler amnesia and wilful forgetting have been little better here. Yet, as I discuss later on, many of us who are settlers have an uncanny ability to compartmentalize Indigenous-settler histories into discrete chunks. Like a Japanese bento box, we are able to keep various aspects of our history separated so that we can potentially enjoy one flavour without it influencing the taste of the other foods, and we can choose the order in which we consume our history, while also ignoring some less palatable dishes (perhaps dismissing them as only garnish). As such, and I will outline this below, not only do we settlers have problems recognizing the IRS system as cultural genocide or genocide, but we also have a bigger problem seeing genocide as being intrinsically and inextricably bound up in the larger settler colonial project that is the creation of Canada.

Lebensborn and Forcible Transfer

Many settler Canadians will find it difficult to understand the IRS system as genocide. Part of this is a result of the long shadow cast by the Holocaust, which has established an archetypal sense of what "real" genocide should look like. Even if we go beyond deliberate mass murder and look at forcible transfer as genocide, the Holocaust precedent still figures prominently. The Holocaust has also given us an archetype of forcible transfer, which has an appreciable effect on how we understand Article 2(e) in the Canadian context.

The *Lebensborn*, or "well of life," program (created in 1935) can be seen as an extreme version of forcible transfer. Details of this organization, a department of Reichsführer-SS Heinrich Himmler's personal staff, emerged during the RuSHA (SS Race and Settlement Main Office) trials of 1947–48. One of *Lebensborn*'s primary goals was to increase the population of so-called Aryan Germans by kidnapping children in countries invaded by Germany, children who physically resembled the Nazi Aryan ideal or, as the Tribunal described them, "'racially valuable children' of foreign nationals." Children were selected from Czechoslovakia, Yugoslavia, Poland, and Norway through an extensive triage process. They were then sent to designated children's centres to be indoctrinated into Nazi

German language and culture, before being farmed out to foster homes, where suitably Aryan parents would adopt them and raise them as their own. In practice, children aged six or younger were preferred as they were more amenable to suggestion and grooming to assume the Nazi ideal. Families were rounded up, and children "bearing the desired characteristics of the Nordic type" were selected.[1] Those who were seen as not racially desirable or who could not be assimilated were often killed either in death camps or by other means.

The history of *Lebensborn* is compelling and disturbing, bringing us into the world of Nazi racial theorists and policymakers. To focus on this unique case is, however, to hold up the exceptional as the rule rather than the extreme example of forcible transfer. There is nothing in the UNGC that states that, for genocide to occur, a transfer must be irrevocable and that a child must forget or lose all contact with their home communities forever. It is also important to note that the *Lebensborn* policies were directed at a comparatively small proportion of target populations, while in Canada and Australia, a larger proportion of child removals targeted Indigenous peoples. The upper range of suspected kidnappings stands at around 250,000 children from the occupied Eastern European countries, with an upper figure for Poland at 100,000. Given that the 1939 population of Poland alone was approximately 34.7 million, this represents a relatively small fraction of the overall population. The Canadian case is different as we have *both* a larger proportion of the targeted group taken *and* a less permanent form of transfer.

Lebensborn became a sort of red herring after the TRC's Final Report appeared, and it was held up by people such as journalist and author Robert MacBain as the archetypal example of forcible transfer. That some Indigenous parents were able to refuse to allow their children to attend residential schools, or were able to somehow withdraw them later, meant that claims of genocidal forcible transfer were not tenable. *Lebensborn* stressed permanence – one was either successfully assimilated or killed. Unlike the parents of Indigenous children, MacBain posits, "The parents of the estimated 400,000 children abducted by the Nazis had no say whatsoever."[2]

In a far more sophisticated legal analysis, but one that contains echoes of the above argument, McGill law professor and former war crimes prosecutor Payam Akhavan casts doubt on the specific intent behind the IRS system, preferring instead the term "persecution," which is legally a crime against humanity, one that exists on the same scale and is of the "same genus as genocide."[3] While persecution and genocide are similar, the key difference between them lies in the specific intent, which must be present in genocide, but not in persecution. Akhavan has tacitly implied that the genocide debate is an unnecessary effort, and he describes being disturbed by "how this polemical debate disregards the deeper meaning of words; the importance of recognition for healing wounds." Cultural genocide, in his particular turn of phrase, is a "mourning metaphor" and "the ghost of proposed crimes past." To focus on this deflects the real issue: "the urgency of national reconciliation with Canada's indigenous people." We should not, he argues, get too focused on "sterile debates on taxonomy."[4]

While he does not directly reference *Lebensborn*, Akhavan backgrounds it as an ideal type against which the IRS system does not measure up. While conceding that the government's IRS policies involved "the forced transfer of children," he draws a legal distinction between acts of genocide and the specific intent behind those acts. The key here is what the government intended to do – did it seek to forcibly transfer children to destroy Indigenous peoples culturally, or to destroy them biologically? One is a far more permanent solution, he argues, than the other:

> In the case of biological destruction, children are permanently separated from a group, with the intention to destroy the group's capacity to physically reproduce itself. In the case of cultural destruction, however, children are separated from a group temporarily or for a prolonged period with the intention to "destroy" the group's cultural identity rather than its reproductive capacity. This is the exact case of residential schools.[5]

Or is it? It is not clear how a group will reproduce itself if it no longer has any group characteristics. Akhavan does not actually explore the effect of the schools on the status Indian birth rate over time. How is he to know that the goals were not also reproductive? Another consideration concerns the base group from which the children were being drawn and to which, if we follow Akhavan, they would return, presumably able to contribute to the group's reproduction. The groups, whether a broad Indigenous category or more focused on individual First Nations, did not remain stable demographically, culturally, or economically during the seven generations of the IRS system.

Certainly, the IRS case differs sharply from *Lebensborn* given that the goal was not to transfer white-looking Indigenous children to increase settler numbers. It was instead designed to transform status Indigenous children from being potential political actors, representing Indigenous nations, into individual (albeit potentially darker-skinned) liberal citizens and consumers within a settler state. We could theoretically say that the IRS system "failed" because Indigenous children went in Indigenous and came out Indigenous, although emotionally and physically damaged from their experiences. The failure would be constituted by the fact that the effort to kill the Indian to save the man did not actually kill the Indian. This, however, is to see Indigenous peoples through some sort of generic lens as status Indians, non-status Indians, Métis, or Inuit and not to actually see them as members of sovereign nations in a political sense.

The Indian Act and settler colonial processes created groups that had little basis in historical reality. "Indigenous peoples" were bound together by the fact of being colonized and were thus subject to similar types of colonial law, created with the goal of taking their lands and controlling their movements, behaviours, and identities. Were we instead to look at the specific fate of individual nations, what becomes clear is that the IRS system imperilled the reproduction of individual nations, coupled with other processes that killed, starved, dislocated, and politically hobbled these nations, thereby inhibiting their capacity to reproduce their numbers demographically, along with their cultures and governance systems.

Akhavan has critiqued Indigenous genocide claims since at least 2012, and his seminal book on genocide was sparse in its analysis of colonialism, colonization, and Indigenous genocide. The exception was his relatively fulsome discussion of a widely discredited, self-published report written in 2001 by former United Church minister Kevin Annett. Rather than engage with more reputable studies of the IRS system and the UNGC, many written by Indigenous peoples, Akhavan chose a straw man, someone who alleged that 50,000 Indigenous children had been killed in residential schools, dubbed the "death camps of the Canadian holocaust."[6] Relying on this report allowed Akhavan to lament that genocide was being appropriated by "a political culture of recognition in which ownership of anguish is ... also a means of achieving a form of celebrity." Genocide, then, was "a much-coveted trophy in a consumer culture of grievance and suffering, alleged or real." Akhavan seemed to be cautioning people like Annett (or was it all genocide claimants?) to forsake "the utilitarian appeal of privileged labels and emotional self-indulgence."[7] This appears to be an almost *reductio ad absurdum* logic, seeking out the most outrageous hyperbole to discredit any finding of genocide. For someone of his stature, devoted to human rights and social justice, this stance is difficult to understand.

Indigenous Peoples as "Victims of Benevolence"

Another type of argument involves seeking a putative balance, positing that the positive elements of the schools have been unfairly submerged under a deluge of negativity. Claims of genocide are thereby critiqued on the basis that those who ran the system were well intentioned. There were some individual bad apples (the argument runs), but the schools responded to problems that already existed in Indigenous communities. In April 2017, Conservative Senator Lynn Beyak was removed from the Standing Senate Committee on Aboriginal Peoples for a series of comments she had made the month before, praising the "kindly and well-intentioned men and women and their descendants," while lamenting that their "remarkable works, good deeds and historical tales in the residential schools" had gone unacknowledged. "Negative reports," she thought, unfairly overshadowed a more balanced picture of the schools.[8] In January 2018, an unrepentant Beyak was ejected from the Conservative caucus in the Senate. Bayek's views have been echoed in the literature for some time, and others from a more academic perspective have equally embraced this need for "balance."

Eric Bays, in his 2009 book, promoted what he called "another picture" of the IRS system. While conceding one picture – some negative experiences in the schools (e.g., "some children were abused") – he nevertheless maintained that the "two pictures need to be held together" to produce a "fair judgment." The other picture is of students who saw their experiences as "generally beneficial." The larger goal was to rehabilitate the motivations of the staff, many of whom, Bays argues, "as faithful Christians, responded to the church's call to help a group of children whose needs were largely ignored by the rest of Canada's population." The argument runs that, unlike mainstream Canadian society, who expressed their "prejudices" by "ignoring the needs of aboriginal peoples entirely," IRS staff cared. They were, Bays averred, "moved by a faith that taught them to care for their neighbour, and to favour those who are disadvantaged and in need."[9]

In his account of the TRC, *Truth and Indignation*, anthropologist Ronald Niezen has also expressed a desire for a more "balanced" picture. Through a range of interviews with former Catholic teachers and administrators, Niezen draws himself into an evolving discussion about the "imbalance" between how the IRS system and its legacies were understood at the TRC and by the wider public. Niezen presents his interviews as "counter narratives to stories of abuse and trauma." He continues, "To those Oblates who had once worked in the schools, there is another history to be constructed out of their very different memories, out of things not being said but that stand out to them: the good intentions, the making do with little, the care, the sacrifice, the love, and hockey."[10]

Niezen attended many of the National Events and numerous regional events, and his work critiques the tone and methodology of the TRC, which, he argues, promoted one particular viewpoint to the practical suppression of other ways of interpreting school experiences. Powerfully emotive and fundamentally negative narratives became "not only 'sayable' (and 'hearable')," but, he observes, "dominant to the point of excluding or overshadowing other forms of remembered experience." A victim-centred narrative became a "protected and protective orthodoxy."[11] Yet the truth, as he sees it, might be different:

> Photographs of children engaged in archery or standing on the shore of a lake holding up an impressive fish make an implicit argument that the intention of the church was not to eliminate aboriginal distinctiveness but to accommodate aboriginal people's core values. Even the formally posed photographs argue obliquely against narratives of suffering. After all, the implicit argument goes, if the children were in such deep pain, why all the smiles?[12]

Niezen highlights a lack of balance and objectivity in the work of the TRC, suggesting that the visual evidence and perceptions excluded from its narrative would provide a more nuanced account. He is not alone. Contributing to the *Dorchester Review* (a journal whose mission is to "engage and challenge the politically correct vision of history often found in the media and in academe"), historian Ken Coates echoed Niezen in 2014, arguing that the IRS system's positive aspects had been downplayed, and "not all students left the residential school broken." The lack of nuance was troubling, he thought, and provided "the country with a distorted view of Indigenous realities." He therefore called for historians to focus on the future and move past the negative history.[13]

Coates questions whether the schools are the central causal factor in all problems experienced by Indigenous peoples. This is because the social problems common to those First Nations communities with many Survivors are also found in communities with few Survivors. In other words, the schools (one presumes the independent variable) may not have caused the social problems (the dependent variable). Given that some Indigenous peoples had positive experiences, the narrative needs to be shaped differently. On balance, then, and despite the fact that "Aboriginal culture was being downplayed, if not suppressed," Coates concludes that "they [First Nations] still viewed the schools as an educational opportunity."[14] The overall suggestion is that we should move on from the negative associations of the schools – to wit: "it is time to refocus attention away from Residential Schools, the devastating impact of which is well known and the constructive elements largely ignored."[15]

I have several problems with these arguments, the first being that, as settler academics, we (I, Niezen, Coates, Akhavan, and others) will be better served (if we have any interest in conciliation at all) to operate from a basis of recognizing our own privileged position within the university system and Canadian society and reflect on who we are and how we approach this history. We might understand that the IRS system was created and maintained to benefit us, and not Indigenous peoples. Settler laws, elected officials, and church leaders created these systems for us, and we continue to benefit from the arrangement (even if Baha'i or of other religions). Our knowledge of the system and its continued legacies was almost non-existent during the 1980s and 1990s, and, according to polling data (which I analyse in the next chapter), it remains outside the frame of reference of most settler Canadians. Certainly, we do not generally use it as the touchstone for understanding our country. That we now know and do not really want to know, and that this knowledge makes us uncomfortable, is not a legitimate reason to treat this as old or imbalanced history that needs to be more palatable for settlers.

Second, we need to be careful about photographic "evidence" from such a highly controlled environment. Unlike the iconic photos of historic atrocities taken by journalists – from the Armenian genocide to the Holocaust and the Vietnam War (the works of Gilles Caron and Nick Ut spring to mind here, as do the four Sonderkommando photos secretly taken at Auschwitz in 1944) – there are few unstaged photographs documenting children's experiences. Instead, as Angel and Wakeham have discussed, the photographic legacies have been skewed since most photographs were taken by school staff and government officials "seeking to produce propagandistic scenes of institutional order." Given this goal, it is not surprising that "there are no photographs of the deaths of thousands of children in residential school custody or the rampant psychological, physical, and sexual abuse that occurred within the schools' walls."[16]

Contra Niezen, the photographs cannot tell the full story, and, indeed, children had days with both smiles *and* considerable pain – they may have been abused yet also found pleasure where they could. The human striving to normalize and seek meaning in any environment does not excuse the abnormality of that environment, as psychiatrist and Holocaust survivor Viktor Frankl ably explored in his 1946 analysis of his experiences at Theresienstadt, Auschwitz, and Dachau. Schissel and Wotherspoon, in an early study, noted that despite the obvious damage the schools inflicted, they could also be venues for making friends and personal connections, and since most of the prominent Indigenous leaders and activists of the 1960s and after had attended the schools, in some cases the schools laid the foundation for political organization.[17]

A third problem relates to the way IRS history is being interpreted here. There have always been, as suggested above, multiple narratives, and most accounts, even the most negative portrayals, mention the positive experiences of some children. We might understand the TRC approach as embodying Indigenous methods of "truth gathering" (as opposed to "truth finding"), where the focus lies in gathering multiple truths without seeking to establish that there is one absolute, correct truth out there.[18] This is important because, while some Indigenous peoples' truths of the schools were positive, they run alongside, but do not undermine, the negative truths of other Survivors.

The TRC certainly heard from Survivors who reported positive experiences, who were grateful for the good teaching they received, and for the many activities they participated in, such as "sports, arts, reading, dancing, writing." Some, as they noted, "chose to stay in school and complete their education. In certain cases, students developed lifelong relationships with their former teachers." Some took up leadership positions as a result of their educational experiences.[19] This more nuanced portrait echoes Miller's observation two decades earlier that some Survivors "firmly deny that their school experience scarred them or their fellow students," while arguing that some teachers were "exceptional individuals who respected Indian ways and made no effort to suppress language and identity."[20]

Of those who better navigated the schools, there seemed to be some common factors, such as parents preparing their children for what to expect. Parents who promoted the ideals of a Western education and provided emotional support helped their children better cope with this period of their lives. In other cases, children fared better if they were sent to a school when they were older, had parents with ties to the school, or had a relative working there. As well, due to the intergenerational legacies of the schools, some children preferred the school environment to their disruptive home life.[21] Survivor Jeanne Rioux recounted a generally positive experience at residential school, certainly when compared with home: "My mother didn't really seem to know how to show affection physically at all so there's a kind of cold atmosphere and my father was absent a lot and he was working." In contrast with her home life: "[It] was a pleasure to be in boarding school. There were a lot of people in the school that were trying to run away constantly but I was happy to be there because it was less hurting and less anger."[22] During the 1930s, a Chilcotin father wrote his son in residential school, "You are lucky to be in school where you get plenty to eat. If you were home you would get hungry many days."[23] This, however, raises the issue of the schools in some cases being *relatively* better than the alternatives. The question here is why the alternatives became so onerous that parents and children sought out residential schooling instead of living together. This brings us to the larger discussion of the colonial context of Indigenous life.

What about Survivors who truly seemed to enjoy their experiences? Playwright and novelist Tomson Highway attended the Oblate-run Guy Hill Indian Residential School in Manitoba from age six to fifteen, and he is notably positive about his experiences, proclaiming the "joy in that school," where he spent "nine of the happiest years of my life." He puts it this way: "There are many very successful people today that went to those schools and have brilliant careers and are very functional people, very happy people like myself."[24]

Highway's recollections might seem to vindicate the notions of Beyak and others, but other stories paint a different picture.

Murdock Sewap attended the same school from 1958. His family was threatened with imprisonment to coerce him and his brother to attend. Sewap was punished for speaking Nêhiyaw and was physically and sexually abused; he recalls being constantly belittled. His head was shaved when he tried to escape, and the legacies of his experiences were destructive.[25] Rosalie Sewap attended from 1959 to 1969 and recounts very negative experiences: "When I was 7 I started being abused by a priest and a nun. They'd come around after dark with a flashlight and would take away one of the little girls almost every night. ... You never really heal from that."[26] In his video story as part of the nindibaajimomin digital storytelling project, Dan Highway describes being "very messed up" by his abusive experiences during his thirteen years at the Guy Hill school.[27]

The tone and focus of these narratives do not influence to any significant extent the discussion of genocide in the schools. First, the fact that some Survivors report positive experiences does not negate the negative experiences of many other Survivors, who emerged with long-term physical and mental challenges. The IAP records indicate clearly that a large proportion of Survivors have endured a range of serious harms. It must also be recognized that children did their best to cope, and this sometimes meant selectively ignoring some aspects of the schools, while remembering others. Survivor Ted Fontaine remarks, "As young children, easily manipulated, we created new connections and rapidly bonded with some of our captors. Being malleable and wanting kindness and love, we slowly came to believe that there was kindness in those we were around every day and attached ourselves to those who looked after us."[28]

Second, even friendly teachers and administrators were still complicit members of a system designed to forcibly remove and transfer Indigenous children. Their kindness rarely extended to aiding escape plans, promoting Indigenous languages or religions, seeking to uphold treaty rights, or in other ways resisting the coercive power of the schools or government. Rather, one sees a sugar-coating of the bitter pill, and the positive memories of many children were influenced by their desire to assimilate and "make it" in mainstream Canadian society once they left school.

Another issue concerns the misguided benevolence of many officials, who, it is claimed, only had the best interests of individual children at heart. This sort of reasoning is misleading: forcible removal can never, under law, be seen as a benevolent act. The core motivation of the UNGC is to protect groups as separate and distinct entities. The claim that Indigenous children were harmed by their membership in their own group and needed to be taken away does not deny the application of the UNGC. Quite the reverse, as legal theorist Kurt Mundorff argues: "Group destruction can never be in the interests of the affected group itself, which according to the Genocide Convention holds a right of and interest in its own existence."[29] Indeed, this quashing of the benevolence defence harkens back to the RuSHA trials, where the court quickly put paid to the defence's argument of "how well these children were treated and of the wonderful care afforded them." Rather, the judges made it clear that "it is no defense for a kidnapper to say he treated his victim well."[30]

Abuse in a Wider Context: Is the Abuse of Indigenous Children Unique?

In the wake of global Catholic abuse scandals, some have questioned whether Indigenous children were targeted because they were Indigenous or because they were isolated and vulnerable. In his preface to the collection *Power through Testimony*, Ronald Niezen makes the case that the abuse of the residential schools was reproduced around the world, and he questions aspects of the TRC's claims:

> The sexual abuse of children is endemic in all institutions in which individuals are given absolute control over the absolutely powerless. Even though it was a central theme in the testimony to the TRC, sexual abuse in institutional settings is a much wider issue than that of the abuse that took place in residential schools.[31]

Niezen's larger point is that while the abuse in the IRS system is atrocious, qualitatively it is not necessarily distinctive given the global nature of Catholic sexual abuse. Here is another example: "This aspect of the abuse of power relations targets children as vulnerable, not Indigenous peoples as subjects of assimilation policy. In a way, the pervasiveness of testimony about sexual abuse in Canada's TRC tells us more about the consequences of institutional failure on a grand scale than about assimilation-oriented Indigenous policy."[32]

Can we make a determination of genocide in a context where thousands of children – Indigenous, European, and many others – have been targeted? Niezen is correct that Catholic abuse has occurred worldwide and constitutes a horror of global proportions. The scandals did not begin with revelations about Indigenous children, however; in 1983, allegations exploded against Gilbert Gauthe, a priest in Henry, Louisiana, who had been sexually abusing children for decades. For the next four years, an average of one case a week of sexual abuse came to light in the United States.[33] The Catholic hierarchy attempted to cover up the truth, often through discrete payouts, and by 1992, Catholic entities in the United States, confronted with hundreds of sexual abuse cases, had paid some $400 million in financial settlements. By 2006, the total amount of the payments had risen to $2.6 billion in that country alone.[34] One US study argued that between 40,000 and 60,000 minors in that country may have been sexually abused by Catholic clergy.[35] In late July 2018, the United States–based cardinal Theodore McCarrick resigned after facing allegations of sexual abuse, an occurrence that paralleled the resignations of bishops in Latin America. Investigations into the sexual abuse of children continue around the world.

The Mount Cashel scandal in Newfoundland was a knock-on effect of the scandals south of the border. Like the US cases, allegations of abuse went back decades, from late 1974, but no allegations were investigated until 1989, when the Royal Newfoundland Constabulary began a serious and in-depth investigation, which resulted in a Catholic-led inquiry. In 1992, the Christian Brothers offered a formal apology, and over the next few years, the number of victims uncovered in the process went from 40 to 130, and over $29 million in compensation was disbursed.[36]

How does this compare with the IRS system? A few key points are in order here.

In the IRS system, the majority of the schools were run by Catholic entities, and there was abuse in other denominational schools as well. To reiterate an earlier point, of the 31,000 claims resolved in the IAP, the TRC noted that "in 21% of the cases, the awards were greater than $150,000. Awards of this size are reflective of the most violent, intrusive, and aggravated acts, and the highest levels of harm."[37] This could include sexual abuse, but not necessarily. The abuse of day scholars (non-resident students) was also part of the Settlement Agreement, although no Common Experience Payments were provided. Someone in the Survivor Class is defined as "a person who attended a federally owned and operated residential school during the day and returned home every night."[38] The process of investigating claims of abuse began in 2012, when the Tk'emlúps te Secwépemc and shíshálh nations, later joined by the Grand Council of the Crees, launched a Day Scholars Class Action suit against the federal government. Ninety-eight First Nations opted into this class action.

Those who attended non-residential schools or non–federally funded residential schools were not eligible for compensation, so we do not have statistics for these children. Given that the statistics for sexual abuse in other countries include children not just in boarding schools but also in day schools, the actual number of Indigenous children who were sexually abused could be considerably higher than the figures presented by the IAP. In addition, under the Settlement Agreement, only a select proportion of Indigenous peoples were entitled to any compensation. It is certainly conceivable that the rate of sexual and other forms of abuse of Indigenous children in state-funded schools, both residential and day, both federal and provincial, could exceed any percentage for any settler students in North America. One can make the inference, then, that Indigenous children were specifically targeted, and in mass numbers out of proportion to their overall share of the Canadian population.

We should be very clear that abuse is not the only issue here. Language, spiritual practices, skin colour, and most aspects of a child's identity were systematically targeted in the residential schools. These types of action were not necessarily visited on other children in other Catholic schools, where the racial, ethnic, religious, and linguistic identities of teacher and student were often the same.

We should also be clear that most settler Canadian children were not forced to attend residential schools and were, therefore, not abused in such schools. Further, there was some level of accountability, in many cases, because the parents or guardians were able to choose school board trustees and other officials and elect other local, provincial, and federal representatives. The right to vote federally was not granted to status Indigenous peoples until 1960 and in many provinces until the mid-1960s (1969 in Quebec). Grant notes another important difference between Mount Cashel and the IRS system in that Mount Cashel was a school for children who had been abandoned, who had no family to care for them. By contrast, "Indian children were not helpless and lonely. They belonged to viable cultures with loving, caring families who provided for their children. Where individual parents could not provide this care, extended families did."[39]

Conclusions

The larger point made in this chapter concerns what we are to make of the genocide lens in this case. Does the fact that other children were abused somehow dilute or mitigate the significance of IRS abuse? I would say no given, and reflecting Grant's observations, that Indigenous children did have homes, families, and communities. They did not need to be sent out to residential schools; they could have stayed with their families and within their communities and could have been schooled in their own traditions, or they could have attended schools located on their reserves, schools that the government and the churches often sought to close down (although they sometimes had conflicting goals with regard to day schools). The vulnerability of the children, which was a permissive cause for them to be abused, was created by the federal government. It was not some accidental by-product of a benign or even neutral system. It was intentional. And to reiterate, the very high numbers are disproportionate when compared with non-Indigenous peoples.

Overall, the arguments against genocide described in this chapter do not involve a denial of the facts so much as conflicting interpretations. A larger problem, with which I deal in the next chapter, involves the search for balance and some form of harmony among shared collective memories of the Canadian past. The forms of what we might call "interpretive denialism" discussed in this chapter relate to how we want to understand the significance of anti-Indigenous crimes in Canadian history. In the next chapter, I explore the most common form of denial – simply ignoring Indigenous history or excising entirely the concept of genocide from our consideration of that history.

chapter eight

Indigenous Peoples and Genocide: Challenges of Recognition and Remembering

Whereas the United Nations Convention on the Prevention and Punishment of the Crime of Genocide states that genocide includes forcibly transferring children from one group to another group, and the actions taken to remove children from families and communities to place them in residential schools meets this definition of genocide ... the second day of June is to be known as "Indian Residential School Reconciliation and Memorial Day."
— Preamble to Bill C-318, 1st Reading, 31 October 2016[1]

The awakening of memories and truths of the residential schools, the Sixties Scoop, and other aspects of settler colonial history have highlighted two distinct narratives. One sees Canadian history as a long process of colonization and genocidal destruction, the other as a long history of progress that can be favourably compared with Western Europe and the United States. There is also a middle ground, where aspects of both narratives blend together, forming both harmonies and dissonances. However, the dissonances seem more palpable in our current political climate. This is nothing new. In a report prepared for the Law Commission of Canada in 1998, Claes and Clifton were clear: "Knowledge of the genocidal intent of the colonisers is well entrenched in aboriginal consciousness, but is still unknown and unrecognised by the larger Canadian public."[2] In 2017, Corntassel and Bird noted that while for Indigenous peoples "the systematic violence and murder of Indigenous peoples has spanned 500-plus years," this was not readily apparent to settlers, for whom "the veneer of the benevolent peacemaker narrative has only begun to be challenged."[3]

This chapter focuses on major gaps in settler knowledge about Indigenous peoples, and it also highlights distractions – how the state presents ways of being Canadian outside of any relationship with Indigenous peoples, while eliding discussion of colonization and genocide. I begin with a discussion of genocide recognition and elision at the provincial and federal levels and then move to examine the Canadian Museum for Human Rights (CMHR). I further this exploration of genocide elision with a larger discussion of how Indigenous peoples have not been fully recognized as political actors in the settler colonial state. In the second half of this chapter, I explore what settlers seem to understand about Indigenous peoples; I first consider a series of recent polls, then examine three governance models and narratives that are deployed, often simultaneously, to define what Canada is and, by omission, what it is not. Much of what has traditionally bound the political and social communities of the state together has excluded Indigenous peoples.

The Politics of Recognizing Genocide

As of 2018, Canada has officially recognized seven distinct genocides, but there has been little effort to recognize Indigenous genocide. Certainly, the Harper government never recognized the IRS system as cultural genocide or genocide. The Liberal Party of Canada seemed more willing to accept cultural genocide and to rhetorically commit to forms of reconciliation. In June 2015, Justin Trudeau agreed that the TRC had presented "the truth of what happened."[4] On its official website during the last election, the party described the IRS system's "legacy of cultural genocide and the ongoing impacts on First Nations, on the Métis Nation and Inuit communities."[5] The Liberal government, however, has been loath to follow up with any substantive genocide recognition project, despite the fact that Liberal

MP Robert-Falcon Ouellette (with Maeengan Linklater) introduced a genocide bill in October 2016 calling for a memorial day. The Trudeau government chose to support an alternative bill, C-369, sponsored by the New Democratic Party (NDP), to recognize a more general National Indigenous Peoples Day, over Bill C-318. In early 2019, Linklater sought to have portions of their bill included in C-369 – specifically, those sections dealing with genocide recognition.

Currently, the federal government and selected provincial and territorial governments recognize the Armenian genocide, the Ukrainian famine genocide (Holodomor), the Holocaust, the Rwandan genocide, the Srebrenica massacres, the mass killing of the Yazidi people, and the mass murder of the Muslim Rohingya in Myanmar. There are no bills related to the crimes of Western settler states; as a result, the genocides of Native Americans and of Australian Aborigines and Torres Strait Islanders are not recognized, nor are the British-made famines in Ireland and India. The deaths of ten million people in the Belgian Congo are not recognized, nor are the mass atrocities committed by the United States in Vietnam, Cambodia, and Laos. None of the recognized genocides acknowledge settler colonialism, nor do they tie colonialism more broadly to genocide and the expansionary goals of European imperial systems.

Instead, genocide recognition bills have tended to reinforce positive narratives of the country, and they do so in three ways. First, they stress the well-meaning, host-like qualities of the settler state, which acts as a haven for survivors, casting genocidal regimes as the antithesis of provincial or national governments and societies. Thus, when the Saskatchewan legislature passed an act commemorating the Holodomor, it argued that "the people of Saskatchewan prize democratic freedoms, human rights and the Rule of Law, appreciate the values of compassion and honesty and cherish the multicultural vibrancy of the province."[6] Similarly, when Parliament approved a national Holodomor Memorial Day, it opined, "Canadians cherish democracy, defend human rights, and value the diversity and multicultural nature of Canadian society."[7] In promoting Armenian Genocide Memorial Day, the Quebec legislature averred that "Quebecers have always rejected intolerance and ethnic exclusion."[8]

Second, recognition is also tacitly offered as an affirmation of victims' groups – indeed, there is a blurring of the border between a group's victimization and its contribution to Canada. Ontario's 2011 Ukrainian Heritage Day Act is premised on the fact that "Ukrainian Canadians have played an important role in the development of Ontario into one of the most desirable places in the world to live and have contributed to making Canada the great country that it is today."[9] In Quebec, the 2001 act creating an Armenian Genocide Memorial Day highlighted how the Armenian community "contributes very actively to the economic, social and cultural development of Québec."[10] When Manitoba recognized the Holodomor, it was partially on the basis that "some survivors ... and their descendants have made their home in Manitoba and have contributed richly to Manitoban society."[11]

The third way in which genocide recognition bills reinforce positive narratives of the country is the alignment of victims' struggles with the larger nation-building goals of the state. Thus, Ontario's *Holocaust Memorial Day Act* of 1988 asserted, "Canada, along with other Allied nations, took part in the armed struggle to defeat Nazism and its collaborators. This event affected the lives of all Ontarians, especially those who fought during World War II and helped liberate the inmates of labour and concentration camps."[12] When Quebec undertook the same process in 1999, the legislature signalled that "many Quebeckers fought and died as members of the Canadian forces that went to war to prevent a Nazi victory."[13]

The most recent federal genocide recognitions were those of the Yazidi mass killings at the hands of the Islamic State, in a bill promoted by Conservative MP Michelle Rempel in October 2016, followed in September 2018 by Liberal MP Andrew Leslie's motion to recognize the genocide of Rohingya Muslims, based on a UN fact-finding mission. Both initiatives are laudable – we expect our governments to condemn genocide. However, this needs to be done not only when it happens in other countries but also when it has been perpetrated here.

Genocide and the Canadian Museum for Human Rights

Silence about Indigenous genocide can have an impact on collective memory and public understandings of history and contemporary society. Sometimes, however, change happens slowly, as we can see with the CMHR. Indeed, from the time it took to write the first draft of this chapter to the last, the museum has moved forward in its recognition of Indigenous genocide.

The CMHR was the first federal museum built since 1967, opening in Winnipeg in September 2014. What began as a public-private partnership among various levels of government and the Asper Foundation eventually became a Crown corporation in 2008, with about half the total budget (some $160 million) coming from a combination of federal, provincial, and municipal sources.[14] The museum became the locus of competition among various groups over how their own histories and legacies of victimization would be represented. Media tycoon Israel Asper's original idea in 2003 was to create a Winnipeg-based version of the United States Holocaust Memorial Museum. This vision evolved to encompass the Holodomor, the Armenian genocide, and other recognized genocides.

The CMHR – an enormous, shining Hershey's kiss of a building – contains 450,000 square feet of interior exhibit space, with the Holocaust and the Holodomor occupying most of the area reserved for genocides. While Canada's Jewish and Ukrainian communities lobbied hard, and were adept at fundraising, Indigenous peoples appeared to have less input and influence. By its very presence, the museum participates in a physical act of settlement given that it is located at the Forks, a historic meeting place where Indigenous peoples have gathered and traded for six millennia. Some 400,000 artefacts were taken from the soil during excavations, a testament to the site's use before colonization.[15] As the museum got off the ground, the Shoal Lake No. 40 community, located northwest of Winnipeg, opened its own museum, drawing attention to the fact that its water had been stolen by the city of Winnipeg, in violation of their treaty rights.[16]

While the Holocaust and Holodomor are front and centre at the museum, Indigenous genocide was studiously avoided for much of the museum's history. In a 2013 statement, then chief executive officer Stuart Murray declined to use the word genocide in exhibit titles, but did promise to use "the term in the exhibit itself when describing community efforts for this recognition." Overall, Murray's position was, "While a museum does not have the power to make declarations of genocide, we can certainly encourage ... an honest examination of Canada's human rights history, in hopes that respect and reconciliation will prevail."[17] The decision not to discuss genocide at the opening provoked considerable outcry and a boycott by some Indigenous groups.

The museum appeared to distance itself from any association with a finding of Indigenous genocide. Métis historian Tricia Logan, who served as the curator of Indigenous content from 2010, writes, "I was consistently reminded that every mention of state-perpetrated atrocity against Indigenous peoples in Canada must be matched with a 'balanced' statement that indicates reconciliation, apology or compensation provided by the government." Contemporary controversies involving Indigenous peoples were inadequately represented. Indeed, when "issues are not reconciled or where accusations of abuse against the government continue to this day, the stories are reduced in scope or are removed from the museum." While Canada's Ukrainian and Jewish communities were relatively settled and affluent, Indigenous peoples did not have the same lobbying power, and as Logan has noted, they confronted a wide range of obstacles, including "ongoing violence, environmental destruction and lack of basic human rights like access to clean water or adequate housing." Indigenous peoples simply did not have the time and energy to devote to extensive lobbying and may have lost out as a result.[18]

On a visit to the CMHR in 2017, I was able to spend a few hours with the curator for Indigenous rights, Karine Duhamel. As we went through the exhibits together, things seemed to have improved since Logan's time, but in the genocide section, not by much. Part of the problem concerned the way that the five (at that time) recognized genocides were canonized in the museum compared to the IRS system and other aspects of colonization. In the genocide gallery, entitled Breaking the Silence, the five genocides stand as pillars. The exhibits do double duty, both as a condemnation of genocidal regimes and as a celebration of Canadian efforts to forestall violent human rights abuses. The Srebrenica exhibit features a bright yellow T-shirt, "worn at the silent march for Srebrenica" in Toronto in 2010. Srebrenica survivor Nazifa Beganovic is quoted: "I moved to Canada. ... My father, my grandfather, my cousins – more than 50 relatives did not make it to safety." Other aspects of the exhibit include captions centred on the theme "Canadians seek accountability." The thrust of the display is that Canada is a haven for genocide survivors and a champion of human rights.

The Rwandan genocide exhibit likewise stresses the goodness of Canadians, under the heading "Canadians call for international responsibility." Here a fax from Roméo Dallaire in 1994 warns of "Hutu plans to exterminate Tutsi," and it is positioned near a photo of Lloyd Axworthy, who is promoting his "responsibility to protect" doctrine. The Holocaust display features a section entitled "Canadians bear witness." In the Holodomor exhibit, a similar series of captions is entitled "Canadians expose and honour truth," which includes Stephen Harper paying his respects at a Ukrainian genocide memorial. In the Armenian genocide display, we have captions entitled "Canadians raise awareness," with Girair Besmadjian quoted as saying, "Seeing Armenian eyes crying is understandable. But seeing the MPs crying – that was the most touching part of all."

There is the sixth exhibit, built into the museum design for the day that another genocide might be recognized. For now, a framed sheet of paper quotes Martin Luther King Jr. in English and French: "We will have to repent in this generation not merely for the hateful words and actions of the bad people but for the appalling silence of the good people." The five exhibit boxes do not change, while unrecognized genocides, massacres, and a range of other human rights abuses are portrayed on enormous, flat-panel tables, where the information, scenes, and text continually move. The attractiveness of these $18,000 panels is that they can easily be adapted, added to, deleted from. The IRS system is represented here, but it comes and goes, competing for screen time with the Cambodian genocide, Mao's Great Leap Forward, the "Ethiopian Red Terror," "State Terrorism in Argentina," "Genocide of the Maya in Guatemala," the "Anfal Campaign," "Afghanistan under Control of the Taliban," and the "Trans-Atlantic Slave Trade."

Murray's promised discussion of IRS genocide, billed as a "National Dialogue," can be found on the flat panels. Front and centre is a 2013 *Globe and Mail* article by Phil Fontaine, Michael Dan, and Bernie Farber, making the case for genocide against Indigenous peoples in Canada. The caption states, "Many Canadians, both Indigenous and non-Indigenous, share the view that Canada's historic treatment of Indigenous peoples should be considered genocide." Indigenous histories can be found on other levels of the museum. These include Jaime Black's *The REDress Project* and a box-like exhibit on the IRS system entitled *Childhood Denied*. There are photos of children at the schools and a large portrait of Duncan Campbell Scott above his famous phrase, "I want to get rid of the Indian problem," in both English and French.

During a more recent visit in late 2018, and after corresponding with Karine Duhamel, it was gratifying to see changes. For example, in the "What Are Human Rights?" gallery, a large section on the Indian Act had been introduced, with titles such as "Act of Oppression" and "Act of Assimilation." There was also a special exhibit on Nelson Mandela, which included comparative references to Indigenous peoples. Apartheid was described as being "firmly rooted in colonial history," alongside a comparative discussion: "As in Canada and other colonized regions, Indigenous communities in South Africa were dispossessed of their lands when Europeans arrived." Another section shows how Canada had problems in its "own backyard," with the "desperate conditions facing Indigenous peoples in Canada." A 2.11-minute video on truth and reconciliation features discussion of both the South African and the Canadian commissions, and it includes commentary by Senator Sinclair. An exhibit on Canadian law now opens with a discussion of Indigenous legal traditions, "which existed long before Europeans arrived, [and] have begun to be asserted in the Canadian legal system."

The caption on the IRS system panel now states, "Many Indigenous and non-Indigenous people argue that the school system was a form of genocide." In the "Defending Sovereignty" area, visitors read, "Reconciliation requires Canadians to confront the truth of these genocidal policies, and to understand how and why First Nations, Métis and Inuit continue to assert their sovereignty and rights." In another section on truth and reconciliation, entitled "Confronting Genocide," the museum observes, "The TRC is just the beginning of the reconciliation process. Recognition that Canada enacted genocidal policies against Indigenous peoples is essential to moving forward."

Part of Duhamel's work has involved preparing Canadians for that forward movement. This is important and laudable work, and while I have singled out the museum here, its previous elision of genocide is hardly unique. Rather, it has echoed a larger problem at work in Canada – widespread settler ignorance and ambivalence towards Indigenous peoples, and a general inability to engage with the legacies and ongoing fallout from genocide.

Settlers and Public Opinions about Indigenous Issues

In late 2016, an Abacus survey was launched as a precursor to Canada's 150th birthday celebrations. When asked to name what made respondents proud to be Canadian, 1,848 participants named 78 things (including Justin Bieber and Conrad Black), but none had anything to do with Indigenous peoples, identities, reconciliation, or nation-to-nation agreements. Instead, at the top and "a source of a great deal of pride for 59% is our 'freedom to live our lives as we see fit.'" In third place was "open-mindedness towards others," followed by "politeness." Canada's "reputation around the world" came in at eighth place, prompting Abacus to remark, "While Canadians embrace humility, it matters to us that the world sees us in a positive light."[19]

In mid-2017, an Innovative Research Group online survey of 1,607 adult respondents offered similar findings; only 43 per cent of respondents reported "having read, seen or heard anything recently concerning Canada's Indigenous peoples." Respondents had no strong opinions on how their federal and provincial governments were dealing with Indigenous issues, although when asked to agree or disagree with the statement, "Canada's Indigenous people should have the same rights as any other Canadian, no more and no less," 69 per cent agreed.[20] Overall, when settlers think of Canada and Canadian identity, more people are likely to name multiculturalism, health care, or maple syrup than Indigenous peoples.

A newer survey conducted by Angus Reid in March 2018 of 2,443 Canadian adults demonstrated a lack of recognition of Indigenous rights. A full 53 per cent of respondents rejected the proposition that "Indigenous Canadians have an inherently unique status because their ancestors were here first," favouring instead the claim that "Indigenous people should have no special status that other Canadians don't have." Another 53 per cent also agreed that "Canada spends too much time apologizing for residential schools – it's time to move on." On the question of whether Indigenous peoples would be better off by "integrating more into broader Canadian society, even if that means losing more of their own culture and traditions," 53 per cent agreed.[21] Overall, more than half of settler Canadians appear to see Indigenous peoples as little different from any other Canadians, they have little knowledge of the IRS system, and they favour "moving on" now that forms of compensation and an apology have been forthcoming.

Media Representations

Mainstream media bears some of the responsibility for this situation, and it has generally failed to report adequately on Indigenous issues. Instead, it tends to either ignore Indigenous peoples or reflect dominant, settler norms that establish them as a problem, while eliding the larger settler colonial context. In their work on media bias and the TRC, Nagy and Gillespie note that mainstream media has, in most cases, promoted reductive frames, focusing on individual Survivor experiences of physical and sexual abuse, trauma, and healing. The media blamed the IRS system primarily for "mistakes," suggesting that, had it operated properly, most of the abuses would not have occurred. Reductively framing stories suggests that the IRS system was a historical arte-fact, a product of mentalities and policies confined to earlier his-torical periods. A reductive lens also ignores Indigenous nations, governments, and self-determining capacities, focusing instead on Survivors as "broken individuals and passive victims who succumb to emotionality." By contrast, an expansive view, which accounted for about 40 per cent of stories, stressed the intercon-nections and continued legacies of all relationships between Indig-enous peoples and settlers. This included territorial dispossession; the imposition of colonial education, justice, governance, and other systems; Indian residential schools; the Sixties Scoop; Indigenous imprisonment; and other forms of structural racism.[22]

Another recent study identified a "depravity narrative" in media reporting, where Indigenous peoples were objectified as problems. Indigenous communities are criticized for being dys-functional, while the structural conditions and the role of con-tinued settler colonialism is rarely, if ever, discussed. This may explain why many Indigenous peoples choose to broadcast their message on social media, blogs, and other independent forms of media less likely to be controlled by settlers.[23] Idle No More largely arose thanks to social media like Facebook and Twitter. Chelsea Vowel and Robert Jago got their start blogging, and radio programs and podcasts such as those by Ryan McMahon, Rosanna Deerchild's *Unreserved*, Eve Tuck's *The Henceforward*, and Rick Harp's *mediaINDIGENA* are popular. Ryerson Univer-sity's Yellowhead Institute engages in policy analysis pertinent to Indigenous peoples. When Indigenous peoples frame, anal-yse, and broadcast their own realities, the result is a considerable expansion and depth of coverage.

A lack of media attention can be coupled with problems with the settler-run educational and training systems, which have not offered much in the way of history or current events about

Indigenous peoples, languages, cultures, or politics. These problems were addressed by the TRC in numerous Calls to Action: 1(iii), 6–12, 16, 53(iii), 55(ii–iii), 57, 59, 61(iii), 62–65, 69(iii), 86, 87, 92(ii). The TRC also highlighted problems of media bias in Calls to Action 84 to 86. These problems may be improving somewhat, especially those dealing with education, although we are very much at the beginning of this process, which seems to progress and regress as governments change. A commitment by Kathleen Wynne's Liberal government in Ontario to revise the social studies and history curricula to add Indigenous content was rolled back once Doug Ford's Progressive Conservatives won the provincial election in 2018. The larger issues, however, concern how the country is imagined and what sorts of divergent, unconscious ideologies animate the decision-making of Indigenous peoples and settlers.

Imagining Canada

Canadian identity has traditionally been constructed on a series of narratives that sideline Indigenous peoples. Dominant modes of thinking include English-French biculturalism and bilingualism, anti-Americanism and pro-British sentiments, and multiculturalism. These ways of imagining and performing Canada are of settler colonial origin, and they often present Indigenous peoples as extraneous to the country's development. This is a conception of Canada that is almost unitary, a society that is more European and Atlanticist than the United States. Expressed here too is a sort of liminality, Canada as a bridge between America and Europe, needing ties with Britain to stave off a cultural, economic, and military hegemon to the south. Continued ties to Britain are obvious. Queen Elizabeth II is our head of state, with her likeness displayed on our banknotes, coinage, and postage stamps. English is our primary official language, and we have Westminster-style legislatures at the federal and provincial levels, the British common law (except in Quebec), and European-derived educational systems as well as towns, cities, rivers, and streets named after their European counterparts.

Being pro-British has also been intimately tied to the need to differentiate Canada from the United States, and as one recent commentary noted, monarchism has served as "a useful form of product differentiation."[24] Indeed, settler Canadians, as Philip Resnick has observed, in contradistinction to Americans, "remain a good deal more European in their sensibilities and will continue to be the more European part of North America into the foreseeable future."[25]

As 2017 and the 150th anniversary of Confederation came around, books promoting the image of Canada as a primarily European society, better and different from the United States, became bestsellers. For the British-born historian Charlotte Gray, the author of *The Promise of Canada*, Canada's attributes shone in relation to others: "less brash than Americans," "less class-conscious than the English," "less clannish than the Chinese," "not as fussy as the French." She concluded with the observation that while Canada did not exhibit the "global swagger" of other Western countries, it did have "what many envy: a society that is progressive and confident, tolerant, and open to the world."[26] Likewise, Mike Myers's humorous romp, entitled simply *Canada*, painted the portrait of a country that forsook revolution and "decided to stay home and live with Mother," a land not of revolutionaries, but "evolutionaries." He concluded his ode with the declaration, "Canada may not have put a man on the moon, but it's been awfully nice to the man on earth. And perhaps that will be Canada's greatest legacy."[27]

These retrospectives also stress the recent origins of the country, a theme picked up by political philosopher Will Kymlicka, who defines Canada as new: "largely ... built by settlers and immigrants who have left the constraints of the old world behind, to start a new life in a new land." He does concede that Canada was not empty when the Europeans arrived, and that colonialism and settlement have "involved many injustices to the indigenous peoples," but this is largely irrelevant to the larger point that Canada is "a young, modern society, free from the old hierarchies, cultural prejudices and embedded traditions of the Old World."[28]

Much of this modern history has been self-congratulatory, revelling in how Canada is fundamentally better than the United States, and has drawn a positive balance between the Old World of Europe and the new world of Canadian opportunity. It has generally paid some small degree of lip service to Indigenous peoples and the IRS system, but only to check a particular historical box before sallying forth with positive narratives of the nation.

National Narratives: Quebec

And then we move to Quebec, where French Canadian nationalism has deflected attention from the need to engage with Indigenous peoples. English-French biculturalism and bilingualism have been based on a partnership theory of Canadian politics, as an official Quebec publication in 2017 explains, whereby the country was the product of a "compact between free and autonomous provinces ... [not] a mere creation of the imperial Parliament."[29] This ideal is complicated by the prior existence of Indigenous nations, possessed of their own territories, governments, world views, and practices, who by their existence problematize some French settler Canadian claims to ersatz Indigeneity. During the hearings of the Royal Commission on Bilingualism and Biculturalism (1963–70), Indigenous peoples, through the National Indian Council of Canada, sought to have the country recognized as having three founding cultures, only to be roundly denounced. Under Pierre Trudeau, only French and English had "collective rights to language," and as Eve Haque notes, "the hegemony of linguistic dualism has not only limited the current conception of multiculturalism but also concretized a racially ordered disparity of rights."[30]

A dominant myth about French settlement concerns how relatively fair and just were early French settlers when compared to the British. Earlier conceptions of French colonial policy and their *mission civilisatrice*, designed to convert and assimilate Indigenous peoples, have been largely downplayed in favour of more positive narratives. This has much to do with the fact that French Canada was colonized by the British, while it simultaneously colonized Indigenous peoples, creating a form of "double colonization."[31]

Some writings on multiculturalism and constitutional history have an unfortunate tendency to parallel Indigenous peoples and

Québécois in ways that are historically inaccurate and misleading. Kymlicka, for example, sees both Indigenous peoples and Québécois as "national minorities," defined as "distinct and potentially self-governing societies incorporated into a larger state." He makes little distinction between the *sui generis* rights of Indigenous peoples and the settler rights of Québécois.[32] Peter Russell draws similar parallels, in one 2012 publication, running together the "unsettled 'national' claims of the Quebecois and the aboriginal peoples" since both had political communities before Confederation and both have resisted British efforts of conquest and assimilation. He observes, "These peoples' only homeland is within the boundaries of Canada, and their consent to be participants in the Canadian state is conditional on having governmental powers sufficient to ensure their survival as distinct societies."[33]

In *Canada's Odyssey* in 2017, Russell described both groups as "holdouts" in the Canadian quest to "belong to a single 'people' whose majority expresses the sovereign will of their nation."[34] He sees both as the targets of the British and both as "founding pillars" of the nation. This is historically misleading because many French Canadians *can* trace their lineage back to specific regions of France, while Quebec was founded with an explicitly *colonial* mandate, which included "l'avancement de la gloire de Dieu, et l'honneur de cette couronne en la conversion des peuples sauvages pour les réduire à une vie civile sous l'autorité de Sa dite Majesté." It was clear from the beginning, as the early French colonizers developed plans to bring over 4,000 settlers to colonize the region, that Indigenous peoples were to be converted and civilized according to French requirements.[35]

What sort of coexistence should there be, then, between these two unassimilated "nations" within Canada? For some in Quebec, Indigenous peoples and their governance systems are presented as a precursor to Quebec nationhood. Narratives of Indigenous helpers and passers of the sovereignty torch are present even in newer publications, such as the Quebec Liberal government's 2017 *Our Way of Being Canadian*. A discussion of a "nation to nation" relationship is subsumed in a repetitious discussion of the French-speaking nation as worthy of extensive recognition and rights to self-preservation. Precisely what sort of nations Indigenous peoples represent is downplayed by the use of innocuous language. The former government's account of when Europeans "discovered" North America acknowledges that "First Nations had already been living there for millennia" and were "already present in all sectors." The Liberal government also recognizes Indigenous peoples as useful helpers for the French: they "would prove vital to ambitious exploration expeditions. Interactions would lead to the sharing of respective know-how."[36]

Bill 99, passed in 2000, remains law in Quebec and sets out the rights of a sovereign Quebec "state" and its dependent Indigenous nations. As such, "the Québec people, in the majority French-speaking, possesses specific characteristics and a deep-rooted historical continuity in a territory over which it exercises its rights through a modern national state." This includes the right of "the Québec people" to "take charge of its own destiny, determine its political status and pursue its economic, social and cultural development." The eleven Indigenous nations predating the formation of the province are recognized as existing "within Québec," and "their right to autonomy within Québec" is likewise based on provincial government recognition. Nothing is said about preserving Indigenous languages or recognizing the political powers of Indigenous nations.[37]

The larger political context here is that successive Quebec governments have not considered themselves bound by the Constitution (and hence Article 35) since they did not sign it. During talks between federal and provincial government leaders and Indigenous leaders in October 2017, former premier Philippe Couillard refused to deal with Indigenous issues unless the federal government agreed to open constitutional talks recognizing Quebec's distinct status. Isadore Day, then Ontario regional chief, described the situation as Quebec holding First Nations "hostage," while Ghislain Picard, chief of the Assembly of First Nations of Quebec and Labrador, critiqued the premier's position that "we are simply not legitimate governments in our own communities."[38]

While eight of the 1982 Constitution's eighty-two sections provide various protections for the French language, no section provides guarantees for Indigenous languages. It is clear, too, that, nationally, a lack of French-language fluency is keeping qualified Indigenous candidates from serving as governor general, sitting on the Supreme Court, or taking up other positions of high office in the settler state. The Indigenous Bar Association took exception to Justin Trudeau's insistence that all Supreme Court nominees must be able to converse and read in French without translation. Their president denounced the policies, given the context of being forced to learn one colonial language at residential school: "And now we have to speak another colonial language – just to get a seat at the table!"[39]

In late 2018, the Coalition Avenir Québec won the provincial election, with François Legault becoming the next premier, at least in part by making promises to instigate "Quebec values" and French-language tests to newcomers. It is unlikely that the status of First Nations will markedly improve under this right-of-centre government.

National Narratives: Multiculturalism

Settler-state governments have long conflated Indigenous hard-territorial and political rights with the softer linguistic and cultural rights provided for racialized communities. Under Pierre Trudeau, liberalism informed *both* the assimilatory 1969 White Paper and his 1971 multicultural policies. White Paper liberalism sought to turn Indigenous peoples into individual citizens who would relinquish their "special status" as a "race apart in Canada" to become instead "Canadians of full status," as Trudeau announced in August 1969. He found it inconceivable "that in a given society one section of the society [should] have a treaty with the other section of the society" given that everyone "must be all equal under the laws."[40] When Indigenous peoples rejected his White Paper, Trudeau responded angrily, "We'll keep them in the ghetto as long as they want."[41]

The state has long viewed multiculturalism as attractive, in part, because of its ability to maintain the dominance of white settlers, who continue to set default Canadian values, while imparting a veneer of toleration. Himani Bannerji observed some time ago that multiculturalism "establishes anglo-Canadian culture as the ethnic core culture while 'tolerating' and hierarchically arranging others around it as 'multiculture.'"[42] To this, Augie Fleras adds that most white Canadians "believe they simply live in a neutral space because whiteness is invisible to them regardless of the domain, from politics to policing, from education to entertainment."[43]

Interestingly, whiteness as an identity is far more visible south of the border, and white Canadian settlers have problems seeing themselves in racial terms. What proportion of each society is white? In 2010, 64 per cent of Americans were identified by the US Census Bureau as "non-Hispanic whites," while in 2011, Statistics Canada identified fully 80 per cent of the population as white. In an August 2017 poll, respondents were asked how they identified ethnically; 54 per cent of Americans identified as either "white" or "Caucasian," versus only 30 per cent of Canadians. The 10 per cent gap in white self-identity in the United States is considerably smaller than the 50 per cent gap in Canada.[44]

As Quebec nationalism has been used as a means of integrating Indigenous peoples, so too has there been a tendency to use multiculturalism to frame Indigenous rights as being somehow analogous to cultural claims made by racialized communities. Amadahy and Lawrence observe that "multiculturalism policy profoundly strengthened Canada's attempts to divest itself of any formal recognition of Indigenous peoples, by creating a playing field where Indigenous peoples could potentially be reduced to 'just another cultural group' within a multicultural mosaic."[45] In a more recent intervention, Nuučaańuł theorist Rachel George articulates similar concerns about narratives of reconciliation, positing that these "seek to divest Indigeneity from Indigenous communities, consuming it as Canada's multicultural identity, and effectively extinguishing Indigenous nationhood."[46]

Multiculturalism can itself encourage new forms of settler colonialism. This is because, for some newcomers, the quest to fit in and become productive members of Canadian society may include mirroring the current population's ignorance of Indigenous issues or even promoting a sort of deflective racism.

Conclusions

Britishness, English-French biculturalism, and multiculturalism have informed the modern face of Canada that we celebrate and project to the outside world. And yet these seemingly benign forms of identity have been created and perpetuated in an environment where Indigenous political agency and territory, as well as the number and power of Indigenous bodies, have been substantially eroded by the state. It would be incorrect to describe the Canadian state as post-genocidal since our current forms of governance are premised on what came after the attempted erasure of Indigenous peoples. The institutions that carried out genocide continue to hold political, economic, and judicial power in Canada. For settlers, the state's recognition of genocide may serve a useful function in catalysing change. Some settlers may never be open to engaging with the issues raised in this book, but there is considerable hope that younger generations will, especially if our educational systems adapt for the better. This is where museums like the CMHR, revisions of school curricula, university commitments to implement the TRC's calls to action, and other educational opportunities can play leading roles. It is also where a stronger focus on political conciliation may prove fundamental to the resurgence of Indigenous nations and a rebalancing of political power in this country. This is the focus of the final chapter.

chapter nine

Conciliation and Moves to Responsibility

Reconciliation sounds nice when discussed in the abstract. But reconciliation, practiced in context, requires that Indigenous peoples reconcile themselves to colonialism. This is hardly a cause for celebration.

    – John Borrows, "Canada's Colonial Constitution" (2017)[1]

Nation to nation means acknowledging the truth of the nations. ... It means funding and supporting models of Indigenous governance most damaged by colonization. *Nation to nation* to me means ensuring that those warrior societies, women societies, two-spirited societies become an active, elevated, treasured and funded portion of Indigenous governance again.

    – Tracey Lindberg, "Reconciliation before Reconciliation" (2017)[2]

What does the future of conciliation look like, especially if we recognize genocide against Indigenous peoples by the Canadian settler state? It is important to acknowledge that many of the institutions, patterns, and processes that led to genocide in the first place continue to inform government policies towards Indigenous peoples. Settler colonialism is still marked by structural violence and the attrition of Indigenous rights. The term *reconciliation* is contested, sometimes critiqued, on the basis that there never was an original "golden era" of conciliation between Indigenous peoples and settlers. Reconciliation may be problematic if we see it only as being about relationships *between* the colonized and the colonizers. This is only one of many types of relationship, and it might be better seen as *conciliation*, creating positive relationships that have not existed before, relationships whose contours are difficult to trace because they will evolve and change with time. If we are to move to responsibility as settlers, genocide recognition may function as one means (alongside others and especially the return of lands) of better situating and contextualizing the role of the settler state, its multiple institutions, and its civil societies in the lives of Indigenous peoples.

Before exploring options for the future, those of us who are settlers can take a few steps back and understand that Indigenous peoples did not *choose* to be colonized. Whatever European-style social contract theory animated the creation of Canada, it did not emerge from Indigenous world views, and it sidelined Indigenous consent. Nor did Indigenous peoples choose to have the British and French create the world's second-largest country at their expense. Indigenous peoples did not ask for the residential school system as it developed, the Indian Act, starvation, the massacre of the buffalo, the outlawing of Indigenous governments and spiritual traditions, forced sterilization, or the creation of the reserve system.

As we contemplate conciliation, those of us who are settlers will need to be open to the full range of potential political, economic, and social changes that may result from Indigenous resurgence. This includes looking at ways to roll back the power of the settler state to ensure that Indigenous rights are fully respected. Those of us who study political systems and how they function will need to better come to terms with how Canadian sovereignty can be unpacked; rendered more porous, more flexible, decentralized, more reflective of Indigenous ways of governance. We also need to be clear that conciliation must never be about coercing anyone into assimilating into the settler state.

Rather, conciliation efforts should support the Indigenous resistance and resurgence occurring across Turtle Island. The NIMMIWG's Interim Report, drafted primarily by Aimée Craft and Paulette Regan, defines *Indigenous resistance* as encompassing activities and strategies that function to "promote decolonization, Indigenous ways of life, values, knowledge, and broader political goals."[3] Jeff Corntassel, in turn, defines *resurgence* as "struggling to reclaim and regenerate one's relational, place-based existence by challenging the ongoing, destructive forces of colonization." This can include, but is not limited to, ceremonies and other methods by which Indigenous peoples engage with the natural world, with which we are interdependent.[4]

In this closing chapter, I consider several dimensions of conciliation and reconciliation. Some aspects may not initially involve building relations *between* Indigenous peoples and settlers. Reflecting the work of some Indigenous thinkers, reconciliation has sometimes entailed Indigenous peoples reconciling with themselves, their communities, and their territories and with the treaties they have formed over millennia with the land, plants, animals, waters – everything around them. Tracey Lindberg has thoughtfully called this "reconciliation before reconciliation." This has sometimes included Indigenous peoples reaffirming treaties with other Indigenous peoples on Turtle Island, with other Indigenous nations, or states, and invigorating forms of diplomacy suppressed under the Indian Act. Indigenous people individually have sometimes reconciled with themselves, as part of their healing journeys, and with their families and communities.[5] Indigenous peoples have and will continue to articulate what can and should be done. Those of us who are settlers would do best to listen and follow their lead.

Reconciliation may also involve those of us who are settlers reconciling with ourselves, documenting the crimes perpetrated by the state and by other settlers against Indigenous peoples. This should include critically engaging with the TRC's ninety-four calls to action and balancing our consumption of mainstream settler–dominated media with Indigenous media and the growing number of publications, blogs, podcasts, and public events on Indigenous issues. It may involve critically interrogating why settlers came to this land in the first place, under what conditions, and what we, our parents, grandparents, or ancestors hoped to achieve.

Conciliation (minus the *re*) may involve renaming schools, public buildings, roads, parks, rivers, and towns, changing coinage and other aspects of what has become normalized as settler identity. More important might be ensuring that Indigenous leaders and historical figures are prominently commemorated. Conciliation may involve European settlers and settlers of racialized origin coming together to sort out what type of society our side of the treaty relationship should become. Fundamentally, settlers may work to roll back the state over the lives of Indigenous peoples. Following Craft and Regan, we can understand *colonialism* as "the attempted or actual imposition of policies, laws, mores, economies, cultures or systems, and institutions put in place by settler governments to support and continue the occupation of Indigenous territories, the subjugation of Indigenous Nations, and the resulting internalized and externalized thought patterns that support this occupation and subjugation." Rolling back involves implementing processes that seek to undo colonialism, and it may be seen as synonymous with the early stages of decolonization, "re-establishing strong contemporary Indigenous Nations and institutions based on traditional values, philosophies, and knowledge systems."[6]

Conciliation between Indigenous peoples and settlers may develop from these processes, and we may evolve relations demarcating some ways that we work together and some ways that we respectfully do not – to honour each other's spaces, places, and sovereignties. This may take generations to achieve, but it is crucial to begin the process now.

Closing Gaps and Conciliation

Closing economic, education, health, and other gaps is an important part of any conciliation process – first, because Indigenous peoples deserve dignity and equality as individuals and as communities. Second, gap-closing may help rebuild the self-determining capacities of Indigenous peoples as nations and political actors so that they can regain what the state sought to dismantle by force, coercion, and genocide. Currently, poverty affects half of First Nations children, while some 130,000 First Nations people need new houses. Our settler state imprisons Indigenous peoples at a rate grotesquely out of proportion to their overall share of the population. Being Indigenous means that you are ten times more likely to be in jail, to have longer sentences, to be in higher-security installations, to be segregated and isolated, and to self-harm. Overall, the life expectancy of Indigenous peoples is considerably lower than that of settlers, as are household incomes, levels of Western education, funding for education, and access to health care. The 2016 census indicates that inadequate housing and other problems on reserves have not improved much, despite a change of government and a myriad of optimistic promises.

Few people would deny that a crisis exists, but "how far" conciliation should go is contested. A June 2016 Environics survey asked settler Canadians what reconciliation meant to them, to which most respondents answered, "closing gaps." "Equality remains a dominant theme," Environics concluded, which it broke down into support for "mutual respect and living together in harmony," with respondents viewing reconciliation as "fair policies" and a "level playing field." Key priorities included ending discrimination, increasing funding for on-reserve housing and schools, safe drinking water, reviving Indigenous languages, and a mandatory curriculum describing Indigenous culture and history.[7] These are important issues that need to be addressed right now.

Yet this is only part of the process – most of the above understandings of reconciliation involve the settler state and its institutions ceding forms of "soft" Indigenous rights, to use Sheryl Lightfoot's terminology. Such rights are soft because they can act to redeem the state and legitimate its ongoing control over Indigenous peoples. These policies can be fundamentally assimilative, changing the balance of who gets what, but they may not alter the system of distribution or the philosophy and institutional structures behind it. Indeed, soft rights may be an invitation to *get settler colonialism right* instead of ending it.[8]

"Hard rights," exemplified by Indigenous self-determination and the return of lands and waters, are less commensurable with the current structures of the settler state, and they remove settlers' ability to exercise "compassion" and paternalism. Instead, hard rights focus on the practice of Indigenous rights and the shifting of the power balance. They potentially question the territorial sovereignty of the settler state. This process reflects how the treaties were originally conceived by their Indigenous signatories – not as surrenders of sovereignty and not as the domestication of their national rights, but as agreements made between legitimate governments representing different sovereign peoples.[9]

Indigenous Lands, Indigenous Law, and Self-Determination

Indigenous-settler conciliation is unlikely to succeed unless the state is able to roll back its illegitimate power over Indigenous peoples. Many Indigenous peoples articulate that this can happen only when Indigenous lands are returned in such a way that First Nations have a sufficient base from which to practise *viable* self-determination on their own terms. Kanien'kehá:ka Elder Ellen Gabriel observes, "Land dispossession remains a key issue as it disrupts the relationship we have with Mother Earth and all our relations." She continues, "The pillars of our identity – our languages, customs, health, ceremonies, and traditional forms of governance – are all inter-related and interdependent upon the health of our environment."[10] Indigenous peoples, Audra Simpson concludes, are best understood as "nationals with sovereign authority over their lives and over their membership and living within their own space."[11] As Simpson articulates, Haudenosaunee have long practised the right of refusal, refusing to recognize that the settler state has *legitimate* control over their lives as nations. They therefore use "every opportunity to remind each other, and especially non-native people, that this is our land, that there are other political orders and possibilities."[12]

Leanne Simpson (Michi Saagiig Nishnaabeg) and Glen Coulthard (Yellowknives Dené) have documented how the settler state's relationships with Indigenous peoples have been structured "primarily through the dispossession of Indigenous bodies from Indigenous lands and by impeding and systemically regulating the generative relationships and practices that create and maintain Indigenous nationhoods, political practices, sovereignties, and solidarities."[13] A key aspect of resurgence is "grounded normativity," which Coulthard defines as "the modalities of Indigenous land-connected practices and longstanding experiential knowledge that inform and structure our ethical engagements with the world and our relationships with human and nonhuman others over time." How can we move forward? Coulthard puts it: "Land has been stolen, and significant amounts of it must be returned. Power and authority have been unjustly appropriated, and much of it will have to be reinstated."[14] This builds on earlier work by Kiera Ladner and Sakej Henderson, who first developed the concept.

Almost 90 per cent of Canada's territory is Crown land, divided between the federal and provincial governments. Overall, reserves comprise a meagre 0.2 per cent of the country's land mass, and while more government funding for services will help in the short term, ultimately the state must give back land. The late Arthur Manuel (of the Ktunaxa and Secwepemc Nations) articulated a vision of how Indigenous self-determination might look.

> These land-bases need to be large enough to protect our languages, cultures, laws and economies. ... That fundamental increase must be made to accommodate Aboriginal and treaty rights to land. These larger land-bases will ultimately be part of Canada's economy. It will provide Indigenous Peoples with the right to make and influence economic development choices because of our increased governance over our larger land base.[15]

Manuel is writing here about Crown-held territory located adjacent to the reserves, or "treaty lands," which Indigenous signatories supposedly "surrendered" in written treaties (where they existed), but which were to be available for traditional activities, such as harvesting, fishing, hunting, and ceremonies. Such rights have been reduced by provincial governments, or the "provincial Crown," which has been delegated power by the federal government to "take up" Indigenous lands for mining, logging, pipelines, and other extractive and industrial activity.[16] This was often done without the consent of First Nations, and sometimes with their active resistance. Many of the creative movements for change have emerged from Indigenous protection of the lands and waters, such as Idle No More, the protectors at Standing Rock, and the Secwepemc Women's Warrior Society, whose Tiny House Warriors movement is blocking the Trans Mountain Pipeline.

Oral histories of the treaties help clarify that Indigenous nations never surrendered their lands, and they had no conception of absolute ownership in the ways understood by British private property norms and laws. Gaining access and control over traditional lands can be a lengthy and expensive process. Successive federal and provincial governments have impoverished some First Nations by holding up land claims in lengthy court cases. Settlements like that of the Nisga'a in 1998 provided them with 8 per cent of the traditional lands they claimed, but the settlement, like later agreements, featured an "extinguishment clause," whereby the parties agreed that this was a "full and final settlement in respect of Aboriginal rights, including Aboriginal title."[17] In June 2018, other nations such as the Lheidli T'enneh voted against a settlement that would have provided them with only 4,330 hectares, a tiny fraction of the over 15,000 square kilometres of territory that comprises their traditional lands. This can hardly be considered a viable settlement.

Negotiation processes are expensive for First Nations because they often have to borrow money from the federal government to negotiate their claims, and this can put them into unsustainable debt. This process is expensive for the settler governments too. In fighting the Tsilhqot'in case, which concluded in 2014, the federal government spent $9 million and eventually lost. Every year, on average, INAC spends over $30 million on litigation services, from a low of $26.5 million in 2007–08 to a high of $36.8 million in 2011–12.[18]

This raises the irony, noted by Ellen Gabriel, that while Justin Trudeau promotes reconciliation in public, "his government has spent more than $700,000 in legal fees fighting a Canadian Human Rights Tribunal order insisting that they stop discriminating against Indigenous children in provision of healthcare."[19] She questions what Indigenous rights mean in the context of widespread settler-government approval for industrial projects on Indigenous territories without Indigenous consent. Indigenous resurgence takes place against the backdrop of some of the most environmentally destructive activities in modern history. Take, for example, the tar sands of northern Alberta, where some 1.2 trillion litres of toxic waste cover over 200 square kilometres. The estimated clean-up costs are over $50 billion and rising, even as Liberal and NDP governments continue to endorse these destructive extraction practices.[20]

Canadian settler courts were not designed to act as bridges or mediators between European and Indigenous legal and governance systems, and they routinely interpret treaties as they would domestic contracts. What has not been undertaken is a systematized process of obtaining sufficient information to understand how much land, and what land, should be set aside to guarantee Indigenous rights. Any such process would involve negotiation and partnership with Indigenous nations.[21] It would also need to reflect the fact that Indigenous populations are some of the fastest growing in Canada and that, thus, the current needs of a community now may be only a fraction of what will be required in the future.

The TRC identified revitalizing Indigenous forms of law as central to any self-determining practices and, hence, any viable form of conciliation. It has promoted the repudiation of the doctrine of discovery and the incorporation of the UNDRIP into domestic law. It has recommended full conciliation of Crown and Indigenous legal orders to create a system in which both are full partners, "including the recognition and integration of Indigenous laws and legal traditions in negotiation and implementation processes involving Treaties, land claims, and other constructive agreements."[22] Indigenous laws and protocols would confirm the resurgence of Indigenous communities as self-determining and may also rectify the power imbalance, thereby creating a more partnership-oriented ethos.

As law professor Val Napoleon (Saulteau First Nation) observes, in most Indigenous nations' legal systems, authority has tended to be decentralized, "operating through horizontal (from the bottom-up) public legal institutions. In each Indigenous society, citizens organized in various ways were, and are, responsible for the maintenance of their legal order." She continues that law for Indigenous peoples is something they *do*, that is practised on a regular basis: "Indigenous peoples apply law to manage all aspects of political, economic, and social life including harvesting fish and game, accessing and distributing resources, managing lands and waters."[23] The challenge for settlers will be not only accepting but also helping to roll back the power of the settler state so that Indigenous peoples have more unencumbered space to exercise self-determination and practise their laws and constitutional orders in ways that work for them.

Relationships, Responsibilities, and Conciliation

Part of any conciliation process, especially after genocide and its continuing effects, is understanding the central importance of treaties, and not only those between Indigenous peoples and the Crown. In a powerful analysis, Heidi Kiiwetinepinesiik Stark (Turtle Mountain Ojibwe) articulates how treaties involved bringing the newcomers into an already existing web of relationships with all creation, those "pre-existing relationships and responsibilities across Anishinaabe *aki* (the Earth) that were impacted by these agreements." As she explains,

> We spoke not only for the land, but also for the newcomers to this land. We vouched for these newcomers. In doing so we became responsible for Americans and Canadians, and how they would relate to aki. We brought them into our long-standing relationships with aki and thus took on responsibility for how they would relate to all of creation.[24]

In consonance with this view, Coulthard is clear that the Indigenous relationship to land is not exclusionary. It is rather "a relationship based on the obligations we have to other people and the other-than-human relations that constitute the land itself."[25] Reconciliation for Indigenous peoples, viewed through this lens, might be seen as a reconnection to land, spirit, and other connections that the settler state has sought to sever. Many other issues regarding reconciliation flow from a return of land. But important in any Indigenous-settler conciliation process is the guarantee that if we cannot live together well, Indigenous peoples have the option of living well apart from the settler state on large, viable territories where they can exercise their right to self-determine their own futures. Otherwise, Indigenous peoples will always be dependent on settler goodwill, which varies considerably with the ideological seasons, from forms of polite paternalism to overt racism. Both are sometimes evident in the same government.

Indigenous Peoples and Settler Democracy

Historically, enfranchisement was more a punishment, a means of disempowering Indigenous leaders, than it was a privilege, and low Indigenous voter turnouts in elections stem, in part, from a desire to remain loyal to the treaties, which affirm the right to self-government. In 1960, John Diefenbaker's Progressive Conservative government unilaterally decided that Indigenous peoples could now be citizens and retain their Indian status. This decision was not exactly generous, as it perpetuated the fiction that Indigenous peoples had consented to both Canadian citizenship and Canada's sovereignty. It was made by the settler state at the same time that it was seeking to prevent Indigenous peoples from claiming rights at the UN level.[26] In the run-up to the patriation of the Constitution in 1982, the National Indian Brotherhood lobbied British MPs to block Pierre Trudeau's constitutional proposals. Legal action took place during this time, leading to the British Court of Appeal decision that, in 1931 (under the Statute of Westminster), the Crown had been effectively "split." Thereafter, the Dominion of Canada had assumed the role of the Crown in all matters taking place on Canadian territory, with the British Crown washing its hands of any responsibility.[27]

With a recent history of Indigenous federal cabinet ministers; MPs across the political spectrum; and Wab Kinew as leader of the NDP in Manitoba, it looked for a time as if Canada might be slowly changing. Indigenous peoples were achieving better representation within settler institutions. While this was a positive development, some have highlighted the potential for "internal exclusion," whereby Indigenous peoples find that their politics, laws, and histories are not taken seriously on their own terms, but are evaluated and judged through a settler lens. Conflicting norms and world views can create major difficulties for Indigenous peoples trying to navigate settler bureaucracies and political systems.[28] Conflicting norms and values were in evidence when former Minister of Justice and Attorney General Jody Wilson-Raybould resigned from the Liberal cabinet over prime ministerial pressure to back off on criminally prosecuting the multinational company SNC-Lavalin. In February 2019 during testimony to the parliamentary justice committee, she articulated that as a Kwakwaka'wakw leader and woman: "I come from a long line of matriarchs and I am a truth teller in accordance with the laws and traditions of our Big House."[29] In a sense, her ethics were incompatible with the way the Trudeau cabinet governed. Jane Philpott also resigned from cabinet soon after for similar reasons.

As we have seen, pro-Indigenous promises and rhetoric may be popular during election campaigns, but they are easily scaled back once a government secures power. The Trudeau Liberals present a rather mixed bag of promises and delivery. They promised to implement UNDRIP, yet took considerable time before they supported Romeo Saganash's Bill C-262, designed to incorporate the declaration into federal legislation. While promising to promote environmental concerns, the government's purchase of the Trans Mountain Pipeline from Kinder Morgan and its crackdown on land protectors looked hypocritical. It appeared equally hypocritical to promise electoral reform that might have resulted in better representation for Indigenous peoples in Parliament, then marshal weak excuses to abandon the process.

At yet another level, the Liberal government initiated a dizzying array of bills, what some have described as the busiest Indigenous legislative agenda in a century. Recently, the government established some sixty confidential "rights and recognition tables" – detailed consultations and negotiations with over three hundred

First Nations communities across the country as well as policy meetings with Indigenous academics and organizations. While the Indian Act may be on the way out sometime after the 2019 federal election, it is not clear that its replacement(s) will offer the hard rights for which activists and leaders have been fighting for decades. There seems to be little discussion of expanding reserves to include the larger treaty lands discussed earlier in this chapter. Nor is there much discussion of recognizing Indigenous political authority to block unwanted pipelines, forestry, tar sands, or other forms of industrial development on traditional lands. Much of the focus seems to be on the delivery of federally funded services by First Nations governments, which may not have much of a say in the design and implementation of the policies themselves. While the end result may be Indigenous governments with more power than they currently have, and better funding, they may only gain powers similar to municipalities, especially if the provinces do not relinquish any of their legislative control.[30]

In 2017, the government released ten principles on its relationship with Indigenous peoples. They make clear that the treaties and nation-to-nation relationships are to be considered domestic relationships with no international dimensions. For example, Principle 4 states that Indigenous self-government is to be conceived as "part of Canada's evolving system of cooperative federalism and distinct orders of government." Decision-making and governance are to be focused on "our shared home." The other "orders of government" with which First Nations are to develop relations are all within the hard container of state sovereignty.[31]

There are certainly many unanswered questions about Liberal policies at the time of writing: What sort of political power will First Nations government gain through this process? Is the federal government willing to negotiate scaling back some provincial powers over Indigenous issues and granting more land, resources, and decision-making to First Nations governments? Will Indigenous land bases expand, together with control over resources and development, if reserves amalgamate with one another or reconstitute to form larger entities? Will First Nations be able to determine who is and who is not a member? These and many other issues remain to be negotiated (or taken off the table, as the case may be).[32] While the Liberals have been criticized for their policies, it is unlikely that the Conservatives would promote a more progressive agenda.

The Return of Complex Sovereignties

Some Indigenous nations are in the process of articulating how their own self-determining capacities can be achieved. This will put some pressure on the settler state. Any viable process of conciliation that fundamentally alters the current power dynamic may result in more complex, overlapping, shared forms of sovereignty, and this may result in what Audra Simpson has described as "sovereignty within multiple sovereignties."[33] Change will mean moving well beyond the Indian Act–based system of over six hundred bands with elected chiefs. But it may also involve changes in provincial territorial organizations. Arthur Manuel was particularly critical of some Indigenous leaders for relying too heavily on settler governments for their power and funding and thus not being fully accountable to the people they are supposed to be serving.[34]

As mentioned in the introduction to this book, RCAP identified between sixty and eighty Indigenous nations that might viably exercise political rights to self-determination if smaller reserves and bands were strategically amalgamated. The logistics of these arrangements would not be for settlers to determine, and RCAP recommended that each band hold a referendum to determine what its members wished to do. Questions of status, group membership, and belonging may also flow from a renewed sense of Indigenous nationhood. At the time of writing, the Liberal government is discussing devolving some federal services to the reserve level, "scaling up" some Indigenous governments, and making other changes. Aspects of these processes are open to public scrutiny; other aspects are lacking in transparency. Negotiations, however, do not seem to include increasing the amount of land for these larger national units, and while some First Nations may wish to amalgamate their reserves with others, others may choose a different path.

Certainly, Indigenous peoples maintained their own sovereign governments for thousands of years, and many considered treaties to be international rather than domestic agreements. Nations engaged in complex trade and military alliances, and they maintained diplomatic protocols and practices over millennia that involved exchanging gifts, holding ceremonies, making treaties, and creating records of diplomatic relationships, many of which are with us still.[35] Contrary to these ancient governance systems, the Westphalian state system is relatively new: it came fully into existence only in the mid-twentieth century; many countries were not formally decolonized until the 1960s, and settler states are still not decolonized. The notion of what states are and how they derive their legitimacy has changed dramatically over the centuries. If we accept, as does Thomas Biersteker, that "concepts of state, sovereignty, and territory are each socially constructed," we create further space for bringing about change.[36]

That change may consist of a return to complex forms of sovereignty, types of Indigenous sovereignty that may move within and outside and between the borders of the Canadian state. If we see the state as a container for multiple forms of sovereignty, that container does not have to be rigid and closed off from other forms. Layers of settler government do not have to exercise forms of absolute control over the territory within that container. Conciliation may involve balancing different political orders, with Indigenous nations exercising the right to use Indigenous passports, such as those used by Haudenosaunee and Haida Gwaii citizens. In time, Indigenous nations may choose to hold dual citizenship with Canada, or hold First Nations citizenship only, perhaps affirmed by Canada through a renewed interpretation of treaties and other international agreements. Indigenous peoples may sign treaties with other Indigenous nations on Turtle Island, outside it, straddling it, or with other countries or entities. An example is the 2014 Buffalo Treaty, which recognizes rights for the buffalo as a wild and free-ranging animal and as a brother, and it pledges to "provide a safe space and environment across our historic homelands, on both sides of the United States and the Canadian border."[37]

Another example is the multinational protest at Standing Rock, which brought together Indigenous peoples from many nations and settlers to fight for Indigenous land against the Dakota Access Pipeline. Protests took place at the Sacred Stone Camp and around the United States, including a national day of action, with peaceful protests in a number of American cities. Indigenous peoples are also practising their right to self-determination in other ways, sometimes at the bargaining table. A more complex understanding of sovereignty might facilitate enhanced international standing for Indigenous nations, enabling them to individually or collectively avail themselves of international legal instruments through the UN system or other fora. As a result, Indigenous nations could represent themselves, either collectively or individually, in new or reformed international bodies and seek action against states (including their own) that have or are continuing to violate their rights and interests.

Genocide Recognition

Much of this book concerns genocide, and one of my goals is to articulate a case for recognizing that genocide occurred (at least) in the Indian residential schools through (at least) the violation of Article 2(e) of the UN Genocide Convention. This is with the obvious caveats that any crimes occurring before 1948 would not, in a strictly legal sense, be interpreted as genocide by a court of law, and that Article 2(e) does not currently form part of Canada's narrow definition of genocide. Nevertheless, legislatures are not bound by such considerations, and half the recognized genocides in this country ended well before the UNGC was in force.

Genocide recognition should be a focus of settler attention, and we should seek this recognition through an act of Parliament; through bills passed by provincial and territorial assemblies, city councils, and municipalities; and through resolutions adopted by teachers' unions, and bar, medical, and other professional associations. These can help remind Canadians that genocide was formative to the creation, expansion, and continued maintenance of our country. Genocide recognition may help those of us who are settlers ensure that the settler state abides by principles of the treaties, the UNDRIP, and international law.

Such recognition should also translate into putting the full definition of genocide into the Criminal Code, something that is almost five decades overdue. Given that the Liberal government has acknowledged that cultural genocide was committed in the IRS system, it would make logical sense (in the spirit of "never again") to also amend the Criminal Code to prohibit cultural genocide. The term could be defined using the 1947 UNGC draft or based on the UNDRIP, given that Bill C-262 has been passed in the House of Commons. The 1994 draft of the UNDRIP (Article 7) outlined prohibitions against cultural genocide, but it did not specifically define the term. The term itself was removed from the declaration, but the crimes outlined in Article 8(2) are very similar to those in the 1994 draft and could constitute the basis for a definition and prohibition of cultural genocide in Canadian criminal law. They are:

(a) Any action which has the aim or effect of depriving [Indigenous peoples] of their integrity as distinct peoples, or of their cultural values or ethnic identities;

(b) Any action which has the aim or effect of dispossessing them of their lands, territories or resources;

(c) Any form of forced population transfer which has the aim or effect of violating or undermining any of their rights;

(d) Any form of forced assimilation or integration;

(e) Any form of propaganda designed to promote or incite racial or ethnic discrimination directed against them.

The revision of the Criminal Code to ensure that the crimes of the past cannot be (under settler law) revisited on Indigenous peoples will send a positive signal; it will also offer a departure from the Harper government's strange approach to the IRS system: apologizing for government excesses in 2008, while keeping the Indian Act provisions that allowed it to happen on the books until 2014. Genocide recognition may not bring substantive changes to how First Nations govern themselves, but it can help lay the basis for a settler society that better understands why such changes to the status quo are necessary. Recognition may also help settlers understand why Crown-Indigenous relations have the power imbalance they do now, and it will help disabuse us of the notion that the Canadian government has always sought to promote the best interests of Indigenous peoples in their policymaking.

Tuck and Yang, in a notable intervention, have called for an "ethic of incommensurability," in which models of decolonization are "not accountable to settlers, or settler futurity," but to "Indigenous sovereignty and futurity." They are clear: "The answers will not emerge from friendly understanding, and indeed require a dangerous understanding of uncommonality that un-coalesces coalition politics – moves that may feel very unfriendly."[38] Unfriendliness may reflect the extreme mismatch in political power between levels of Canadian government and Indigenous nations, and it also reflects the long-term legacies of genocide. Genocide in its many forms has been a useful expedient for settler governments to deprive Indigenous peoples of their lands, identities, practices, and lives. Canada's world-class standard of living (for settlers) still relies on the exploitation of Indigenous lands and bodies. Giving back land, resources, and political power will invariably be a central component of any successful conciliation strategy.

The Settlers' Right of Refusal

Those of us who are settlers and who are dissatisfied with the current state of government policies and institutions can practise refusal – refusing to condone our government's ongoing colonial activities. We can, as Barker and Lowman have argued, "disrupt settler colonial spaces." This can include such examples as failing "to uphold settler colonial relationships, to fail to properly inhabit and embody settler colonial structures, systems, and stories, and by necessity find ways to build relationships differently." The authors call for settlers to work with Indigenous peoples to come up with creative ways to roll back the state and strengthen Indigenous self-determining capacities, to "work to create a broad base, to build communities that undertake these efforts together."[39] If the settler state is made up of practices, we can practise sovereignty differently. For some, this may involve personal sacrifice, as it did for Anglican priest Emilie Smith and for Steve Heinrichs, director of Indigenous-settler relations for the Mennonite Church. Both of these settler-activists stood with Indigenous peoples in protesting the expansion of the Kinder Morgan Pipeline. They were arrested in April 2018 on charges of "contempt" and sentenced to imprisonment in British Columbia.

An important change we can make now as settlers is to work to repatriate land to First Nations. Several settlers in 2017 undertook this process, starting with British Columbia rancher Kenneth Linde, who donated three hundred acres of land to the Esk'etemc First Nation. Peterborough-based teacher Janice Keil started the process of repatriating one hundred acres of family-owned land to the Alderville First Nation in Ontario. Both donors have described these efforts as acts of reconciliation. The provincial and federal governments can work to streamline this process (known as the Addition to Reserve policy) as it can take well over a decade for a reserve to expand its territorial base, and it involves negotiation with municipal and provincial authorities. Further, Indigenous peoples have only usufructuary rights to reserve lands (that is, they have the right to enjoy the use of them without owning them), all of which is considered to be "held" by the Crown, even new lands purchased by First Nations in treaty settlements.

The contours of Indigenous self-determination and the exercise of hard rights will be different for each Indigenous nation, and nations are invariably going to change and evolve as they seek to overcome centuries of colonization and genocide. There will be no one universal solution and no one way of establishing certainty about what conciliation and/or reconciliation will look like. Conciliation will be part of long-term relationship building and not a terminus. This is something few of us will see in our lifetimes at a national level, but we need to promote positive change now so that our children and grandchildren will hopefully see the benefits instead of the harms of our actions today.

Notes

Epigraph

1 Notes of the Aboriginal Healing Foundation Regional Gathering, Vancouver Friendship Centre, Moncton, 23 November 2000.

Introduction: The Sleeping Giant Awakens

1 Library and Archives Canada, Indian Affairs, RG 10, vol. 6462, file 888-1, part 2.
2 "St. George's School – Lytton, BC," Anglican Church of Canada, accessed 15 October 2017, http://www.anglican.ca/tr/histories/st-georges-school-lytton/.
3 UN Web TV, Permanent Forum on Indigenous Issues – 17th session, 5th plenary meeting, 18 April 2018, video, http://webtv.un.org/watch/5th-plenary-meeting-permanent-forum-on-indigenous-issues-17th-session/5772804133001/?term=[2:28:06].
4 Canada, Department of Canadian Heritage, "Canada's 2017 Country Report to the International Holocaust Remembrance Alliance (IHRA)," 20 March 2018, https://www.canada.ca/en/canadian-heritage/services/canada-holocaust/international-remembrance-alliance/canada-report-2011-2017.html.
5 Kiera L. Ladner, "150 Years and Waiting: Will Canada Become an Honourable Nation?," in *Surviving Canada: Indigenous Peoples Celebrate 150 Years of Betrayal*, ed. Kiera L. Ladner and Myra J. Tait, Kindle (Winnipeg: ARP Books, 2017), chap. 10.
6 Nancy Macdonald, "Canada's Prisons Are the 'New Residential Schools,'" 18 February 2016, http://www.macleans.ca/news/canada/canadas-prisons-are-the-new-residential-schools/.

7 Mary Jane Logan McCallum, "Starvation, Experimentation, Segregation, and Trauma: Words for Reading Indigenous Health," *Canadian Historical Review* 98, no. 1 (2017): 102.

8 Michael Dan, "Seeking the Right Word for a History of Suffering," *Ottawa Citizen*, 9 April 2014, http://www.ottawacitizen.com/opinion/oped/Seeking+right+word+history+suffering/9719245/story.html.

9 Nancy Macdonald, "Saskatchewan: A Special Report on Race and Power," *Maclean's* magazine, 29 July 2016, http://www.macleans.ca/news/canada/saskatchewan-a-special-report-on-race-and-power/.

10 Gloria Galloway and Dakshana Bascaramurty, "Census 2016," *Globe and Mail*, 25 October 2017, accessed 15 October 2017, https://beta.theglobeandmail.com/news/national/census-2016-highlights-diversity-housing-indigenous/article36711216/?ref=http://www.theglobeandmail.com&.

11 Pamela D. Palmater, *Beyond Blood: Rethinking Indigenous Identity* (Vancouver: University of British Columbia Press, 2011).

12 On the gender of settler states, see Audra Simpson, "The State Is a Man: Theresa Spence, Loretta Saunders and the Gender of Settler Sovereignty," *Theory & Event* 19, no. 4 (2016).

13 Interview 5, National Residential School Survivors Society, Sault Ste. Marie, ON, 4 August 2011.

14 Canada, National Inquiry into Missing and Murdered Indigenous Women and Girls, *Our Women and Girls Are Sacred: Interim Report* (Vancouver: National Inquiry into Missing and Murdered Indigenous Women and Girls, 2017), 7–8.

15 Julie Jai, "Bargains Made in Bad Times: How Principles from Modern Treaties Can Reinvigorate Historic Treaties," in *The Right Relationship: Reimagining the Implementation of Historical Treaties*, ed. John Borrows and Michael Coyle, 105–48 (Toronto: University of Toronto Press, 2017), 121–2.

16 Truth and Reconciliation Commission of Canada, *Canada's Residential Schools: The Métis Experience*, vol. 3 of the Final Report of the Truth and Reconciliation Commission of Canada (Montreal and Kingston: McGill-Queen's University Press, 2015), 3, 4 (quote), 21–9, 45, 55. See also Larry N. Chartrand, Tricia E. Logan, and Judy D. Daniels, *Métis History and Experience and Residential Schools in Canada* (Ottawa: Aboriginal Healing Foundation, 2006).

17 Senator Murray Sinclair, interview by the author, Ottawa, 30 October 2017.

18 Truth and Reconciliation Commission of Canada, *Canada's Residential Schools: The Inuit and Northern Experience*, vol. 2 of the Final Report of

the Truth and Reconciliation Commission of Canada (Montreal and Kingston: McGill-Queen's University Press, 2015), 3–4, 18, 27, 74–5, 187.

19 Chelsea Vowel, *Indigenous Writes: A Guide to First Nations, Métis & Inuit Issues in Canada* (Winnipeg: Highwater Press, 2016), 16.

20 Dylan Robinson, "Intergenerational Sense, Intergenerational Responsibility," in *Arts of Engagement*, ed. Dylan Robinson and Keavy Martin (Waterloo, ON: Wilfrid Laurier University Press, 2016), 63.

21 Aaron Mills, "What Is a Treaty: On Contract and Mutual Aid," in *The Right Relationship: Reimagining the Implementation of Historical Treaties*, ed. John Borrows and Michael Coyle (Toronto: University of Toronto Press, 2017), 210.

22 Truth and Reconciliation Commission of Canada, *The Survivors Speak: A Report of the Truth and Reconciliation Commission of Canada* (Winnipeg: Truth and Reconciliation Commission of Canada, 2015), xiii.

23 Theodore Fontaine, *Broken Circle: The Dark Legacy of Indian Residential Schools* (Vancouver: Heritage House, 2010), 120.

24 Arthur Bear Chief, *My Decade at Old Sun, My Lifetime of Hell* (Edmonton: AU Press, 2016), 7.

25 Truth and Reconciliation Commission of Canada (TRC), *Canada's Residential Schools: The History, Part 1; Origins to 1939*, vol. 1 of the Final Report of the Truth and Reconciliation Commission of Canada (Montreal and Kingston: McGill-Queen's University Press, 2015), 56.

26 John Milloy, "Indian Act Colonialism: A Century of Dishonour, 1869–1969," research paper (Ottawa: National Centre for First Nations Governance, 2008), 7.

27 TRC, *The History, Part 1*, 83. I am grateful to Doug Smith for his detailed comments and suggestions on the history of the IRS system.

28 James Daschuk, *Clearing the Plains: Disease, Politics of Starvation, and the Loss of Aboriginal Life* (Regina: University of Regina Press, 2013), 183. Robert Innes sees starvation policies on the Plains as a clear example of genocide: "genocide occurred in the early 1880s in Treaty 4 territory; a genocide that killed hundreds and perhaps thousands of First Nations and Métis people": Robert Innes, "Historians and Indigenous Genocide in Saskatchewan," *Shekon Neechie: An Indigenous History Site*, 21 June 2018, https://shekonneechie.ca/2018/06/21/historians-and-indigenous-genocide-in-saskatchewan/.

29 Sinclair, interview.

30 Truth and Reconciliation Commission of Canada, *Canada's Residential Schools: The History, Part 2; 1939 to 2000*, vol. 1 of the Final Report of

the Truth and Reconciliation Commission of Canada (Montreal and Kingston: McGill-Queen's University Press, 2015), 10, 55.

31 John Borrows, "Canada's Colonial Constitution," in *The Right Relationship: Reimagining the Implementation of Historical Treaties*, ed. John Borrows and Michael Coyle (Toronto: University of Toronto Press, 2017), 25–6.

32 Howard Adams, *A Tortured People: The Politics of Colonization* (Penticton, BC: Theytus Books, 1995), 62–3, 66, 75.

33 Canada, Royal Commission on Aboriginal Peoples, *Looking Forward, Looking Back*, vol. 1 of the Final Report of the Royal Commission on Aboriginal Peoples (Ottawa: Government of Canada, 1996), 366–7.

34 Michael Ferguson, *Spring Report of the Auditor General of Canada* (Ottawa: Office of the Auditor General of Canada, 2013), http://www.oag-bvg .gc.ca/internet/English/parl_oag_201304_06_e_38191.html.

35 Kathleen Mahoney, "The Settlement Process: A Personal Reflection," *University of Toronto Law Journal* 64, no. 4 (2014): 510–2.

36 James R. Miller, "Reconciliation with Residential School Survivors: A Progress Report," in *Aboriginal Policy Research: Voting, Governance, and Research Methodology*, ed. Jerry White, Julie Peters, and Dan Beavon (Toronto: Thompson Educational Publishing, 2010), 138.

37 Thomas McMahon, "'And Then the Pope Died': The Timeline for How Canada Reached a Settlement Agreement on Indian Residential Schools," *SSRN* (1 July 2017): 6–7, 23–6, https://ssrn.com/abstract= 2995639 or http://dx.doi.org/10.2139/ssrn.2995639.

38 Thomas McMahon, "The Horrors of Canada's Tort Law System: The Indian Residential School Civil Cases," *SSRN* (2017): 1, 40.

39 McMahon, "'And Then the Pope Died,'" 4.

40 Ibid., 77–8.

41 Indigenous and Northern Affairs Canada, "Prime Minister Harper Offers Full Apology on Behalf of Canadians for the Indian Residential Schools System," 11 June 2008, https://www.aadnc-aandc.gc.ca/eng/ 1100100015644/1100100015649.

42 McMahon, "'And Then the Pope Died,'" 77–8.

43 Thomas McMahon, "The Final Abuse of Indian Residential School Children: Deleting Their Names, Erasing Their Voices and Destroying Their Records after They Have Died and without Their Consent," *SSRN* (2017): 4.

44 Maura Forrest, "A Decade after Payouts Began, Residential School Survivors Still Await Settlements," 2 August 2017, accessed 22 June 2017, http://nationalpost.com/news/politics/a-decade-after-payouts -began-residential-school-survivors-still-await-settlements/wcm/ 9f2539ea-c8e8-478a-b695-8398a990e027.

45 "Indian Residential Schools (Update)," Assembly of First Nations, accessed 22 June 2017, http://www.afn.ca/policy-sectors/indian -residential-schools/.

46 James R. Miller, *Residential Schools and Reconciliation: Canada Confronts Its History* (Toronto: University of Toronto Press, 2017), 257.

47 Eve Tuck and K. Wayne Yang, "Decolonization Is Not a Metaphor," *Decolonization* 1, no. 1 (2012): 1.

1. Understanding Genocide: Raphael Lemkin, the UN Genocide Convention, and International Law

1 Senator Murray Sinclair, interview by the author, Ottawa, 30 October 2017.

2 Jason Warick, "Family Stands behind School Survivor," *Star Phoenix*, 23 June 2012, http://www2.canada.com/saskatoonstarphoenix/news/ story.html?id=386a1264-e857-4c63-9b70-3be2d8e79cd0.

3 William A. Schabas, *Genocide in International Law: The Crime of Crimes*, 2nd ed. (Cambridge: Cambridge University Press, 2009), 10–11.

4 Dirk A. Moses, "Conceptual Blockages and Definitional Dilemmas in the 'Racial Century': Genocide of Indigenous Peoples and the Holocaust," in *Colonialism and Genocide*, ed. Dirk A. Moses and Dan Stone (New York: Routledge, 2013), 162–4.

5 Alexander Laban Hinton, "Critical Genocide Studies," *Genocide Studies and Prevention* 7, no. 1 (2012): 13.

6 Raphael Lemkin, *Axis Rule in Occupied Europe: Laws of Occupation – Analysis of Government – Proposals for Redress* (Washington, DC: Carnegie Endowment for International Peace, 1944), 27–8.

7 Dan Stone, "Raphael Lemkin on the Holocaust," *Journal of Genocide Research* 7, no. 4 (2005): 540.

8 Raphael Lemkin, "Genocide," *American Scholar* 15, no. 2 (1946): 227–30.

9 Raphael Lemkin, "Transcript of Interview of Raphael Lemkin," 12 June 1947, Raphael Lemkin Collection, box 6, folder 1, American Jewish Archives, Cincinnati, OH.

10 Raphael Lemkin, "Stop Genocide Now," n.d., Raphael Lemkin Collection, box 7, folder 3, American Jewish Archives, Cincinnati, OH.

11 UN Secretariat, Convention on the Prevention and Punishment of the Crime of Genocide, First Draft, May 1947, UN Doc. E/447, http://www .preventgenocide.org/law/convention/drafts/.

12 John Docker, "Raphael Lemkin's History of Genocide and Colonialism," in *Paper for United States Holocaust Memorial Museum* (Washington, DC: Center for Advanced Holocaust Studies, 2004), 3.

13 UN General Assembly, Convention on the Prevention and Punishment of the Crime of Genocide, Resolution 260 A (III), 9 December 1948, http://www.ohchr.org/EN/ProfessionalInterest/Pages/CrimeOf Genocide.aspx.

14 *Prosecutor v. Radovan Karadžić*, case no. IT-95-5/18-T, Public Redacted Version of Judgment Issued on 24 March 2016, 208–9.

15 Ben Kiernan, *Blood and Soil: A World History of Genocide and Extermination from Sparta to Darfur* (New Haven, CT: Yale University Press, 2008), 18–20.

16 Ibid.

17 Schabas, *Genocide in International Law*, 308.

18 Ibid., 268–70.

19 Ibid.

20 Caroline Fournet, *Genocide and Crimes against Humanity* (London: Bloomsbury, 2013), 130.

21 *Prosecutor v. Radislav Krstic*, case no. IT-98-33-A, judgment issued on 19 April 2004, 2–3, http://www.icty.org/x/cases/krstic/acjug/en/krs -aj040419e.pdf.

22 Payam Akhavan, *Reducing Genocide to Law: Definition, Meaning, and the Ultimate Crime* (Cambridge: Cambridge University Press, 2012), 48–9.

23 Payam Akhavan, "Cultural Genocide: Legal Label or Mourning Metaphor?," *McGill Law Journal* 62, no. 1 (2016): 250.

24 *Prosecutor v. Radovan Karadžić*, 205.

25 Akhavan, "Cultural Genocide," 251–2.

26 *Prosecutor v. Radovan Karadžić*, 205–7.

27 Schabas, *Genocide in International Law*, 201.

28 Raphael Lemkin, "Manuscript on Genocide," 2 February 1951, Raphael Lemkin Collection, box 7, folder 3, American Jewish Archives, Cincinnati, OH.

29 Raphael Lemkin, "Paper on Genocide 2," n.d., Statements and Memoranda, box 7, folder 6, American Jewish Archives, Cincinnati, OH.

30 Raphael Lemkin, "Memorandum on Action against Genocide," 16 November 1949, roll 3, Raphael Lemkin Collection (bulk 1941–51), American Jewish Historical Society, New York.

31 Raphael Lemkin, letter to L.K. Garrison, 20 December 1949, roll 3, Raphael Lemkin Collection (bulk 1941–51), American Jewish Historical Society, New York.

32 *Prosecutor v. Blagojević & Jokić*, case nos. joined: IT-02-53, IT-01-44, IT-98-33/1, judgment issued on 17 January 2005, para. 666.

33 University of Oslo, The Faculty of Law, "Rome Statute of the International Criminal Court (ICC)," enacted 17 July 1998, in force 1 July 2002, https://www.jus.uio.no/english/services/library/treaties/04/4-06/icc_statute.xml.

34 Hirad Abtahi and Philipppa Webb, *The Genocide Convention: The Travaux Préparatoires*, vol. 2 (Leiden, Netherlands: Martinus Nijhoff, 2008), 1509.

35 Hirad Abtahi and Philipppa Webb, *The Genocide Convention: The Travaux Préparatoires*, vol. 1, 1224–5.

36 Akhavan, "Cultural Genocide," 259–60.

37 Canada, Parliament, House of Commons, Standing Committee on External Affairs and National Defence, Minutes of Proceedings and Evidence, issue nos. 1–12 (1952): 232.

38 Karen Stote, *An Act of Genocide: Colonialism and the Sterilization of Aboriginal Women* (Blackpoint, NS: Fernwood, 2015), 142.

39 Ibid., 143.

40 Criminal Code (RSC, 1985, c. C-46), s. 318, 2004, c. 14, s. 1.

41 Crimes Against Humanity and War Crimes Act, SC 2000, c. 24, s. 3.

42 *R. v. Therese Malboeuf* [2005] SKQB 543, 2005.

43 Ibid., para. 69.

44 Ibid., para. 73.

45 Tamara Starblanket, "Genocide: Indigenous Nations and the State of Canada" (master's thesis, University of Saskatchewan, 2014), 40, https://oatd.org/oatd/record?record=handle%5C%3A10388%5C%2FE TD-2014-06-1625. For further support of the same perspective, see Stote, *An Act of Genocide*, 149.

46 Abtahi and Webb, *The Genocide Convention*, vol. 1, 889.

47 Ibid., 890.

48 Douglas Irvin-Erickson, *Raphaël Lemkin and the Concept of Genocide* (Philadelphia: University of Pennsylvania Press, 2017), 160.

49 Ibid., 193.

50 Eliza Novic, *The Concept of Cultural Genocide: An International Law Perspective* (Oxford: Oxford University Press, 2016), 29.

51 Akhavan, "Cultural Genocide," 253–4.

52 Ibid., 254–6.

2. Pluralists, Indigenous Peoples, and Colonial Genocide

1 Joseph P. Gone, "Colonial Genocide and Historical Trauma in Native North America," in *Colonial Genocide and Indigenous North America*, ed. Alexander Laban Hinton, Andrew Woolford, and Jeff Benvenuto (Durham, NC: Duke University Press, 2014), 275, 278.

2 Ibid., 278.
3 Ann Curthoys and John Docker, "Defining Genocide," in *The Historiography of Genocide*, ed. Dan Stone, 9–41 (London: Palgrave Macmillan, 2008).
4 Michael A. McDonnell and A. Dirk Moses, "Raphael Lemkin as Historian of Genocide in the Americas," *Journal of Genocide Research* 7, no. 4 (2005): 502.
5 Raphael Lemkin, *Axis Rule in Occupied Europe: Laws of Occupation, Analysis of Government, Proposals for Redress* (Clark, NJ: Lawbook Exchange, 2005), ix.
6 Raphael Lemkin, "The Genocide Convention before the U.S.A. Senate, Undated," 1948–51, Statements and Memoranda, Raphael Lemkin Collection, box 6, folder 2, American Jewish Archives, Cincinnati, OH.
7 Andrew Woolford, "Decriminalizing Settler Colonialism: Entryways to Genocide Accusation and Canadian Absolution" (presentation to the "Entryways, Criminalization and Criminal Governance" symposium, University of Alberta, Edmonton, 22–23 January 2016), 16.
8 Dan Eshet, *Totally Unofficial: Raphael Lemkin and the Genocide Convention*, Making History Series (Brookline, MA: Facing History and Ourselves Foundation, 2007), 43.
9 John Docker, "Raphael Lemkin's History of Genocide and Colonialism" (paper presented at the United States Holocaust Memorial Museum, Washington, DC, 26 February 2004), 64.
10 Ibid., 73.
11 Anton Weiss-Wendt, "Hostage of Politics: Raphael Lemkin on 'Soviet Genocide,'" *Journal of Genocide Research* 7, no. 4 (2005): 551–9.
12 Raphael Lemkin, "Letter to Salvatore Parisi, 17 February, 1950," roll 3, Raphael Lemkin Collection (bulk 1941–51), American Jewish Historical Society, Cincinnati, OH.
13 Weiss-Wendt, "Hostage of Politics," 551–9.
14 Douglas Irvin-Erickson, *Raphaël Lemkin and the Concept of Genocide* (Philadelphia: University of Pennsylvania Press, 2017), 9.
15 Tony Barta, "Relations of Genocide: Land and Lives in the Colonization of Australia," in *Genocide and the Modern Age: Etiology and Case Studies of Mass Death*, ed. Isidor Wallimann and Michael N. Dobkowski (Westport, CT: Greenwood Press, 1987), 239–40.
16 Ibid.
17 Daniel Francis, *The Imaginary Indian: The Image of the Indian in Canadian Culture* (Vancouver: Arsenal Pulp Press, 1992), 58–9.

18 Dominion of Canada, *Annual Report of the Department of Indian Affairs for the Year Ended June 30, 1906* (Ottawa: Indian Affairs, 1906), xxii.

19 Sherene Razack, *Dying from Improvement: Inquests and Inquiries into Indigenous Deaths in Custody* (Toronto: University of Toronto Press, 2015), 193.

20 Andrew Woolford, *This Benevolent Experiment: Indigenous Boarding Schools, Genocide, and Redress in Canada and the United States* (Winnipeg: University of Manitoba Press, 2015), 40.

21 Sheri P. Rosenberg, "Genocide Is a Process, Not an Event," *Genocide Studies and Prevention* 7, no. 1 (2012): 20.

22 Rob Nixon, *Slow Violence and the Environmentalism of the Poor* (Cambridge, MA: Harvard University Press, 2011), 33. My thanks to Pauline Wakeham for introducing me to Nixon's work.

23 David Stewart, "The Red Man and the White Plague," *Canadian Medical Association Journal* (December 1936): 674–5.

24 Robert Davis and Mark Zannis, *The Genocide Machine in Canada: The Pacification of the North* (Montreal: Black Rose Books, 1973), 175–6.

25 Menno Boldt, *Surviving as Indians: The Challenge of Self-Government* (Toronto: University of Toronto Press, 1993), 61.

26 Roland Chrisjohn and Sherri Young, *The Circle Game: Shadow and Substance in the Residential School Experience in Canada* (Penticton, BC: Theytus Books, 1997), 17.

27 Andrea Bear Nicholas, "Canada's Colonial Mission: The Great White Bird," in *Aboriginal Education in Canada: A Study in Decolonization*, ed. K.P. Binda and S. Calliou (Mississauga, ON: Canadian Educators' Press, 2001), 10–11.

28 Dean Neu and Richard Therrien, *Accounting for Genocide: Canada's Bureaucratic Assault on Aboriginal Peoples* (Halifax: Fernwood Publishing, 2003), 22.

29 Ibid., 25.

30 Leroy Little Bear, *Naturalizing Indigenous Knowledge: Synthesis Paper* (Saskatoon: University of Saskatchewan, Aboriginal Education Research Centre; Calgary: First Nations and Adult Higher Education Consortium, 2009), 8.

31 Lisa Monchalin, *The Colonial Problem: An Indigenous Perspective on Crime and Injustice in Canada* (Toronto: University of Toronto Press, 2016), 27.

32 Robert J. Miller, Jacinta Ruru, Larissa Behrendt, and Tracey Lindberg, *Discovering Indigenous Lands: The Doctrine of Discovery in the English Colonies* (Oxford: Oxford University Press, 2010), 89–90.

33 Blair Stonechild, *The Knowledge Seeker: Embracing Indigenous Spirituality* (Regina: University of Regina Press, 2016), 3.
34 Andrew Woolford, "Ontological Destruction: Genocide and Canadian Aboriginal Peoples," *Genocide Studies and Prevention* 4, no. 1 (2009): 89.
35 Truth and Reconciliation Commission of Canada, *Canada's Residential Schools: Reconciliation*, vol. 6 of the Final Report of the Truth and Reconciliation Commission of Canada (Montreal and Kingston: McGill-Queen's University Press, 2015), 103.
36 Lynne Kelly, *The Memory Code* (Crows Nest, AU: Allen & Unwin, 2016).
37 Tasha Hubbard, "'Kill, Skin, and Sell': Buffalo Genocide," in *Colonial Genocide in Indigenous North America*, ed. Alexander Laban Hinton, Andrew Woolford, and Jeff Benvenuto (Durham, NC: Duke University Press, 2014), 294, 302.
38 Ibid., 301.
39 Sylvia McAdam (Saysewahum), *Nationhood Interrupted: Revitalizing nêhiyaw Legal Systems* (Vancouver: University of British Columbia Press, 2015), 44.
40 Matthew Wildcat, "Fearing Social and Cultural Death: Genocide and Elimination in Settler Colonial Canada – An Indigenous Perspective," *Journal of Genocide Research* 17, no. 4 (2015): 391–409.
41 Robert Alexander Innes, *Elder Brother and the Law of the People: Contemporary Kinship and Cowessess First Nation* (Winnipeg: University of Manitoba Press, 2013), 7.
42 Robert Alexander Innes, "Multicultural Bands on the Northern Plains and the Notion of Tribal History," in *Finding a Way to the Heart: Writings on Aboriginal and Women's History of Canada; In Honour of Sylvia Van Kirk*, ed. Robin J. Brownlie and Valerie J. Korinek (Winnipeg: University of Manitoba Press, 2012), 123.
43 Ibid., 124–5, 131.
44 James Daschuk, *Clearing the Plains: Disease, Politics of Starvation, and the Loss of Aboriginal Life* (Regina: University of Regina Press, 2013), 36, 40.
45 Michael Cachagee, interview by the author, Sault Ste. Marie, ON, 4 August 2011.
46 Andrew Woolford, "Truth Unspoken: Residential Schools, Genocide and the Truth and Reconciliation Commission of Canada" (paper prepared for the 2011 meetings of the International Association of Genocide Scholars, Buenos Aires, Argentina, 19–23 July), 15.
47 Patrick Wolfe, "Settler Colonialism and the Elimination of the Native," *Journal of Genocide Research* 8, no. 4 (2006): 388.

3. Forcible Transfer as Genocide in the Indian Residential Schools

1 Arthur Fourstar, interview by Legacy of Hope Foundation, Nipawin, SK, 25 February 2008.

2 J.R. Miller, *Shingwauk's Vision: A History of Native Residential Schools* (Toronto: University of Toronto Press, 1996), 141–2.

3 James R. Miller, review of *Colonial Genocide in Indigenous North America*, by A.J. Woolford, J. Benvenuto, and A.L. Hinton, eds., *BC Studies: British Columbian Quarterly* 191 (Autumn 2016): 175–7.

4 *Prosecutor v. Radislav Krstic*, case no. IT-98-33-A, judgment issued on 19 April 2004, 10, http://www.icty.org/x/cases/krstic/acjug/en/krs -aj040419e.pdf.

5 Shirley Scott, "Why Wasn't Genocide a Crime in Australia? Accounting for the Half Century Delay in Australia Implementing the Genocide Convention," *Australian Journal of Human Rights* 10, no. 1 (2004): 170. For the whole report, see https://www.humanrights.gov.au/publications/ bringing-them-home-report-1997.

6 Daniel N. Paul, *We Were Not the Savages: Collision between European and Native American Civilizations*, 3rd ed., First Nations History series (Halifax: Fernwood, 2006).

7 Brian Titley, *A Narrow Vision: Duncan Campbell Scott and the Administration of Indian Affairs in Canada* (Vancouver: University of British Columbia Press, 1986), 34.

8 Kurt Mundorff, "Other Peoples' Children: A Textual and Contextual Interpretation of the Genocide Convention, Article 2(e)," *Harvard International Law Journal* 50, no. 1 (Winter 2009): 96.

9 Miller, *Residential Schools and Reconciliation*, 257.

10 Dean Neu and Richard Therrien, *Accounting for Genocide: Canada's Bureaucratic Assault on Aboriginal Peoples* (Halifax: Fernwood Publishing, 2003), 103.

11 Eliza Novic, *The Concept of Cultural Genocide: An International Law Perspective* (Oxford: Oxford University Press, 2016), 45.

12 Canada, Royal Commission on Aboriginal Peoples (RCAP), *Looking Forward, Looking Back*, vol. 1 of the Final Report of the Royal Commission on Aboriginal Peoples (Ottawa: Government of Canada, 1996), 316.

13 Agnes Grant, *No End of Grief: Indian Residential Schools in Canada* (Winnipeg: Pemmican Publications, 1996), 84.

14 Nicholas Flood Davin, *Report on Industrial Schools for Indians and Half-Breeds* (Ottawa: Canadian Institute for Historical Microproductions, 1979), microfiche, 10–11.

15 Celia Haig-Brown, *Resistance and Renewal: Surviving the Indian Residential School* (Vancouver: Arsenal Pulp Press, 1988), 29.

16 Grant, *No End of Grief*, 64.

17 J.R. Miller, *Reflections on Native-Newcomer Relations* (Toronto: University of Toronto Press, 2004), 191.

18 Ibid., 195.

19 Grant, *No End of Grief*, 65.

20 Haig-Brown, *Resistance and Renewal*, 29.

21 RCAP, *Looking Forward, Looking Back*, vol. 1, 314.

22 Ibid., 312.

23 John Milloy, *A National Crime: The Canadian Government and the Residential School System, 1879 to 1986* (Winnipeg: University of Manitoba Press, 1999), 30.

24 Truth and Reconciliation Commission of Canada (TRC), *Canada's Residential Schools: The History, Part 1; Origins to 1939*, vol. 1 of the Final Report of the Truth and Reconciliation Commission of Canada (Montreal and Kingston: McGill-Queen's University Press, 2015), 197–8.

25 David J. Hall, "Clifford Sifton and Canadian Indian Administration 1896–1905," in *As Long as the Sun Shines and Water Flows*, ed. Ian A.L. Getty and Antoine S. Lussier (Vancouver: University of British Columbia Press, 1983), 128.

26 Titley, *A Narrow Vision*, 32, 33.

27 Ibid., 34.

28 Miller, *Native-Newcomer Relations*, 35.

29 Andrew Woolford, *This Benevolent Experiment: Indigenous Boarding Schools, Genocide, and Redress in Canada and the United States* (Winnipeg: University of Manitoba Press, 2015), 54. For a similar discussion of the tensions between "throne and altar," see Miller, *Native-Newcomer Relations*, 209–10.

30 TRC, *Canada's Residential Schools: The History, Part 1*, 198–200.

31 Report from the Methodist Church Missionary Department, 12 September 1911, Indian Affairs, RG 10, vol. 6040, file 160.

32 Letter from Glen Campbell, 23 October 1912, Indian Affairs, RG 10, vol. 6039, file 160.

33 TRC, *Canada's Residential Schools: The History, Part 1*, 201–2; Milloy, *A National Crime*, 70–1.

34 "An Act to Amend the Indian Act, 1920," *Canadianhistory.ca*, https://canadianhistory.ca/act-to-amend-the-indian-act-1920.

35 Bill C-428: An Act to amend the Indian Act (publication of by-laws) and to provide for its replacement, SC 2014, c. 38, accessed 20 September 2017, https://laws-lois.justice.gc.ca/eng/acts/I-5.3/index.html.

36 Indian Act, RSC, 1985, c. I-5, accessed 20 September 2017, https://laws
-lois.justice.gc.ca/eng/acts/I-5/index.html.
37 Titley, *A Narrow Vision*, 90–1.
38 Ibid., 92–3.
39 Grant Charles and Mike DeGagné, "Student-to-Student Abuse in the
Indian Residential Schools in Canada: Setting the Stage for Further
Understanding," *Child and Youth Services* 34, no. 4 (2013): 346.
40 Elizabeth Comack, "Colonialism Past and Present: Indigenous Human
Rights and Canadian Policing," in *Indivisible: Indigenous Human Rights*,
ed. Joyce Green (Blackpoint, NS: Fernwood Publishing, 2014), 64.
41 Constance Deiter, *From Our Mothers' Arms: The Intergenerational Impact
of Residential Schools in Saskatchewan* (Etobicoke, ON: United Church
Publishing House, 1999), 15–16.
42 Notes of the Aboriginal Healing Foundation Regional Gathering,
Vancouver Friendship Centre, Vancouver, 26 October 2006.
43 Truth and Reconciliation Commission of Canada (TRC), *The Survivors
Speak: A Report of the Truth and Reconciliation Commission of Canada*
(Winnipeg: Truth and Reconciliation Commission of Canada, 2015), 13.
44 Arthur Bear Chief, *My Decade at Old Sun, My Lifetime of Hell* (Edmonton:
AU Press, 2016), 20.
45 TRC, *The Survivors Speak*, 23.
46 Bud Whiteye, *A Dark Legacy: A Primer on Indian Residential Schools in
Canada*, 3rd ed. (Walpole Island, ON: self-pub., 2004).
47 TRC, *Canada's Residential Schools: The History, Part 1*, 256–7.
48 Agnes Grant, *Finding My Talk: How Fourteen Native Women Reclaimed
Their Lives after Residential School* (Calgary: Fifth House, 2004), 21–2.
49 TRC, *Canada's Residential Schools: The History, Part 1*, 258–62.
50 Ibid., 167.
51 David B. MacDonald, "Reconciliation after Genocide in Canada:
Towards a Syncretic Model of Democracy," *AlterNative: An International
Journal of Indigenous Peoples* 9, no. 1 (2013): 60–73.
52 TRC, *Canada's Residential Schools: The History, Part 1*, 127–8.
53 Neu and Therrien, *Accounting for Genocide*, 298–9.
54 TRC, *Canada's Residential Schools: The History, Part 1*, 264–5.
55 Ibid., 612.
56 Eviatar Zerubavel, *Time Maps: Collective Memory and the Social Shape of
the Past* (Chicago: University of Chicago Press, 2003), 89–91.
57 Fred Kelly, "Confessions of a Born Again Pagan," in *From Truth to
Reconciliation: Transforming the Legacy of Residential Schools*, ed. Marlene
Brant Castellano, Linda Archibald, and Mike DeGagné, Aboriginal

Healing Foundation Research Series (Ottawa: Aboriginal Healing Foundation, 2008), 26.

58 Andrea Bear Nicholas, "Canada's Colonial Mission: The Great White Bird," in *Aboriginal Education in Canada: A Study in Decolonization*, ed. K.P. Binda and S. Calliou (Mississauga, ON: Canadian Educators' Press, 2001), 9–20, 22.

59 L. O'Connor, M. O'Neal, L. Dolha, and J. Ada, *Dark Legacy: Systemic Discrimination against Canada's First Peoples* (Vancouver: Totem Pole Books, 2010), 25–6.

60 Dennis George Greene, interview by Legacy of Hope Foundation, Vancouver, 20 February 2006.

61 Robert Tomah, interview by Legacy of Hope Foundation, Prince George, BC, 10 May 2006.

62 Terry Glavin and Former Students of St. Mary's, *Amongst God's Own: The Enduring Legacy of St. Mary's Mission* (Mission, BC: Longhouse Publishing, 2002), 57.

63 Lucille Mattess, interview by Legacy of Hope Foundation, Winnipeg, 1 May 2007.

64 TRC, *Canada's Residential Schools: The History, Part 1*, 599.

65 Truth and Reconciliation Commission of Canada (TRC), *Truth and Reconciliation Commission of Canada: Interim Report* (Winnipeg: Truth and Reconciliation Commission of Canada, 2012), 22–3.

66 Bev Sellars, *They Called Me Number One: Secrets and Survival at an Indian Residential School* (Vancouver: Talon Books, 2012).

67 TRC, *The Survivors Speak*, 66–7.

68 TRC, *Interim Report*, 24–5.

69 Randy Fred, foreword to Haig-Brown, *Resistance and Renewal*, 11.

70 Glavin and Former Students of St. Mary's, *Amongst God's Own*, 61.

71 TRC, *The Survivors Speak*, 51.

72 Ibid.

73 Milloy, *A National Crime*, 38.

74 Grant, *No End of Grief*, 193.

75 Miller, *Shingwauk's Vision*, 203; Miller, *Native-Newcomer Relations*, 208.

76 Joanna Rice, "Indian Residential School Truth and Reconciliation Commission of Canada," *Cultural Survival Quarterly Magazine* (March 2011), https://www.culturalsurvival.org/publications/cultural -survival-quarterly/indian-residential-school-truth-and-reconciliation.

77 TRC, *Canada's Residential Schools: The History, Part 1*, 400.

78 Ibid., 405.

79 Survivor interview 4, National Residential School Survivors Society, Sault Ste. Marie, ON, 4 August 2011.

80 Melvin Jack, interview by Legacy of Hope Foundation, Whitehorse, 23 March 2007.

81 Suzanne Fournier and Ernie Crey, *Stolen from Our Embrace: The Abduction of First Nations Children and the Restoration of Aboriginal Communities* (Vancouver: Douglas & McIntyre, 1997), 62.

82 Velma Page, interview by Legacy of Hope Foundation, Nanaimo, BC, 24 March 2008.

83 Milloy, *A National Crime*, 30.

84 TRC, *Canada's Residential Schools: The History, Part 1*, 602–3.

85 Letter from Hayter Reed to Joseph Hugonnard, 20 May 1891, Indian Affairs, RG 10, vol. 3675, file 11.

86 TRC, *Canada's Residential Schools: The History, Part 1*, 602–3.

87 Letter from Hayter Reed to Joseph Hugonnard, 20 May 1891.

88 TRC, *Canada's Residential Schools: The History, Part 1*, 607, 610, 613.

89 Grant, *Finding My Talk*, 5.

90 TRC, *Canada's Residential Schools: The History, Part 1*, 654–6, 658.

91 Dian Million, *Therapeutic Nations: Healing in an Age of Indigenous Human Rights* (Tucson: University of Arizona Press, 2013), 44.

92 Howard Adams, *Prison of Grass* (Calgary: Fifth House Publishers, 1989), 15.

93 Shalene Jobin, "Double Consciousness and Nehiyawak (Cree) Perspectives: Reclaiming Indigenous Women's Knowledge," in *Living on the Land: Indigenous Women's Understanding of Place*, ed. Nathalie Kermoal and Isabel Altamirano-Jiménez (Edmonton: AU Press, 2016), 40.

94 Ibid., 45–6.

95 Bear Chief, *My Decade at Old Sun*, 67.

96 David Striped Wolf, interview by Legacy of Hope Foundation, Calgary, 16 June 2007.

97 Elder Campbell Papequash, *The Yearning Journey: Escape from Alcoholism* (Norquay, SK: Seven Generation Helpers Publishing, 2011), 43.

98 Adams, *Prison of Grass*, 16.

99 William George Lathlin, interview by Legacy of Hope Foundation, The Pas, SK, 14 March 2007.

100 Lorna Rope, interview by Legacy of Hope Foundation, Regina, 2007.

101 UN General Assembly, Convention on the Prevention and Punishment of the Crime of Genocide, Resolution 260 A (III), 9 December 1948, http://www.ohchr.org/EN/ProfessionalInterest/Pages/CrimeOfGenocide.aspx.

4. The Sixties and Seventies Scoop and the Genocide Convention

1 Interview 3, day 1, National Residential School Survivors Society, Sault Ste. Marie, ON, 1 August 2011.
2 Ibid.
3 For a discussion, see John Borrows, *Canada's Indigenous Constitution* (Toronto: University of Toronto Press, 2010).
4 For details, see the Sixties Scoop class action, accessed 15 October 2017, https://sixtiesscoopclaim.com/.
5 Chelsea Vowel, *Indigenous Writes: A Guide to First Nations, Métis, and Inuit Issues in Canada* (Winnipeg: Portage and Main Press, 2016), 181.
6 Truth and Reconciliation Commission of Canada, *Canada's Residential Schools: The History, Part 2; 1939 to 2000*, vol. 1 of the Final Report of the Truth and Reconciliation Commission of Canada (Montreal and Kingston: McGill-Queen's University Press, 2015).
7 John Leslie, "The Indian Act: An Historical Perspective," *Canadian Parliamentary Review* 25, no. 2 (2002): 25–6.
8 Assembly of First Nations, *Breaking the Silence: An Interpretive Study of Residential School Impact and Healing as Illustrated by the Stories of First Nation Individuals* (Ottawa: Assembly of First Nations, 1994), 17–18.
9 Suzanne Fournier and Ernie Crey, *Stolen from Our Embrace: The Abduction of First Nations Children and the Restoration of Aboriginal Communities* (Vancouver: Douglas & McIntyre, 1997), 82.
10 Lauren Pelley, "Indigenous Children Removed from Homes in the 1960s Begin to Heal," *Toronto Star*, 2 November 2015, https://www.thestar.com/news/canada/2015/11/02/indigenous-children-removed-from-homes-in-the-19Sixties-just-now-beginning-to-heal.html.
11 L.J. O'Connor and Morgan O'Neal, *Dark Legacy: Systemic Discrimination against Canada's First Peoples* (Vancouver: Totem Pole Books, 2009), 36; Raven Sinclair, "Identity Lost and Found: Lessons from the Sixties Scoop," *First Peoples Child & Family Review: A Journal on Innovation and Best Practices in Aboriginal Child Welfare Administration, Research, Policy & Practice* 65 (2007): 66.
12 Karen Dubinsky, "A Haven from Racism? Canadians Imagine Interracial Adoption," in *Lost Kids, Vulnerable Children and Youth in Twentieth-Century Canada and the United States*, ed. Mona Gleason, Tamara Myers, Leslie Paris, and Veronica Strong-Boag (Vancouver: University of British Columbia Press, 2010), 18.
13 Vowel, *Indigenous Writes*, 182.

14 Gary Mason, "The Punishing Sixties Scoop," *Globe and Mail*, 6 February 2017, https://beta.theglobeandmail.com/opinion/the-punishing -sixties-scoop/article34051027/?ref=https://www.theglobeandmail .com&.

15 Dubinsky, "A Haven from Racism?," 19.

16 Bev Sellars, *Price Paid: The Fight for First Nations Survival* (Vancouver: Talon Books, 2016), 104.

17 Fournier and Crey, *Stolen from Our Embrace*, 88–9.

18 Donna Carreiro, "Indigenous Children for Sale: The Money behind the Sixties Scoop," *CBC News*, 28 September 2016, http://www.cbc .ca/news/canada/manitoba/sixties-scoop-americans-paid-thousands -indigenous-children-1.3781622.

19 Fournier and Crey, *Stolen from Our Embrace*, 89.

20 Anne Bokma, "Confronting the Sixties Scoop," *United Church Observer*, April 2015, http://www.ucobserver.org/justice/2015/04/sixties_ scoop/.

21 Christine Smith McFarlane, "A Legacy of Canadian Child Care Surviving the Sixties Scoop," *Briarpatch Magazine*, 1 September 2012, https://briarpatchmagazine.com/articles/view/a-legacy-of-canadian -child-care.

22 Government of Manitoba, Aboriginal Justice Implementation Commission, *The Justice System and Aboriginal People*, vol. 1 of the Report of the Aboriginal Justice Inquiry of Manitoba (Winnipeg, 1999), http:// www.ajic.mb.ca/volume1/chapter14.html#6.

23 Vowel, *Indigenous Writes*, 183.

24 Gloria Galloway and Dakshana Bascaramurty, "Census 2016," *Globe and Mail*, 25 October 2017, accessed 15 October 2017, https://beta .theglobeandmail.com/news/national/census-2016-highlights -diversity-housing-indigenous/article36711216/?ref=http://www .theglobeandmail.com&.

25 Margaret D. Jacobs, *A Generation Removed: The Fostering and Adoption of Indigenous Children in the Postwar World* (Lincoln: University of Nebraska Press, 2014), 6–9.

26 Emily Alston-O'Connor, "The Sixties Scoop: Implications for Social Workers and Social Work Education," *Critical Social Work* 11, no. 1 (2010): 4.

27 Jo-Ann Episkenew, *Taking Back Our Spirits: Indigenous Literature, Public Policy and Healing* (Winnipeg: University of Manitoba Press, 2009), 67.

28 Linda Liebenberg and Michael Ungar, *Resilience in Action* (Toronto: University of Toronto Press, 2010), 296.

29 Senator Murray Sinclair, interview by the author, Ottawa, 30 October 2017.

30 Ibid.

31 Ibid.

32 Eliza Novic, *The Concept of Cultural Genocide: An International Law Perspective* (Oxford: Oxford University Press, 2016), 40.

33 Robert Manne, *In Denial: The Stolen Generations and the Right* (Melbourne: Black, 2001), 17, 39; Paul Bartrop, "The Holocaust, the Aborigines, and the Bureaucracy of Destruction: An Australian Dimension of Genocide," *Journal of Genocide Research* 3, no. 1 (2001): 75–87.

34 Manne, *In Denial*, 27; Bartrop, "The Holocaust," 77; Colin Tatz, "Confronting Australian Genocide," *Aboriginal History* 25 (2001): 16–36.

35 Stuart MacIntyre and Anna Clark, *The History Wars* (Melbourne: Melbourne University Press, 2004), 154.

36 Australian Human Rights Commission, *Bringing Them Home: Report of the National Inquiry into the Separation of Aboriginal and Torres Strait Islander Children from Their Families* (Sydney: Australian Human Rights Commission, 1997), 190.

37 Ibid., 237.

38 Ibid., 237–8.

39 Ibid., 238.

40 Ibid.

41 Ibid., 27.

42 Ann Curthoys and John Docker, "Genocide and Colonialism," *Australian Humanities Review*, http://australianhumanitiesreview .org/2002/09/01/genocide-and-colonialism/.

43 Ben Kiernan, "Cover-Up and Denial of Genocide: Australia, the USA, East Timor, and the Aborigines," *Critical Asian Studies* 34, no. 2 (2002): 179.

44 Fournier and Crey, *Stolen from Our Embrace*, 81.

45 Chris Benjamin, *Indian School Road: Legacies of the Shubenacadie Residential School* (Halifax: Nimbus Publishing, 2014), 169.

46 Sinclair, "Identity Lost and Found," 65.

47 O'Connor and O'Neal, *Dark Legacy*, 37–8.

48 Shandra Spears, "Strong Spirit, Fractured Identity: An Ojibway Adoptee's Journey to Wholeness," in *Racism, Colonialism and Indigeneity in Canada*, ed. Martin Cannon and Lina Sunseri (Don Mills, ON: Oxford University Press, 2011), 128–9.

49 "About the Sixties Scoop Class Action," accessed 22 June 2017, https:// sixtiesscoopclaim.com/about-the-ontario-sixties-scoop-claim-registration -as-a-class-member/.

50 Dubinksy, "A Haven from Racism?," 22–3.
51 Sellars, *Price Paid*, 103.

5. The Truth and Reconciliation Commission of Canada and the Question of Genocide

1 Dr. Marie Wilson, interview by the author, Yellowknife, 31 August 2018.
2 Senator Murray Sinclair, interview by the author, Ottawa, 30 October 2017.
3 Truth and Reconciliation Commission of Canada (TRC), "Our Mandate," accessed 22 June 2017, http://www.trc.ca/about-us/our -mandate.html.
4 Sinclair, interview.
5 Wilson, interview.
6 Kathleen Mahoney, "The Settlement Process: A Personal Reflection," *University of Toronto Law Journal* 64, no. 4 (2014): 519.
7 Canada, Royal Commission on Aboriginal Peoples, *Looking Forward, Looking Back*, vol. 1 of the Final Report of the Royal Commission on Aboriginal Peoples (Ottawa: Government of Canada, 1996), 366–7.
8 Aaron Wherry, "What He Was Talking about When He Talked about Colonialism," *Maclean's*, 1 October 2009, http://www.macleans.ca/ uncategorized/what-he-was-talking-about-when-he-talked-about -colonialism/.
9 Ronald Niezen, *Truth and Indignation: Canada's Truth and Reconciliation Commission on Indian Residential Schools* (Toronto: University of Toronto Press, 2013), 43–8.
10 Mahoney, "The Settlement Process," 509–10.
11 "Schedule 'D' Independent Assessment Process (IAP) for Continuing Indian Residential School Abuse Claims," Residential School Settlement: Official Court Notice, 3–4, accessed 22 June 2017, http://www .residentialschoolsettlement.ca/Schedule_D-IAP.PDF.
12 Paul Barnsley, "Survivors 'Falling through the Cracks' of Indian Residential Schools Settlement Agreement," *APTN National News*, 19 June 2017, http://aptnnews.ca/2017/06/19/survivors-falling -through-the-cracks-of-indian-residential-schools-settlement -agreement/.
13 TRC, "Our Mandate."
14 Ibid.
15 Suzanne Fournier and Ernie Crey, *Stolen from Our Embrace: The Abduction of First Nations Children and the Restoration of Aboriginal Communities* (Vancouver: Douglas & McIntyre, 1997), 75.

16 Dian Million, *Therapeutic Nations: Healing in an Age of Indigenous Human Rights* (Tucson: University of Arizona Press, 2013), 79.

17 TRC, "Our Mandate."

18 Thomas L. McMahon, "The Final Abuse of Indian Residential School Children: Deleting Their Names, Erasing Their Voices and Destroying Their Records after They Have Died and without Their Consent," *SSRN* (2017): 66.

19 Ibid., 71.

20 Ibid., 4, 10.

21 Ibid.

22 Sinclair, interview.

23 "Chairman Quits Troubled Residential-School Commission," *CBC News*, 20 October 2008, accessed 22 June 2017, http://www.cbc .ca/news/canada/chairman-quits-troubled-residential-school -commission-1.704043.

24 Mark Kennedy, "Truth Seeker: Murray Sinclair's Relentless Quest for the Facts about Residential Schools," *Ottawa Citizen*, 22 May 2015, http://ottawacitizen.com/news/politics/truth-seeker-murray -sinclairs-relentless-quest-for-the-truth-about-residential-schools.

25 Shari Narine, "TRC Back on Track with New Appointments," *Windspeaker* 27, no. 4 (2009), http://www.ammsa.com/publications/ windspeaker/trc-back-track-new-appointments.

26 Danielle Metcalfe-Chenail, "A Conversation between Shelagh Rogers and the Honourable Justice Murray Sinclair," in *In This Together: Fifteen Stories of Truth & Reconciliation*, ed. Danielle Metcalfe-Chenail (Victoria: Brindle & Glass Publishing, 2016), 186–8.

27 "Lift Each Other Up: An Interview with Chief Wilton Littlechild," *Cultural Survival Quarterly Magazine* 35, no. 1 (March 2011), https:// www.culturalsurvival.org/publications/cultural-survival-quarterly/ lift-each-other-interview-chief-wilton-littlechild.

28 Michael Ferguson, *2013 Spring Report of the Auditor General of Canada*, http://www.oag-bvg.gc.ca/internet/English/parl_oag_201304_06_e_ 38191.html.

29 Government of Canada, "Population of the Federal Public Service by Department," accessed 22 June 2017, https://www.canada.ca/en/ treasury-board-secretariat/services/innovation/human-resources -statistics/population-federal-public-service-department.html.

30 TRC, "Our Mandate."

31 Ry Moran, "Truth and Reconciliation Commission," *Canadian Encyclopedia*, accessed 22 June 2017, http://www.thecanadianencyclopedia.ca/en/

article/truth-and-reconciliation-commission/; Truth and Reconciliation Commission of Canada (TRC), *Canada's Residential Schools: Reconciliation*, vol. 6 of the Final Report of the Truth and Reconciliation Commission of Canada (Montreal and Kingston: McGill-Queen's University Press, 2015), 177.

32 TRC, *Canada's Residential Schools: Reconciliation*, 173.

33 Ferguson, *2013 Spring Report of the Auditor General*.

34 Ibid.

35 Moran, "Truth and Reconciliation Commission."

36 J.R. Miller, *Shingwauk's Vision: A History of Native Residential Schools* (Toronto: University of Toronto Press, 1996), 10.

37 Agnes Grant, *No End of Grief: Indian Residential Schools in Canada* (Winnipeg: Pemmican Publishing, 1996), 24–5.

38 Harold Cardinal, *The Unjust Society* (Vancouver: Douglas & McIntyre, 1999), xiv–xv.

39 Assembly of First Nations, *Human Rights Report to Non-governmental Organizations: Redress for Cultural Genocide; Canadian Residential Schools* (Ottawa: Assembly of First Nations, 2002), 3; underlining in original.

40 Sam McKegney, *Magic Weapons: Aboriginal Writers Remaking Community after Residential School* (Winnipeg: University of Manitoba Press, 2007), 28.

41 Gregory Younging, "Inherited History, International Law, and the UN Declaration," in *Response, Responsibility, and Renewal*, ed. Gregory Younging, Jonathan Dewar, and Mike DeGagné (Ottawa: Aboriginal Healing Foundation, 2009), 331.

42 Paulette Regan, *Unsettling the Settler Within: Indian Residential Schools, Truth Telling, and Reconciliation in Canada* (Vancouver: University of British Columbia Press, 2010), 10.

43 Sinclair, interview.

44 Truth and Reconciliation Commission of Canada, *They Came for the Children: Canada, Aboriginal Peoples, and Residential Schools* (Winnipeg: Truth and Reconciliation Commission of Canada, 2012), 85–6.

45 Ibid.

46 J.R. Miller, *Residential Schools and Reconciliation: Canada Confronts Its History* (Toronto: University of Toronto Press, 2017), 257.

47 Sinclair, interview.

48 Wilson, interview.

49 Phil Fontaine and Bernie Farber, "What Canada Committed against First Nations Was Genocide. The UN Should Recognize It," *Globe and Mail*, 14 October 2013, http://www.theglobeandmail.com/globe-debate/

what-canada-committed-against-first-nations-was-genocide-the-un
-should-recognize-it/article14853747/.

50 Marites Sison, "Holocaust Survivor Offers Message of Hope," *Anglican Journal*, 19 September 2013, http://www.anglicanjournal.com/articles/ holocaust-Survivor-offers-message-of-hope#sthash.0yCRQWql.dpuf.

51 "The Justice Murray Sinclair Interview," *Red Man Laughing*, 20 May 2015, http://www.redmanlaughing.com/listen/2014/5/red-man- laughing-the-justice-murray-sinclair-interview.

52 Sean Fine, "Chief Justice Says Canada Attempted 'Cultural Genocide' on Aboriginals," *Globe and Mail*, 28 May 2015, https://www .theglobeandmail.com/news/national/chief-justice-says-canada -attempted-cultural-genocide-on-aboriginals/article24688854/.

53 Wilson, interview.

54 Truth and Reconciliation Commission of Canada, *Honouring the Truth, Reconciling for the Future: Summary of the Final Report of the Truth and Reconciliation Commission of Canada* (Winnipeg: Truth and Reconciliation Commission of Canada, 2015), 1.

55 Ibid.

56 Ibid., 264.

57 Dylan Robinson, "Intergenerational Sense, Intergenerational Responsibility," in *Arts of Engagement*, ed. Dylan Robinson and Keavy Martin (Waterloo, ON: Wilfrid Laurier University Press, 2016), 60.

58 Timothy J. White, "The Impact of British Colonialism on Irish Catholicism and National Identity: Repression, Reemergence, and Divergence," *Études irlandaises* 35, no. 1 (2010): 21–37.

6. The TRC and Indigenous Deaths, inside and outside the Residential Schools

1 Canada, Parliament, House of Commons, Debates, 39th Parliament, 1st Session, No. 139, 24 April 2007, http://www.ourcommons.ca/ DocumentViewer/en/39-1/house/sitting-139/hansard.

2 Alexandra Maass, "Perspectives on the Missing," in *Missing Persons: Multidisciplinary Perspectives on the Disappeared*, ed. Derek Congram (Toronto: Canadian Scholars' Press, 2016), 33.

3 House of Commons, Debates, 24 April 2007.

4 Maass, "Perspectives on the Missing," 18–21, 23.

5 Alexandra Maass, "Questions and Responses Re: TRC Missing Children Projects, October 30, 2017," interview by the author, Ottawa.

6 Truth and Reconciliation Commission of Canada, *Honouring the Truth, Reconciling for the Future: Summary of the Final Report of the Truth and*

Reconciliation Commission of Canada (Winnipeg: Truth and Reconciliation Commission of Canada, 2015), 95–6.

7 Truth and Reconciliation Commission of Canada (TRC), *Canada's Residential Schools: Missing Children and Unmarked Burials*, vol. 4 of the Final Report of the Truth and Reconciliation Commission of Canada (Montreal and Kingston: McGill-Queen's University Press, 2015), 58.

8 Ry Moran, "Truth and Reconciliation Commission," *Canadian Encyclopedia*, accessed 22 June 2017, http://www.thecanadianencyclopedia.ca/en/article/truth-and-reconciliation-commission/.

9 Marie Wilson, foreword to *Missing Persons: Multidisciplinary Perspectives on the Disappeared*, ed. Derek Congram (Toronto: Canadian Scholars' Press, 2016), xiv.

10 Maass, "Perspectives on the Missing," 29.

11 TRC, *Missing Children*, 22–3.

12 Ibid., 23, 26.

13 Truth and Reconciliation Commission of Canada, *They Came for the Children: Canada, Aboriginal Peoples, and the Residential Schools* (Winnipeg: Truth and Reconciliation Commission of Canada, 2012), 31.

14 Suzanne Fournier and Ernie Crey, *Stolen from Our Embrace: The Abduction of First Nations Children and the Restoration of Aboriginal Communities* (Vancouver: Douglas & McIntyre, 1997), 50.

15 Canada, Royal Commission on Aboriginal Peoples, *Looking Forward, Looking Back*, vol. 1 of the Final Report of the Royal Commission on Aboriginal Peoples (Ottawa: Government of Canada, 1996), 340; Truth and Reconciliation Commission, *Truth and Reconciliation Commission of Canada: Interim Report* (Winnipeg: Truth and Reconciliation Commission of Canada, 2012), 29.

16 TRC, *Missing Children*, 29.

17 Ibid., 32.

18 Michelle M. Robinson, "Dying to Learn: Infectious Disease and Death among the Children in Southern Alberta's Indian Residential Schools, 1889–1920" (master's thesis, Laurentian University, 2008).

19 Truth and Reconciliation Commission of Canada (TRC), *Canada's Residential Schools: The History, Part 1; Origins to 1939*, vol. 1 of the Final Report of the Truth and Reconciliation Commission of Canada (Montreal and Kingston: McGill-Queen's University Press, 2015), 544–5.

20 TRC, *Missing Children*, 28.

21 Ibid., 10.

22 Basil Ambers, interview by Legacy of Hope Foundation, Nanaimo, BC, 2008.

23 Bev Sellars, "Bev Sellars," in *Residential Schools: The Stolen Years*, ed. Linda Jaine (Saskatoon: University of Saskatchewan Press, 1993), 125.

24 Alexandra Maass, interview by the author, Ottawa, 15 November 2017.

25 Annis Gregory Aleck, *Almost a Born Loser!* (Bloomington, IN: Xlibris, 2011), 526.

26 Interview 6, National Residential School Survivors Society, Sault Ste. Marie, ON, 5 August 2011.

27 Aaron Smale, "Our Stolen Generation: A Shameful Legacy," *The Spinoff* (blog), 14 November 2017, https://thespinoff.co.nz/atea/14-11-2017/our-stolen-generation-a-shameful-legacy/.

28 Senator Murray Sinclair, interview by the author, 30 October 2017.

29 William Schabas, *Genocide in International Law: The Crime of Crimes* (Cambridge: Cambridge University Press, 2009), 269.

30 TRC, *Missing Children*, 10–1.

31 Ibid., 63–8.

32 Ibid., 50–1.

33 Ian Mosby and Tracey Galloway, "'Hunger Was Never Absent': How Residential School Diets Shaped Current Patterns of Diabetes among Indigenous Peoples in Canada," *CMAJ* 189, no. 32 (2017): 1044–5.

34 See Ian Mosby, *Food Will Win the War: The Politics, Culture, and Science of Food on Canada's Home Front* (Vancouver: University of British Columbia Press, 2014), 199–201; Ian Mosby, "Administering Colonial Science: Nutrition Research and Human Biomedical Experimentation in Aboriginal Communities and Residential Schools, 1942–1952," *Social History* 46, no. 91 (May 2013).

35 David Stewart, "The Red Man and the White Plague," *Canadian Medical Association Journal* (December 1936): 675.

36 Canada, Department of Indian Affairs, "Supplementary Estimates 1907–1908," RG 10, vol. 3957, file 140, 754–1, Library and Archives Canada, quoted in Robinson, "Dying to Learn," 78–9.

37 E.L. Ross and A.L. Paine, "A Tuberculosis Survey of Manitoba Indians," *Canadian Medical Association Journal* (December 1939): 180.

38 TRC, *Canada's Residential Schools: The History, Part 1*, 123–4.

39 Jeff Corntassel and Christine Bird, "Canada: Portrait of a Serial Killer," in *Surviving Canada: Indigenous Peoples Celebrate 150 Years of Betrayal*, ed. Kiera Ladner and Myra Tait, Kindle (Winnipeg: ARP Books, 2017), 193.

40 Achille Mbembe, "Necropolitics," *Public Culture* 15, no. 1 (2003): 11–40.

41 "Unmarked Graves of Children from Residential School Found beneath RV Park," *CTV News*, 31 August 2018, https://www.ctvnews.ca/

canada/unmarked-graves-of-children-from-residential-school-found
-beneath-rv-park-1.4076698.

42 Nancy Macdonald, "Sen. Murray Sinclair on Truth and Reconciliation's
Progress," *Maclean's*, 1 June 2016, http://www.macleans.ca/news/
canada/sen-murray-sinclair-on-the-progress-of-truth-and
-reconciliation/.

7. Genocide and the Politics of Memory: Discussing Some Counterarguments

1 "The RuSHA Case," vol. 4 of *Trials of War Criminals before the Nuernberg Military Tribunals*, Military Tribunal no. 1, case 8 (Washington, DC: U.S. Government Printing Office), 635, 675, 681–2.

2 Robert MacBain, "TRC's Own Report Contradicts Claim," *Winnipeg Free Press*, 13 June 2016, http://www.winnipegfreepress.com/opinion/
analysis/trcs-own-report-contradictsclaim-of-an-act-of-genocide
-382650271.html.

3 Payam Akhavan, "Genocide: Legal Label or Mourning Metaphor?,"
McGill Law Journal 62 (2016): 265.

4 Payam Akhavan, "Cultural Genocide: When We Debate Words, We Delay Healing," *Globe and Mail*, 10 February 2016, http://www
.theglobeandmail.com/opinion/cultural-genocide-when-we-debate
-words-we-delay-healing/article28681535/.

5 Akhavan, "Genocide," 263.

6 For a discussion, see David B. MacDonald, "First Nations, Residential Schools, and the Americanization of the Holocaust: Rewriting Indigenous History in America, Australia, and Canada," *Canadian Journal of Political Science* 40, no. 4 (December 2007): 1006–7.

7 Payam Akhavan, *Reducing Genocide to Law: Definition, Meaning, and the Ultimate Crime* (Cambridge: Cambridge University Press, 2012), 124.

8 Kristy Kirkup, "Lynn Beyak Removed from Senate Committee over Residential School Comments," *Globe and Mail*, 5 April 2017, https://
www.theglobeandmail.com/news/politics/beyak-removed-from
-senate-committee-over-residential-school-comments/article34610016/.

9 Eric Bays, *Indian Residential Schools: Another Picture* (Ottawa: Baico Publishing, 2009), iii–vi.

10 Ronald Niezen, *Truth and Indignation: Canada's Truth and Reconciliation Commission on Indian Residential Schools* (Toronto: University of Toronto Press, 2013), 142.

11 Ibid., 58–9.

12 Ibid., 133.

13 Crystal Fraser and Ian Mosby, "Setting Canadian History Right? A Response to Ken Coates' 'Second Thoughts about Residential Schools,'" *ActiveHistory.ca* (blog), http://activehistory.ca/papers/paper-20/.

14 Kenneth Coates, "Second Thoughts about Residential Schools," *Dorchester Review* 4, no. 2 (2014): 26.

15 Ibid., 27–8.

16 Naomi Angel and Pauline Wakeham, "Witnessing *in Camera:* Photographic Reflections on Truth and Reconciliation," in *Arts of Engagement*, ed. Dylan Robinson and Keavy Martin (Waterloo, ON: Wilfrid Laurier University Press, 2016), 94.

17 Bernard Schissel and Terry Wotherspoon, *The Legacy of School for Aboriginal People: Education, Oppression and Emancipation* (Toronto: Oxford University Press, 2002), 37–8.

18 Canada, National Inquiry into Missing and Murdered Indigenous Women and Girls, *Our Women and Girls Are Sacred: Interim Report* (Vancouver: National Inquiry into Missing and Murdered Indigenous Women and Girls, 2017), 57–8.

19 Truth and Reconciliation Commission of Canada, *They Came for the Children: Canada, Aboriginal Peoples, and Residential Schools* (Winnipeg: Truth and Reconciliation Commission of Canada, 2012), 45.

20 J.R. Miller, *Shingwauk's Vision: A History of Native Residential Schools* (Toronto: University of Toronto Press, 1996), 205.

21 Agnes Grant, *No End of Grief: Indian Residential Schools in Canada* (Winnipeg: Pemmican Publishing, 1996), 29.

22 Truth and Reconciliation Commission of Canada, *The Survivors Speak: A Report of the Truth and Reconciliation Commission of Canada* (Winnipeg: Truth and Reconciliation Commission of Canada, 2015), 186.

23 Truth and Reconciliation Commission of Canada, *Truth and Reconciliation Commission of Canada: Interim Report* (Winnipeg: Truth and Reconciliation Commission of Canada, 2012), 46.

24 Joshua Ostroff, "Tomson Highway Has a Surprisingly Positive Take on Residential Schools," *Huffington Post*, 15 December 2015, http://www.huffingtonpost.ca/2015/12/15/tomson-highway-residential-schools_n_8787638.html.

25 Jonathan Naylor, "Surviving a Dark Canadian Chapter," *Reminder* (online newspaper), 28 August 2009, http://www.thereminder.ca/news/local-news/surviving-a-dark-canadian-chapter-1.1535836#sthash.teFIlpl7.dpuf.

26 Alice Zoo, "The Legacy of the Indian Residential Schools as Seen in Photos," *Feature Shoot*, 22 November 2016, http://www.featureshoot

.com/2016/11/the-legacy-of-the-indian-residential-schools-as-seen-in
-photos/.

27 Dan Highway, "Biography," *Nindibaajimomin: A Digital Storytelling
Project for Children of Residential School Survivors* (website), accessed
22 June 2017, http://nindibaajimomin.com/stories/dan-highway/.

28 Theodore Fontaine, "Killing the Indian in the Child," in *Manitowapow:
Aboriginal Writings from the Land of Water*, ed. Niigaanwewidam James
Sinclair (Winnipeg: Portage & Main Press, 2011), 178.

29 Kurt Mundorff, "Other Peoples' Children: A Textual and Contextual
Interpretation of the Genocide Convention, Article 2(e)," *Harvard
International Law Journal* 50, no. 1 (Winter 2009): 118–19.

30 "The RuSHA Case," 676–7.

31 Ronald Niezen, foreword to *Power through Testimony: Reframing
Residential Schools in the Age of Reconciliation*, ed. Brieg Capitaine
and Karine Vanthuyne (Vancouver: University of British Columbia
Press, 2017), viii.

32 Ibid.

33 Mary Gail Frawley-O'Dea, preface to *Predatory Priests, Silenced Victims:
The Sexual Abuse Crisis and the Catholic Church*, ed. Mary Gail Frawley-
O'Dea and Virginia Goldner (New York: Routledge, 2007), xi–xiv.

34 Alexander Stille, "What Pope Benedict Knew about the Abuse in the
Catholic Church," *New Yorker*, 14 January 2016, http://www.newyorker
.com/news/news-desk/what-pope-benedict-knew-about-abuse-in-the
-catholic-church.

35 Virginia Goldner, "Introduction: The Catholic Sexual Abuse Crisis," in
*Predatory Priests, Silenced Victims: The Sexual Abuse Crisis and the Catholic
Church*, ed. Mary Gail Frawley-O'Dea and Virginia Goldner (New York:
Routledge, 2007), 7.

36 Jenny Higgins, "Mount Cashel Orphanage Abuse Scandal,"
Newfoundland and Labrador Heritage (website), accessed 22 June 2017,
http://www.heritage.nf.ca/articles/politics/wells-government-mt
-cashel.php; Rob Antle, "N.L. Settles Mount Cashel Abuse Claim for
$750K," *CBC News*, 16 November 2016, http://www.cbc.ca/news/
canada/newfoundland-labrador/john-doe-mount-cashel-christian
-brothers-suit-settled-1.3843286.

37 Truth and Reconciliation Commission of Canada, *Canada's Residential
Schools: The History, Part 2; 1939 to 2000*, vol. 1 of the Final Report of
the Truth and Reconciliation Commission of Canada (Montreal and
Kingston: McGill-Queen's University Press, 2015), 405.

38 See http://justicefordayscholars.com/.

39 Grant, *No End of Grief*, 23.

8. Indigenous Peoples and Genocide: Challenges of Recognition and Remembering

1 Bill C-318: An Act to establish Indian Residential School Reconciliation and Memorial Day, 1st Reading, 31 October 2016, 42nd Parliament, 1st Session, 2015–16, https://www.parl.ca/DocumentViewer/en/42-1/bill/C-318/first-reading.

2 Rhonda Claes and Deborah Clifton, "Needs and Expectations for Redress of Victims of Abuse at Residential Schools," in *Final Report Submitted to the Law Commission of Canada by Sage* (Ottawa: Law Commission of Canada, 1998), 30.

3 Jeff Corntassel and Christine Bird, "Canada: Portrait of a Serial Killer," in *Surviving Canada: Indigenous Peoples Celebrate 150 Years of Betrayal*, ed. Kiera Ladner and Myra Tait, Kindle (Winnipeg: ARP Books, 2017), 205.

4 Hymie Rubenstein and Rodney A. Clifton, "Cultural Genocide and the Indian Residential Schools," *C2C Journal*, 9 November 2015, http://www.c2cjournal.ca/2015/11/cultural-genocide-and-the-indian-residential-schools/.

5 Liberal Party of Canada, "Words Are Not Enough: It's Time for Real Action to Repair the Harm Caused by Residential Schools," *Liberal.ca* (website), accessed 2 June 2017, https://www.liberal.ca/petitions/truth-and-reconciliation-on-residential-schools/.

6 Saskatchewan, Legislative Assembly, The Ukrainian Famine and Genocide (Holodomor) Memorial Day Act, *Statutes of Saskatchewan*, c. U-0.1, 14 May 2008, http://www.publications.gov.sk.ca/details.cfm?p=25192.

7 Ibid.

8 Quebec, National Assembly, Act to Proclaim Armenian Genocide Memorial Day, *Statutes of Quebec*, c. J-0.2, http://legisquebec.gouv.qc.ca/en/showdoc/cs/J-0.2/20031210.

9 Ontario, Legislative Assembly, Bill 155: An Act to proclaim Ukrainian Heritage Day, 39th Legislature, 2nd Session, 2011, http://www.ontla.on.ca/web/bills/bills_detail.do?locale=en&BillID=2459&detailPage=bills_detail_the_bill.

10 Quebec, National Assembly, Act to Proclaim Armenian Genocide Memorial Day.

11 Manitoba, Legislative Assembly, Bill 217: The Ukrainian Famine and Genocide Memorial Day Act, 39th Legislature, 2nd Session, 2007, http://web2.gov.mb.ca/bills/39-2/pdf/b217.pdf.

12 Ontario, Legislative Assembly, Bill 66: An Act to proclaim Holocaust Memorial Day – Yom ha-Shoah in Ontario, 36th Legislature, 2nd Session,

1998, http://www.ontla.on.ca/web/bills/bills_detail.do?locale=en&Bill ID=1735&ParlSessionID=36:2&isCurrent=false.

13 Quebec, National Assembly, Bill 198, An Act to proclaim Holocaust-Yom Hashoah Memorial Day in Québec, 36th Legislature, 1st Session, 1999, http://www.assnat.qc.ca/en/travaux-parlementaires/projets-loi/projet-loi-198-36-1.html.

14 Catherine D. Chatterley, "Canada's Struggle with Holocaust Memorialization: The War Museum Controversy, Ethnic Identity Politics, and the Canadian Museum for Human Rights," *Holocaust and Genocide Studies* 29, no. 12 (2015): 189–211.

15 Travis Wysote, "'Risk Your Life Accessing the Museum': The Canadian Museum for Human Rights and the Question of Indigenous Genocide(s)" (master's thesis, McGill University, Art History and Communications, April 2015), http://www.academia.edu/25143102/_RISK_YOUR_LIFE_ACCESSING_THE_MUSEUM_The_Canadian_Museum_for_Human_Rights_and_the_Question_of_Indigenous_Genocide_s, 30–1.

16 Erica Lehrer, "Thinking Through the Canadian Museum for Human Rights," *American Quarterly* 67, no. 4 (December 2015): 1196.

17 Rita Kaur Dhamoon, "Re-presenting Genocide: The Canadian Museum of Human Rights and Settler Colonial Power," *Journal of Race, Ethnicity and Politics* 1 (2016): 10–11.

18 Tricia Logan, "National Memory and Museums," in *Remembering Genocide*, ed. Nigel Eltringham and Pam MacLean (New York: Routledge, 2014), 120, 125.

19 Bruce Anderson and David Coletto, *The True North, Friendly & Free: What Makes Us Proud to Be Canadian* (Ottawa: Abacus Data, 2016), http://abacusdata.ca/the-true-north-friendly-free-what-makes-us-proud-to-be-canadian/.

20 "New Poll on Indigenous Issues Shows Lack of Engagement and Dissatisfaction with Governments," *Innovative Research Group*, 20 June 2017, http://innovativeresearch.ca/indigenous-issues-ctm-may-2017/.

21 "Canadians on Indigenous Issues: Focus on Reserves Final Survey Questionnaire – Post Pre-Test Feedback," 19 March 2018; "Truths of Reconciliation: Canadians Are Deeply Divided on How Best to Address Indigenous Issues," 6 June 2018. Both are available at Angus Reid Institute, http://angusreid.org/indigenous-canada/.

22 Rosemary Nagy and Emily Gillespie, "Representing Reconciliation: A News Frame Analysis of Print Media Coverage of Indian Residential Schools," *Transitional Justice Review* 1, no. 3 (2015): 11–13, 22.

23 Hayden King, "Media's Indigenous Coverage Has Always Been Slanted," *Toronto Star*, 31 July 2017, https://www.thestar.com/news/insight/2017/07/31/medias-indigenous-coverage-has-always-been-slanted-and-its-still-scant-says-writer-hayden-king.html.

24 Conrad Black and F.H. Buckley, "Four Pillars," *Dorchester Review* 4, no. 2 (Autumn/Winter 2014): 3.

25 Philip Resnick, *The European Roots of Canadian Identity* (Peterborough, ON: Broadview Press, 2005), 76.

26 Charlotte Gray, *The Promise of Canada: 150 Years – People and Ideas That Have Shaped Our Country* (Toronto: Simon & Schuster Canada, 2016), 54, 324.

27 Mike Myers, *Canada* (Toronto: Doubleday Canada, 2016), 38, 277.

28 Will Kymlicka, "Being Canadian," in *Ethics in Canada: Ethical, Social and Political Perspectives*, ed. Karen Wendling (Don Mills, ON: Oxford University Press, 2015), 175.

29 Government of Quebec, *Quebecers: Our Way of Being Canadian; Policy on Québec Affirmation and Canadian Relations* (Quebec City: Ministère du Conseil exécutif Gouvernement du Québec, 2017), 19.

30 Eve Haque, "The Bilingual Limits of Canadian Multiculturalism: The Politics of Language and Race," in *Critical Inquiries: A Reader in Studies of Canada*, ed. Lynn Caldwell, Carrianne Leung, and Daryl Leroux (Halifax: Fernwood Publishing, 2013), 31–2.

31 Darryl Leroux, "The Many Paradoxes of Race in Québec: Civilization, Laïcité and Gender (In)Equality," in *Critical Inquiries: A Reader in Studies of Canada*, ed. Lynn Caldwell, Carrianne Leung, and Darryl Leroux (Halifax: Fernwood Publishing, 2013), 54–5.

32 Will Kymlicka, *Multicultural Citizenship* (Oxford: Oxford University Press, 1995), 19.

33 Peter Russell, "Can Canadians Be a Sovereign People? The Question Revisited," in *Constitutional Politics in Canada and the United States*, ed. Stephen L. Newman (Albany, NY: SUNY Press, 2012), 28.

34 Peter Russell, *Canada's Odyssey: A Country Based on Incomplete Conquests* (Toronto: University of Toronto Press, 2017), 3.

35 W.J. Eccles, "Sovereignty-Association, 1500–1783," *Canadian Historical Review* 65, no. 4 (1984): 481–2.

36 Government of Quebec, *Our Way of Being Canadian*, 5–6.

37 Act Respecting the Exercise of the Fundamental Rights and Prerogatives of the Québec People and the Québec State, *Statutes of Quebec*, E-20.2, http://legisquebec.gouv.qc.ca/en/ShowDoc/cs/E-20.2.

38 Jorge Barrera, "Quebec Wants to Reopen Constitution before Dealing with Indigenous Rights," *APTN National News*, 3 October 2017, http://

aptnnews.ca/2017/10/03/quebec-wants-to-reopen-constitution-before
-dealing-with-indigenous-rights/.

39 Cristin Schmitz, "Insistence on French for SCC Judges Could Block
Historic Appointment of First Indigenous Judge," *Lawyers Daily*,
1 August 2017, https://www.thelawyersdaily.ca/articles/4316/
insistence-on-french-for-scc-judges-could-block-historic-appointment
-of-first-indigenous-judge-.

40 Pierre Elliott Trudeau, "Justice in Our Time (Excerpt)," in *Ethical Issues:
Perspectives for Canadians*, ed. Eldon Soifer (Toronto: Broadview Press,
2009), 631–2.

41 Pauline Comeau and Aldo Santin, *The First Canadians: A Profile of
Canada's Native People Today* (Toronto: James Lorimer, 1995), 10.

42 Himani Bannerji, *The Dark Side of the Nation: Essays on Multiculturalism,
Nationalism and Gender* (Toronto: Canadian Scholars' Press, 2000), 78.

43 Augie Fleras, *Racisms in a Multicultural Canada: Paradoxes, Politics, and
Resistance* (Waterloo, ON: Wilfrid Laurier University Press, 2014), 86.

44 Terry Glavin, "Are White Canadians Becoming Conscious of Their
Whiteness?," *Maclean's*, 28 August 2017, www.macleans.ca/society/are
-white-canadians-getting-conscious-of-their-whiteness/.

45 Zainab Amadahy and Bonita Lawrence, "Indigenous Peoples and Black
People in Canada: Settlers or Allies?," in *Breaching the Colonial Contract:
Anti-colonialism in the U.S. and Canada*, ed. Arlo Kempf (Berlin: Springer
Science + Business Media, 2009), 115.

46 Rachel George, "Inclusion Is Just the Canadian Word for Assimilation:
Self-Determination and the Reconciliation Paradigm in Canada," in
Surviving Canada: Indigenous Peoples Celebrate 150 Years of Betrayal, ed.
Kiera L. Ladner and Myra J. Tait (Winnipeg: ARB, 2017), 49–62.

9. Conciliation and Moves to Responsibility

1 John Borrows, "Canada's Colonial Constitution," in *The Right Relationship:
Reimagining the Implementation of Historical Treaties*, ed. John Borrows and
Michael Coyle (Toronto: University of Toronto Press, 2017), 33.

2 CBC Radio, "Reconciliation before Reconciliation with Dr. Tracey Lindberg,"
Ideas with Paul Kennedy, 21 June 2017, http://www.cbc.ca/radio/ideas/
reconciliation-before-reconciliation-with-dr-tracey-lindberg-1.3948075.

3 Canada, National Inquiry into Missing and Murdered Indigenous
Women and Girls (NIMMIWG), *Our Women and Girls Are Sacred: Interim
Report* (Vancouver: National Inquiry into Missing and Murdered
Indigenous Women and Girls, 2017), 85.

4 Jeff Corntassel, "Re-envisioning Resurgence: Indigenous Pathways to Decolonization and Sustainable Self-Determination," *Decolonization* 1, no. 1 (2012): 89.

5 CBC Radio, "Reconciliation before Reconciliation."

6 NIMMIWG, *Our Women and Girls Are Sacred*, 83.

7 Environics, *Canadian Public Opinion on Aboriginal Peoples* (Toronto: Environics Institute for Survey Research, 2016), 34–6.

8 Sheryl Lightfoot, *Global Indigenous Politics: A Subtle Revolution* (New York: Routledge, 2016), 29–30.

9 Ibid.

10 Katsi'tsakwas Ellen Gabriel, "Untethering Colonial Rule for Canada's 150th Birthday," *National Observer*, 1 July 2017, http://www .nationalobserver.com/2017/07/01/opinion/untethering-colonial-rule -canadas-150th-birthday.

11 Audra Simpson, *Mohawk Interruptus: Political Life across the Borders of Settler States* (Durham, NC: Duke University Press, 2014), 16.

12 Audra Simpson, "The Ruse of Consent and the Anatomy of 'Refusal': Cases from Indigenous North America and Australia," *Postcolonial Studies* 1 (2017): 5.

13 Glen Coulthard and Leanne Betasamosake Simpson, "Grounded Normativity/Place-Based Solidarity," *American Quarterly* 68, no. 2 (2016): 254.

14 Glen Coulthard, *Red Skin, White Masks: Rejecting the Colonial Politics of Recognition* (Minneapolis: University of Minnesota Press, 2014), 13, 168. See also Kiera L. Ladner, "Governing within an Ecological Context: Creating an Alternative Understanding of Blackfoot Governance," *Studies in Political Economy* 70 (2003), and Marie Battiste and James (Sakej) Youngblood Henderson, *Protecting Indigenous Knowledge and Heritage* (Edmonton: Purich Publications, 2000).

15 Arthur Manuel, "Until Canada Gives Indigenous People Their Land Back, There Can Never Be Reconciliation," *rabble.ca* (blog), 18 January 2017, http://rabble.ca/blogs/bloggers/views-expressed/2017/01/ until-canada-gives-indigenous-people-their-land-back-there-ca.

16 Shin Amai, "Consult, Consent, and Veto: International Norms and Canadian Treaties," in *The Right Relationship: Reimagining the Implementation of Historical Treaties*, ed. John Borrows and Michael Coyle (Toronto: University of Toronto Press, 2017), 396.

17 Peter Russell, *Canada's Odyssey: A Country Based on Incomplete Conquests* (Toronto: University of Toronto Press, 2017), 430–1.

18 "Backgrounder – INAC Legal Fees," Indigenous Affairs and Northern Development Canada, accessed 22 June 2017, https://www.aadnc-aandc.gc.ca/eng/1359569904612/1359569939970.

19 Gabriel, "Untethering Colonial Rule for Canada's 150th birthday."

20 Brent Patterson, "NAFTA Compounds 1.2 Trillion Litres of Toxic Petrochemical Waste in Tar Sands Tailings Ponds," *Council of Canadians*, 13 July 2017, https://canadians.org/blog/nafta-compounds-12-trillion-litres-toxic-petrochemical-waste-tar-sands-tailings-ponds.

21 Shin Imai, "Consult, Consent, and Veto: International Norms and Canadian Treaties," in *The Right Relationship*, ed. Michael Coyle and John Borrows (Toronto: University of Toronto Press, 2017), 399.

22 Truth and Reconciliation Commission of Canada, *Canada's Residential Schools: Reconciliation*, vol. 6 of the Final Report of the Truth and Reconciliation Commission of Canada (Montreal and Kingston: McGill-Queen's University Press, 2015), 37–8.

23 Val Napoleon, "What Is Indigenous Law? A Small Discussion," research paper (Victoria: Indigenous Law Research Unit, Faculty of Law, University of Victoria, 2016), https://www.uvic.ca/law/assets/docs/ilru/What%20is%20Indigenous%20Law%20Oct%2028%202016.pdf.

24 Heidi Kiiwetinepinesiik Stark, "Changing the Treaty Question: Remedying the Right(s) Relationship," in *The Right Relationship: Reimagining the Implementation of Historical Treaties*, ed. John Borrows and Michael Coyle (Toronto: University of Toronto Press, 2017), 256, 268.

25 Harsha Walia, "'Land Is a Relationship': In Conversation with Glen Coulthard on Indigenous Nationhood," *rabble.ca* (blog), 21 January 2015, http://rabble.ca/columnists/2015/01/land-relationship-conversation-glen-coulthard-on-indigenous-nationhood.

26 Joseph H. Carens, *Culture, Citizenship, and Community: A Contextual Exploration of Justice as Evenhandedness* (Oxford: Oxford University Press, 2000), 179–80.

27 Russell, *Canada's Odyssey*, 477–8.

28 Toby Rollo, "Mandates of the State: Canadian Sovereignty, Democracy and Indigenous Claims," *Canadian Journal of Law and Jurisprudence* 27 (2014): 227, 232.

29 Cassandra Szklarski, "What Are the Indigenous 'Big House' Laws That Jody Wilson-Raybould Invoked?," *Huffington Post Canada*, 2 March 2019, https://www.huffingtonpost.ca/2019/03/01/what-are-indigenous-big-house-laws-jody-wilson-raybould_a_23682457/.

30 Hayden King and Shiri Pasternak, "Canada's Emerging Indigenous Rights Framework: A Critical Analysis," *Yellowhead Institute Special Report*, 5 June 2018, https://yellowheadinstitute.org/wp-content/uploads/2018/06/yi-rights-report-june-2018-final-5.4.pdf.

31 Canada, Department of Justice, "Principles Respecting the Government of Canada's Relationship with Indigenous Peoples," 2017, http://www.justice.gc.ca/eng/csj-sjc/principles-principes.html.

32 For a detailed discussion on these topics with Rick Harp, Hayden King, and Shiri Pasternak, see *MediaIndigena*, podcasts 124 (20 July 2018) and 125 (27 July 2018), https://www.mediaindigena.com/.

33 Audra Simpson, *Mohawk Interruptus: Political Life across the Borders of Settler States* (Durham, NC: Duke University Press, 2014), 187.

34 Arthur Manuel and Grand Chief Ronald Derrickson, *The Reconciliation Manifesto: Recovering the Land, Rebuilding the Economy* (Toronto: Lorimer, 2017).

35 Hayden King, "The Erasure of Indigenous Thought in Foreign Policy," *OpenCanada.org* (blog), 31 July 2017, https://www.opencanada.org/features/erasure-indigenous-thought-foreign-policy/.

36 Thomas J. Biersteker, "State, Sovereignty and Territory," in *Handbook of International Relations*, ed. Walter Carlsnaes, Thomas Risse, and Beth A. Simmons (London: Sage, 2013), 245.

37 "The Buffalo: A Treaty of Co-operation, Renewal and Restoration," *American Bison Society*, accessed 22 June 2017, http://www.ambisonsociety.org/Buffalo-Treaty-2nd-Anniversary.aspx.

38 Eve Tuck and K. Wayne Yang, "Decolonization Is Not a Metaphor," *Decolonization* 1, no. 1 (2012): 35.

39 Adam J. Barker and Emma Battell Lowman, "The Spaces of Dangerous Freedom: Disrupting Settler Colonialism," in *The Limits of Settler Colonial Reconciliation: Non-Indigenous Peoples and the Responsibility to Engage*, ed. Sarah Maddison, Tom Clark, and Ravi de Costa (Singapore: Springer Nature, 2016), 198–9.

Index